"The Spiritual Exercises of Ignatius is one of very [...] at reliably guides those who have seriously put their c[...] ve Christians endlessly talk about becomes the real [...] us guides the disciple into experience of the things we [...] ils of what is experienced. But for most, trying to take the Exercises straight is [...] the airplane when it is already a hundred feet off the ground. Larry Warner's *Journey with Jesus* effectively brings the Exercises within reach of any disciple of Jesus ready to work with grace to turn life in the kingdom of the heavens with Jesus into their actual existence."

Dallas Willard, author of *Renovation of the Heart*

"In *Journey with Jesus,* Larry Warner has retrieved a five-hundred-year-old spiritual practice and revealed its practical significance for Christians of the twenty-first century. This insightful and reader-friendly presentation of the Spiritual Exercises of Ignatius of Loyola is the product of more than ten years' experience. To follow his wisdom and experience in *Journey with Jesus* is to discover the transforming power of the life of Jesus."

Albert Haase, O.F.M., author of *Coming Home to Your True Self*

"Larry Warner has done us a great service by translating a complex sixteenth-century retreat manual (The Spiritual Exercises of St. Ignatius) into a highly useable format that brings alive this spiritual treasure. Warner makes it possible for twenty-first-century people to engage in the Ignatian exercises that lead one into a living relationship with Jesus. I am impressed that he has been able to remain true to the original nature of the exercises even while recasting them into a contemporary context. This is not the first attempt at updating the Exercises . . . but it is, to my mind, the best such effort."

Richard Peace, Fuller Theological Seminary

"Larry Warner brings the Exercises alive by providing the guidance, expertise and wisdom necessary to navigate the Exercises well. In both the practical and spiritual aspects of this volume, Larry leads you . . . before a God who, in the work of Christ, shows that his love is truly enough."

Kyle Strobel, cofounder of Metamorpha.com

"Contained in these pages is an experience of a lifetime, guided by a seasoned master who knows the Spiritual Exercises so well that they're his second language. Drink deeply and enjoy this adventure with Jesus."

Jan Johnson, author of *Spiritual Disciplines Companion* and *Invitation to the Jesus Life*

"I have witnessed over the past years numerous students using these exercises to open their personal life to Jesus at a deep emotional level and experience the meaning of the gospel and the Scripture from the inside out. This is spiritual reading of the Word in its most meaningful sense. The reader will particularly benefit from Warner's spiritual advice that comes from years of experience with others on the journey in praying over the life of Christ."

John Coe, director, Institute for Spiritual Formation, Talbot School of Theology

"This book needs a warning label: 'Caution—serious engagement with the practices, disciplines and techniques set forth in this book will be destructive to everything in your life that is not yet conformed to the image of Jesus.' Warner has provided an invaluable resource for any who desire to live in loving union with God and to live Christlike lives in the world. Here the Spiritual Exercises of Ignatius have been made accessible to contemporary believers . . . in a manner that facilitates their use in any sincere desire to know God and live with Jesus."

Robert Mulholland, author of *The Deeper Journey*

formatio

TRADITION. EXPERIENCE.
TRANSFORMATION.

Formatio books from InterVarsity Press follow the rich tradition of the church in the journey of spiritual formation. These books are not merely about being informed, but about being transformed by Christ and conformed to his image. Formatio stands in InterVarsity Press's evangelical publishing tradition by integrating God's Word with spiritual practice and by prompting readers to move from inward change to outward witness. InterVarsity Press uses the chambered nautilus for Formatio, a symbol of spiritual formation because of its continual spiral journey outward as it moves from its center. We believe that each of us is made with a deep desire to be in God's presence. Formatio books help us to fulfill our deepest desires and to become our true selves in light of God's grace.

LARRY WARNER

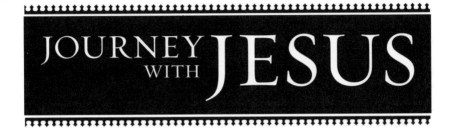
JOURNEY WITH JESUS

IVP Books

An imprint of InterVarsity Press
Downers Grove, Illinois

InterVarsity Press
P.O. Box 1400, Downers Grove, IL 60515-1426
World Wide Web: www.ivpress.com
E-mail: email@ivpress.com

©2010 by Larry Warner

All rights reserved. No part of this book may be reproduced in any form without written permission from
InterVarsity Press.

InterVarsity Press® is the book-publishing division of InterVarsity Christian Fellowship/USA®, a movement of
students and faculty active on campus at hundreds of universities, colleges and schools of nursing in the United States
of America, and a member movement of the International Fellowship of Evangelical Students. For information
about local and regional activities, write Public Relations Dept., InterVarsity Christian Fellowship/USA, 6400
Schroeder Rd., P.O. Box 7895, Madison, WI 53707-7895, or visit the IVCF website at <www.intervarsity.org>.

All Scripture quotations, unless otherwise indicated, are taken from the Holy Bible, New International Version®.
NIV®. Copyright ©1973, 1978, 1984 by International Bible Society. Used by permission of Zondervan Publishing
House. All rights reserved.

The poem "The Cross" by Lois A. Cheney is taken from God Is No Fool (Nashville: Abingdon, 1969), p. 105. It is
reprinted here by permission of the author.

Design: Cindy Kiple

Images: gravel pathway: Clayton Bastiani/Trevillion Images
        decorative border: iStockphoto

ISBN 978-0-8308-3541-6

Printed in the United States of America ∞

green
press
INITIATIVE   InterVarsity Press is committed to protecting the environment and to the responsible use of natural
          resources. As a member of Green Press Initiative we use recycled paper whenever possible. To learn
          more about the Green Press Initiative, visit <www.greenpressinitiative.org>.

Library of Congress Cataloging-in-Publication Data

Warner, Larry, 1955-
 Journey with Jesus: discovering the Spiritual exercises of Saint
Ignatius / Larry Warner.
    p. cm.
  Includes bibliographical references (p.   ).
  ISBN 978-0-8308-3541-6 (pbk.: alk. paper)
  1. Ignatius, of Loyola, Saint, 1491-1556. Exercitia spiritualia. 2.
Spiritual exercises. I. Title.
  BX2179.L8W27 2010
  248.3—dc22
                                                                        2010014318

P	20	19	18	17	16	15	14	13	12	11	10	9	8	7	6	5	4	3	2	1
Y	27	26	25	24	23	22	21	20	19	18	17	16	15	14	13	12	11	10

This book is dedicated to the students, faculty and staff of the Institute of Spiritual Formation at Biola University from 2007 to 2010 who allowed me to journey with them through the Spiritual Exercises of St. Ignatius of Loyola. This book is an outflow of our times together in class and spiritual direction. Thank you for permitting me to be a part of your journey with Jesus. I count it an honor and privilege to have been able to journey with you through the Exercises and to be given a front-row seat from which to watch what God was doing in and through you during that season of your life.

CONTENTS

INTRODUCTION

THIS BOOK, AN ADAPTATION OF the Spiritual Exercises of St. Ignatius, was written to help you to enter into a holistic, life-transforming journey toward Christlikeness. This is not another book about the methods or techniques of Christian formation but a vehicle that enables you to come before God through the Gospel narratives in order to meet Jesus again for the first time. If you have grown weary of hearing and reading about spiritual formation and are ready to dive heartfirst into a spiritual formation experience, this book may be the right book for you. In fact, near the end of this introduction, you will find a list of statements under the heading "Is This Book for You?" that will help you determine just that.

If you are continuing to read through this introduction, then you are feeling a pull toward, or at least an interest in, the journey set down in the pages of this book. *A Journey with Jesus* is not for spectators but for those with a hunger for something deeper, a yearning to walk with Jesus (not just read about Jesus), a desire to embrace more of what God has for you, a longing to be equipped to partner with what God is doing in and through you, a willingness to get down and get dirty with God, Jesus and yourself. These desires will serve you well as you embark on the adventure of faith contained within these pages. But I am getting ahead of myself. Let us continue with the introduction.

TWO WORLDS COLLIDE

This book is an outgrowth of two worlds colliding: my twenty-first-century world of Protestant Christianity and a set of writings from the counter-reformation period of the sixteenth century: the Spiritual Exercises of St. Ignatius of Loyola. The catalyst for this colliding of worlds were the words of Dallas Willard in his book *The Divine Conspiracy.* While reading it, I ran across a sentence that momentarily caught my attention and was then forgotten. Yet unbeknownst to me, that sentence would be used by God to fuel my exploration of the sixteenth-century writings that form the foundation and essence for what will be found, entered into and experienced in the pages of this book. Willard suggested that the Spiritual Exercises of Ignatius would be a good template for creating a curriculum for Christlikeness.

> If you . . . make necessary adjustments to the content . . . you will see [the Spiritual Exercises of Ignatius] offer in substance . . . a curriculum, a course for training, for life on the rock. And that is why, century after century, they have exercised incredible power over all who open themselves up to them as disciples of Jesus.

Though at the time I had no idea what the Spiritual Exercises of Ignatius was, these words of Willard would be used by God to open me up to the richness and value contained in these writings of Ignatius at the appropriate time.

It turned out that the "appropriate time" came about five years later, when I felt God's prompting to pursue training in the art of spiritual direction. I hesitantly moved forward and eventually enrolled in a training program at a Catholic university. As I began the course, I discovered that the Exercises would serve as the foundation for my training. It was at this point that my Protestant world and the sixteenth-century writings of Ignatius began to collide.

Over the next two years, as I worked my way through the Exercises, I began to fall in love with the various types of prayer that compose them. The prayer styles enabled me to come before God with a new openness and honesty, to be with God and to hear from God in ways I never had before. I was also delighted by the emphasis on the person of Jesus. He was presented in the Exercises not as a subject to be studied, but as a person to dialogue with, learn from and walk alongside. I began to see and experience firsthand what Willard had alluded to in his book regarding the use of the Exercises as a curriculum for Christlikeness. As I spent time with Jesus in the Exercises, my spirit was enlivened and my heart transformed. The wisdom and insight contained in them, as well as the holistic emphasis on body, mind and spirit, made so much sense to me.

In the years following the spiritual direction program, I began introducing people to the Exercises and experimenting with many of the prayer styles incorporated throughout them. I watched and observed how the Exercises helped people to reconnect with Jesus and with themselves in life-giving ways. After a couple years of doing this, I was asked to coauthor a book titled *Imaginative Prayer for Youth Ministry,* which was drawn from material found in the Exercises.

A little more than four years ago, a professor and administrator of an evangelical seminary asked me, "If you could teach anything you wanted to in the area of spiritual formation, what would you like to teach?" I heard myself saying, "I would love to lead an interactive class based on the Exercises, because I have come to appreciate them as a powerful tool for spiritual formation." Now, as they say, "the rest is history." I am finishing my fourth year at that seminary, leading deans, professors, administrative staff and seminarians through the Exercises and again seeing lives touched and transformed by God using them. The material that composes much of this book flows out of my experience leading people through the Exercises at that seminary.

ABOUT THE EXERCISES

For nearly five hundred years, the Spiritual Exercises of Ignatius have been a tool for spiritual formation into Christlikeness. During those years their popularity has ebbed and flowed, but they are now experiencing a revival of sorts within both Protestant and Catholic circles. I believe this is in large part due to the renewed emphasis on spiritual formation, as well as the desire many Christians have to experience the person of Jesus in meaningful ways, thus making the Exercises the prefect choice.

My attraction to the Exercises flows from the fact that they were not written by a theologian or scholar but by Ignatius long before he received any formal religious education. These writings are an outpouring from Ignatius's own conversion and subsequent experience of walking with God (see biography on p. 263). Ignatius took notes on what happened as he walked with God, on what he read and on what others taught him along the way, and he eventually compiled all that into a manual of sorts that became known as the Spiritual Exercises of St. Ignatius of Loyola.

The Exercises were crafted by Ignatius to help people, all people, to encounter Jesus. So strong was his passion for giving the Exercises to others so they might know Jesus that he willingly went to jail on a number of occasions for leading people through them. The emphasis of the Exercises is growth and development into internal conformity to Christ, freedom in Christ and greater intimacy and union with God. These Exercises are built on a twofold foundation of Scripture and Jesus, with the vast majority of the material being drawn from the Gospels. The trajectory of the Exercises follows Jesus' life—birth, early ministry, passion and resurrection—using the relevant biblical narratives to guide retreatants through the life of Christ.

Once the sole property of Catholics, more and more Protestants are discovering the treasure chest of spiritual formation tools contained in these ancient writings and are beginning to make use of them as never before. Rather than seeking to make use of these tools independent from the Exercises, this book keeps the tools firmly situated within the intended structure of the Exercises. This will enable you to get a sense of their original intention and use as you journey through them and will also familiarize you with them so you can wisely continue to make use of them once you have completed your time in the Exercises.

The sections of the Spiritual Exercises of St. Ignatius of Loyola used in this book are paraphrases based on the literal translation of the Spanish autograph by Father Elder Mullan (1914) and the translation of David Fleming, both of which where published in Fleming's *Draw Me into Your Friendship*, and the translation of George Ganss found in his book *The Spiritual Exercises of Saint Ignatius*. For the most part, the text of the Exercises is not quoted here in *A Journey with Jesus*, but functional equivalents were chosen. References in the notes referring to these paraphrases and quotes are from Fleming's book.

ADAPTABILITY

Jesus had radically changed Ignatius's life, and he wanted others to have the opportunity to experience that change for themselves. Thus Ignatius designed the Exercises so they would be accessible to all people who desired to walk more closely with Jesus, no matter their station or vocation in life.

Traditionally, when people speak of the Spiritual Exercises of Ignatius, they are referring to a format of a thirty-day experience in which a retreatant would remove himself from his ordinary responsibilities and withdraw to a retreat center or monastery. During this time the retreatant would spend five one-hour periods in prayer each day, beginning at midnight. He would also meet daily with a spiritual director.

But this was not the only method Ignatius made available to those desiring to journey through the Exercises. He was well aware that the thirty-day method would make it nearly impossible for many to take advantage of this remarkable means of spiritual formation, so he provided two other methods for people to journey through the Exercises. One of these is known as the "19th Annotation," which allows those involved in "public affairs or pressing occupations" to journey through the Exercises. This type of experience in the Exercises is also referred to as "the Spiritual Exercises made in everyday life." It is this form of the Exercises that is found in this book.

I want to assure you that this book is not a watered-down version of the Spiritual Exercises of Ignatius. Its form is in harmony with Ignatius's original intention, and there is ample evidence that he made use of this mode of giving the Exercises to others. Although this is seemingly less intense and demanding than the thirty-day retreat, do not think using the 19th Annotation is easy or is used by God in less significant or transforming ways.

I have journeyed with a few people who had experienced the thirty-day retreat and then went through the nine-month journey as well. As

I spoke with them, there were aspects of the 19th Annotation journey that were far more difficult in their own way than some aspects of the thirty-day retreat. These individuals also commented on the value of journeying through the Exercises in the midst of life and how that experience naturally led to them making many of the practices an ongoing part of the rhythm of their life long after the Exercises were over. The question of how to take the practices back into the "real" world was not one they had to deal with in the abstract, but rather one that was lived out naturally each and every day.

Although this book has sought to retain the spirit of the Exercises, it also differs from the original Exercises in a number of ways. First, the fact that you—the one who may soon be journeying through the Exercises—are holding this book containing them is a major deviation from tradition. Traditionally, the only person in possession of the Exercises was the person who was journeying with you through them as your spiritual director. This is because the written Exercises were really a manual to be used to guide someone. The director would speak about the part of the Exercises you needed to know, but you would not be given the manual.

The Exercises were not to be journeyed through alone, and this is the danger inherent in producing a book like this. As with the original version, this adaptation is not to be journeyed through without the help of a spiritual director. A spiritual director plays an extremely important role in helping you to get the most out of the Exercises, while also assisting you so you do not fall into the snares that are common to many who take this journey, including Ignatius. So, when the time comes for you to enter into the Exercises, I strongly urge you to seek out a director who will make this journey with you. If I could make it a criminal offense to go through the Exercises without a spiritual director, I would.

Another difference in this adaptation is the inclusion of some quotes, optional exercises and prayers to bring greater variety to your time in the Exercises and to create a little extra space and freedom for you from time to time. Also added are questions that follow the Scripture passages for each day and were not part of the original Exercises. These are provided to help you explore and interact with the text. All these additions to the Exercises are a result of my journey through them with others and are provided to enhance your experience in them.

Finally, in the body of the Exercises is a voice in the form of text boxes sprinkled throughout. This voice serves as a guide. These were not part of the original Exercises but were added as I discovered some of the difficulties those going through the Exercises often have. They are provided to help you deal with these common struggles. They are not there to replace the need for a spiritual director but to augment the director's role.

These adaptations to the Exercises as found in this book have sought to keep intact the essence and genesis of the Spiritual Exercises of Ignatius while also providing ongoing guidance and direction as you journey through them. These additional pieces are in harmony with the spirit with which Ignatius penned the original Exercises.

BENEFITS OF THE EXERCISES

Walking with Jesus. It was my desire to walk with Jesus that helped me to fully engage in the Exercises and journey through them. This has also been true for those with whom I have journeyed through the Exercises. They each have had a deep yearning to walk with Jesus, to know and experience Jesus in an interactive and personal way. That is exactly what the Exercises help to facilitate.

The goal of the prayer practices found in the Exercises is not to learn more about Jesus but rather to personally walk with Jesus, meet Jesus and interact with Jesus. The daily prayer practices and the use of the Gospel narratives are intended to engender encounter with Jesus so that you will begin to know Jesus more clearly, love Jesus more dearly and follow Jesus more nearly. In fact, to know Jesus more clearly, love Jesus more dearly and follow Jesus more nearly is the stated purpose of Week 2* of the Exercises. The sections that follow Week 2 continue the journey with Jesus, walking with Jesus to the cross (Week 3) and journeying with the resurrected Christ (Week 4). The thrust of the Exercises is

---

*Please note that *Week* (with a capital *W*) does not refer to a seven-day period but rather to a section or movement within the Exercises. Each Week has its own focus.

encountering the person of Jesus, fostering a deeper relational knowing of him and a greater desire and the freedom to say yes to him. This daily walking with, encountering and fixing your eyes on Jesus is one of the great benefits for those who journey through the Exercises. If you have this same desire to be with Jesus, this book will help you do just that.

Finding God in all things. Another result of the days, weeks and months spent in the Exercises is a greater awareness of God in the ordinary stuff of everyday life. In fact, those who study Ignatius's Exercises use the phrase "finding God in all things" as the quintessential summary of them. The daily prayer practices each morning, afternoon and evening, when truly entered into, birth a growing awareness of God within you and around you. Your spirit becomes sensitized to the movements of God in and through the circumstances and relationships of your life. You gradually begin to develop the spiritual eyesight needed to see "the invisible which is eternal rather than merely the visible which is temporal" (to paraphrase the apostle Paul's words). You will see your times in the Word, at work, at school, at home and with others through new eyes. And you will begin to realize that it is through these various realities that you are provided with the opportunity to experience God and partner with God's Spirit in being more and more conformed to the image of Jesus.

This "finding God in all things" is another of the benefits that gradually become internalized over the course of your time in the Exercises and will continue to be a part of internal awareness long after you have finished your journey through the Exercises. You are equipped to live life with the ongoing awareness that in God you live, move and have your being, come what may.

Developing prayer practices. Finally, as you journey through the Exercises, you will participate in a wide variety of prayer practices. These practices may initially feel cumbersome but eventually will become part of the fabric of your experience in the Exercises and in your life. Though these prayer practices are tied to Ignatius's Exercises, their value extends beyond the Exercises, and they can be spiritual formation tools that will continue to be a part of your life, shaping and molding you into Christlikeness long after the Exercises are over. Many of those who have made use of these prayer practices long after finishing the formal exercises also have introduced some of these practices to family and friends.

IS THIS BOOK FOR YOU?

Prayerfully and honestly work through the statements below, asking God to reveal to you if this book is the right spiritual formation vehicle for you at this time.

1. You have a strong desire to know Jesus more intimately, love Jesus more fully and follow Jesus more wholeheartedly.

2. You have a longing for a deeper, richer and more expansive relationship with God.

3. You desire to live with an internalized awareness that in God you live, move and have your being, and to find God in all things.

4. You have the desire, time (fifty to seventy-five minutes a day, seven days a week for about nine months) and space in your life to fully engage in the Exercises.

5. You are willing to be open and honest with God, your spiritual director and yourself as you journey through these Exercises.

6. You are willing to follow Jesus during good times and difficult times.

7. You are open to having your theology and image of Jesus challenged and expanded.

8. You yearn to walk with Jesus through the Gospel narratives in a holistic and interactive way rather than merely read about Jesus.

9. You are willing to say no to whatever holds you back from spiritual freedom.

10. You desire to enter into a spiritual practice that will help you better partner with what God is doing in you to conform you to the image of Christ.

11. You long for a vehicle that will help you to be more consistent and intentional in spending time with Jesus and connecting with God throughout the day.

12. You sense the gentle invitation of God to enter into the Spiritual Exercises of St. Ignatius of Loyola.

If there is a yes that rises from deep within you as you read through the above list, or if you sense the quivering of excitement beginning to grow in your spirit as you consider the possibility of walking with Jesus through the Gospels, or if it is not so dramatic but simply a gentle knowing that this is for you, I strongly encourage you to embark on this journey.

If none of the above is the case, this may not be the right vehicle for you at this time. God works uniquely with each person, and the important thing is not that you are doing this or that, but that you are where God wants you. If this is not the right timing for you, please do not forget about the Spiritual Exercises of Ignatius of Loyola, for there may very well be a time that these Exercises will be the exact vehicle for spiritual formation God desires you to embrace.

FOLLOWING THE RHYTHM

As you read through this introduction, you may be getting eager to embark on your journey through the Exercises. Please resist this temptation and slowly make your way through part 1, which offers an overview of what your daily time with God will look like, important tips on getting the most out of the Exercises, an explanation of the methods you will use to interact with God through the Scriptures, an expanded daily rhythm template and some down-to-earth explanations of prayer practices, journaling, the importance of a spiritual director and tips on how to find a spiritual director.

Skipping over part 1 could very well rob you of many of the benefits associated with going through the exercises and open you up to a greater degree to the struggles that can be experienced by those who go through the Exercises. Part 1 will help you be prepared for what will likely arise during your journey through the Exercises, while also providing excellent tips so you can maximize your experience. You will find that once you are familiar with it, part 1 will be a place you will revisit throughout your journey through the Exercises, a place filled with wisdom and insight to be drawn upon and used time and time again.

The Spiritual Exercises of St. Ignatius of Loyola have been a valuable spiritual formation tool for almost five hundred years, and in this book, great care has been taken to remain true to the original form and spirit of the Exercises, while also making them readily accessible for those in our day and age who are hungering for more from their Christian life. These exercises will bring you face to face with Jesus, helping you to love Jesus more dearly, follow Jesus more closely and love God and others as never before. Do not grow weary or lose heart as you journey through the Exercises, but keep your eyes on Jesus, the author and perfecter of your faith, who journeys with you, guiding, directing, enlightening and empowering you.

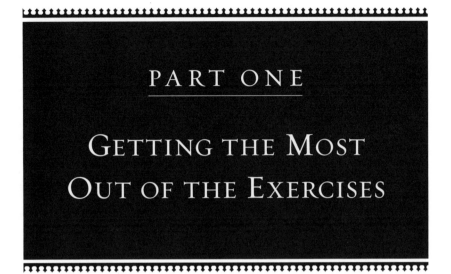

PART ONE

GETTING THE MOST
OUT OF THE EXERCISES

1

THE DAILY ELEMENTS

OF THE EXERCISES

THIS SECTION PROVIDES AN OVERVIEW of what a normal day in the Exercises will look like, while also explaining the components involved. If you desire further elaboration on a specific component, you will be directed where to find this information at the end of the component's summary. The format below will appear at the beginning of each week. As your journey continues, you will naturally flow through your time in the daily prayer practices, but at first it can seem overwhelming.

You are expected to spend fifty to seventy-five minutes in the Exercises each day. This period is comprised of the parts delineated below, including the General Examen of Conscience, which is done at noontime and in the evening. There are no individual periods listed for the components (except for the examen; five to fifteen minutes). You proceed as God guides and directs. Some days it may take you a long time to slow down; other days you may spend a long time journaling or sitting in silence with God. There is flexibility within this structure so that you may be free to connect with God as God leads and directs you. The structure keeps you on track and provides you ample opportunity to linger along the way.

If possible, begin each new section of the Exercises on Mondays. This way Sunday, which can be a very busy and demanding day, is a review or repetition day—something easier to enter into on a busy day than a new meditation. But by all means, feel free to choose any day to be your beginning day.

DAILY ELEMENTS

Opening. Your time each day begins with the opening, which is designed to prepare you to enter into the presence of God and ready you for the assigned meditation for the day. This opening format is made of several components and will remain unchanged in structure for the most part throughout your time in the Exercises.

Prayer. The opening begins with you coming into God's presence, remembering who you are and who God is. Seek to foster an attitude of respect and also ask God for help throughout your day. This opening is referred to as preparatory prayer and involves a conscious effort to present yourself before God "as living sacrifices, holy and pleasing to God" (Rom 12:1) and ready yourself to be present to God.

This is also the time to practice the prayer of recollection. Recollection involves a profound turning of the self at its root toward God, in order to allow God to mark, mold and shape you.

The prayer of recollection involves orienting all that you are, just as you are, to God. This means remembering and reflecting on who you are, on your struggles and difficulties with yourself and with God, and on who this God is into whose presence you are entering. The preparatory prayer and the prayer of recollection provide the foundation on which your daily prayer time is built. It is not to be hurried through. This is all part of offering yourself to God as a living and holy sacrifice, which is pleasing to God.

Slowing down. The next step will be the slowdown. The goal of the slowdown is to settle down and settle into this time with God. (There are a number of suggestions regarding how to conduct a slowdown under "Slowing Down" below.)

Ask for desired grace. The desired grace is what you will be asking God for—not demanding from God, but asking God for. The grace will change from time to time but, as a rule, each section has one or two graces you will be asking God for each time you enter the day's meditation. The graces asked for are the very things that the daily meditations in each section are meant to foster within you. The specific grace you will ask for will be noted at the beginning of each new week.

Ask God to guide and direct you. Finally, you will close this opening segment by asking God to guide and direct you through your time.

As you can see, throughout this opening you will be continuing to present yourself before God and to convey your need for God and your desires to God. This opening should be fully entered into and not rushed through. Some days you may want to linger as you initially come before God, while other days you may need to take a few minutes to begin to slow yourself down internally. God may very well meet you during the beginning, so seek to be truly present to God and yourself as you make your way through the opening each day.

Daily exercise. Each day you will be provided the subject matter of the meditation and the suggested way to interact with that subject matter. Often questions will be furnished to help you interact with material for your prayer time. The questions are not a part of the original Exercises and are given as an aid, a prompt, a suggestion, not as an assignment to complete.

Sometimes there will be prayers to pray during this time in addition to the mediation, prayers such as the Lord's Prayer or the Soul of Christ. Often you will be invited to pray to God and/or Jesus in what is called a colloquy, a "little conversation." These will all be outlined in your daily exercise material.

Journaling. Some people also find it helpful to journal during this time. After your meditation time (or during it), take time to journal. (For additional information and tips, see "Journaling" below.)

Closing. When you have finished the prayer time and journaling, you will take a few moments to be with God, seeking to be present to the One who is always present to you, taking time to soak in God's love for you, God's presence within you. The time here often lengthens as you journey through the Exercises. When you are ready, you will conclude your time with prayer. This concludes your prayer time in the Exercises.

Noontime and evening examen. This brings you to the General Examen of Conscience, or what is commonly referred to as the prayer of examen. You will be given questions at the beginning of each section to use during step 3 of the examen. These questions apply to the material you spent time with during the morning prayer time. The examen takes five to fifteen minutes and is prayed twice a day. Please make sure you read the section on the prayer of examen (see "Prayer of Examen" below).

Weekly review/repetition days. One or two days each week are review days. If you start going through the exercises for the week beginning on Monday (called day 1), your review/repetition day will usually be every Thursday (day 4) and will definitely be every Sunday (day 7). Feel free to switch the midweek review/repetition day around a little. It is best to have them on day 3, 4 or 5 of the week. These days afford you the opportunity to go back and explore passages you felt strongly drawn to or resistant toward. These can be very powerful and insightful days that lead to new personal as well as divine discoveries.

The outline above is the daily rhythm you will be following throughout your time in the Exercises. There will be minor changes made from time to time: the grace will change, and the questions for the examen will change with each section. There will also be new additions, which will be highlighted and explained at the beginning of the section in which they appear. It is helpful to read the grace and the examen every time you move into a new section of the Exercises.

SLOWING DOWN

How you enter into the exercises is very important. It sets the tenor of your time with God. The slowdown is a time of personal preparation before entering into your daily time with God. It is a time to ready your heart, mind and spirit to come before God, be open to God and listen for the still small voice of God. Though the methods below are not a part of Ignatius's Exercises, they emphasize the need for preparation when you come into God's presence.

Below are three methods to help you slow down and be present to God and yourself. Each method contains common elements of breathing (focus on body), letting go of thoughts, worries and pressures (focus on mind, heart), and prayer (focus moves from self to God). These elements will help prepare you to be open to what God has for you. Remember to go slowly. Intentionally making this step a part of your daily experience will make a huge difference as you continue your journey through the Exercises.

1. Start by getting into a comfortable position. Once you are comfortable, begin to take slow, deep breaths. Breathe in enough air to expand your chest. Breathe in through your nose and out through your mouth. As you continue taking slow, deep breaths, allow your mind to slow down, letting go of thoughts and worries. Release the tension of your body. Let the stress flow from your muscles. Allow your body to relax.

Continue taking slow, deep breaths in through your nose and out through your mouth as you imagine that God is breathing life, love and peace into you with each breath you take. As you breathe out, imagine stress, anxiety, fear and any feelings that weigh you down leaving you. Feel yourself sinking deeper and deeper into the presence of God.

Conclude this time with a silent prayer, offering yourself to God, asking that God would guide and direct you through the exercise and requesting the desired grace for the day. (Allow at least three to five minutes for this method.)

2. (This slowdown step is similar to the previous, but it adds hand movements combined with deep breathing.) Start by getting into a comfortable position, then begin to take slow, deep breaths. Breathe in enough air to expand your chest. Breathe in through your nose and out through your mouth. As you continue taking slow, deep breaths, allow your mind to slow down, letting go of thoughts and worries. Release the tension of your body. Let the stress flow from your muscles. Continue taking slow, deep breaths in through your nose and out through your mouth.

As you continue to slowly and deeply breathe, turn your hands over, palms down. Imagine yourself dropping those things that are weighing you down: your worries, concerns and frustrations, the things that bring you emotional discomfort or pain. When you feel you've been able to let these things go, turn your hands over, palms up. This represents your readiness to enter into imaginative prayer and to receive what God has for you.

Conclude this time with a silent prayer, offering yourself to God, asking that God would guide and direct you and requesting the desired grace for the day. (Allow at least three to five minutes for this method.)

3. This method may or may not be combined with the breathing techniques of the above slowdown methods. The difference here is that instead of imagining you are breathing out your worries and concerns or dropping them to the ground, you write them on a piece of paper and then put the paper somewhere out of sight until you are done with the exercises. This way you have told yourself, "I am not going to think about all this now, but I will be able to, if I so choose to, after I am finished with my time with God in the exercises." When you are done writing out your worries and concerns, come to God, asking God to guide you through the exercise and also requesting the desired grace for the day.

Don't be afraid to explore different ways of doing the slowdown, and put into practices what is most helpful to you. The slowdown's purpose is to help you to let go of those things in your mind and heart that would hinder your ability to be present to God. Whatever means you use to help you to do this is great.

Caution: At some points in your journey, you may be convinced that those things that surface during the slowdown are the things you should be spending your prayer time pondering. Resist this temptation, because it will take you away from the rhythm and flow of what God is doing through your journey, take you away from what God called you to be present to.

Also do not get stuck in trying to get the slowdown right. Slow down your inner being the best you can and move on, trusting that God will honor the intention of your heart.

PRAYER OF EXAMEN

As you journey through the Exercises, you will be asked to do a prayer of examen at noontime and in the evening. The noontime examen helps you to reconnect with God after your initial morning time in the Exercises, while the evening examen is designed to help you bookend your day with time spent with God. You will follow the traditional format for the examen outlined below and use the assigned examen questions from the daily exercises during step 3. The examen should take no longer than fifteen minutes and can be completed within a much shorter time frame.

The prayer of examen over time will enable you to become more aware and sensitive to the reality of living, moving and being in God's presence (Acts 17:28) and alert to the invitations that flow from God to you throughout your day. Make sure you become familiar with the prayer of examen and endeavor to quickly make it a part of your daily experience in the Exercises. This prayer practice will have an extraordinary impact on your experience and will assist you in "finding God in all things," which is a desired outcome of your time in the Exercises.

The examen was the central element of Ignatian spirituality. Ignatius would give permission to his followers to refrain from various types of prayers for a season, but not from the prayer of examen. This prayer is steeped in biblical tradition. The essence of the examen is not external change but internal transformation. It is not another avenue of self-scrutiny but rather an opening to divine awareness. The goal of the examen is to gradually develop an internalized openness and sensitivity to the promptings and invitations of God throughout the course of your day. It is an aid to finding God in all things and becoming aware of the disordered attachments within you that hinder your freedom to say yes to God.

The origins for the prayer of examen are traced back to the Psalms, in particular Psalm 139:23-24, in which David asked God to "search me, O God, and know my heart; test me and know my anxious thoughts. See if there is any offensive way in me, and lead me in the way everlasting." The prayer of examen was birthed from this passage.

There are two examens in Ignatius's Exercises: the Daily Particular Examen of Conscience and the General Examen of Conscience/ Consciousness. As indicated by the name, the Particular Examen of Conscience is highly focused, while the General Examen of Conscience involves an overall sense of an entire day or other period.

General Examen of Conscience. Listed below are the steps for the General Examen of Conscience, which captures the essence of Psalm 139:23-24. It is a five-step form of the examen you will be using as you proceed through the Exercises.

1. Give thanks to God for what you have received. This causes you to focus on God and God's goodness and grace, and on the greatness of God.

2. Ask God to reveal your sins to you. This may seem moralistic and externally driven, but that is not the case. According to Ignatius's rules for discernment, the focus is not on the external sin but on the roots from which that weed sprouted. It also affirms that you cannot do this alone but only as God gives insight and illumination.

3. Examine how you lived this day, looking at your thoughts, words and deeds. During this step you will use the examen questions given in the daily/weekly exercises. This step helps you to discover how you might have missed God today so that tomorrow you will have a better chance of connecting with God and with what God is up to.

4. Ask forgiveness, expressing sorrow for your sins while recalling to mind God's love and grace. This provides the opportunity to soak in God's grace, forgiveness, mercy and love.

5. Ask God for the grace to amend your ways and more fully live out of a sense of connection with God. In this step you are once again affirming your need for God and dependence on God. You begin to internalize that it is not up to you and your effort, for "apart from [Jesus] you can do nothing" (Jn 15:5).

When the General Examen of Conscience is regularly practiced, it generates an internal spiritual sensitivity to the movements and invitations of God, while fostering a greater awareness of God's love, grace and forgiveness and your dependency on God. (This prayer can be done in five to fifteen minutes. The key is being totally open and honest with God and yourself.)

As you go through the Exercises, you will be making use of the General Examen of Conscience. The questions you will use for step three of this examen are provided to you weekly and are designed to help you to explore your day in light of the grace you have asked God for and the focus of the meditation time for that particular day. As you go through the Exercises, you will make use of a modified General Examen of Conscience.

Particular Examen of Conscience. The second type of examen prayer, the Particular Examen of Conscience, is highly focused and is meant to be prayed three times throughout the day. You will practice this prayer style in the morning shortly after rising, again right after lunch and the third time after dinner. This prayer's focus is on a fault or sin over which you desire to gain victory.

In the first prayer time, you ask God for the grace to deal with the fault or sin the coming day. At the examen time following lunch, you ask God for the grace to reveal your shortcomings in the previous period, ask for forgiveness of that fault or sin, and then ask God for the grace to amend your ways. (This follows the structure of the General Examen of Conscience, steps 1 through 5.) You then write down your failures and repeat this process during the examen time after dinner, again writing down your failures.

This entire prayer process is repeated the next day and the next, with charting to compare periods, days and weeks with each other. The charting aspect of this prayer can be overwhelming, but when practiced, it is a helpful aid in discovering trends and formulating plans to better partner with God at times of great difficulty. The Particular Examen of Conscience might be a tool you will find helpful if God brings something to your mind and heart to work on as you journey through the Exercises. However, remember—and this is essential—it is not the outward action that is the real concern, but the internal roots (thoughts, desires and so on) that need to be your focus.

As I have journeyed with individuals through the Exercises, I have found that the examen is the single most important factor in deepening the experience of the Exercises. I have also noticed that this practice, although it takes only a few minutes, is the hardest for those going through the Exercises to do regularly. This is not because it is difficult, but because people tend to forget it.

JOURNALING

Journaling is part of the DNA of the Exercises, for the Exercises themselves are a by-product of Ignatius's discipline of journaling. Journaling is strongly encouraged and considered an important component of the Exercises, even though it was not an original element of them. A journal helps preserve this unique journey you are embarking on and may become a treasured possession, a spiritual snapshot of a significant piece of your spiritual journey. Journaling is yet another way to open yourself up to God as you journey through the Exercises.

Morton Kelsey writes, "Without a journal . . . we remain out of touch with large parts of ourselves." Journaling is an excellent tool for becoming honest with God and yourself. The discipline of journaling helps you

- pay attention to God. It is a way of hearing and responding to God.
- process what is going on inside. It slows you down enough to notice what is happening within.
- listen to and learn about yourself and God, giving direction and insight to live a more authentic life.
- understand your unfolding story and discover where God is in that story.
- put feelings into words.
- develop your thinking and lead to the generation of new thoughts, extending your knowledge in new ways.
- record your growth into Christlikeness.
- serve as marks on your spiritual wall, recording and denoting growth.
- gain perspective, encouragement and hope, and combat desolation.

Journaling tips.
Choosing a journal. There are many styles of journals: bound, loose leaf, spiral, lined, blank, small, large, leather, pressed cardboard, recycled paper—and the list goes on. The important thing is to choose a journal

that works for you. I have used many types, but I now use an 8 1/2-by-11 spiral notebook with no lines. The spiral design allows me to fold my journal over; the blank page gives me freedom and plenty of room for artistry; and the size allows me to get into a flow and keep writing without constantly turning pages. There are many people who journal on computers, which I find limiting because I can take my hardcopy journal anywhere and can even glue notes and other things in it. But the choice is yours.

Incorporating creativity. Journal as you can, not as you think you should. Journaling needs to flow out of your creative, free self without restraint, fear or performance anxiety. Seek to approach journaling as a child entering into a time of mystery, a time when you are not sure what will happen yet you are excited about the possibilities. It is best to approach journaling as a dynamic adventure, seeing where it leads you, rather than as a prescribed, static act.

Write as little or as much as you like, but also feel free to draw, paint or make collages. Do not worry about spelling, sentence structure, grammar and the like. Experiment with different ways of journaling: write in crayon with your nondominant hand, write prayers, paraphrase a passage, write a letter to God, write a letter from God, paint, use clay. The possibilities are endless, so give yourself permission to explore and experiment as you journal.

I suggest that, as you journal, you have on hand a box containing colored markers, pencils, crayons, construction paper, a glue stick, a pair of scissors or even watercolors. Sometimes images and colors communicate what words cannot. Also, the use of art can release emotions that are hard for you to get in touch with or communicate. Do not use the excuse that you are not good at art. Instead give it a go, focusing on God's grace and love rather than on your perceived weakness. See God as your heavenly Parent, who receives your art project with great joy and delight, not because of your skill but because of God's great love of you and delight in you.

From time to time experiment with colors. Even something as simple as writing a word or phrase that God has brought to mind in big, colored letters can become a powerful expression of what is going on within you. Step out and have fun, not trying to be a great artist but entering into and enjoying the creative process, knowing whatever you end up with is received by God as a precious expression of your heart and thus cherished by God and firmly affixed on the gigantic refrigerator of heaven.

Addressing emotion. Use journaling as a time to become aware of your feelings. Are you in the midst of consolation or desolation? Expressing your feelings will provide something to share with your spiritual director or listener when you get together, and it will help you know what might be a good focus. Ignatius tells us that prior consolations are a great resource during times of desolation, and journaling can help you to recall previous consolations. As you journal through times of desolation, God can bring insight that can enable you to escape the despair and discouragement desolation can bring and will help stir the embers of faith, hope and love that remain in your heart.

In the Exercises, Ignatius attaches great importance to the emotional affect of the retreatant. If you struggle with articulating your feelings, do not give up; instead give grace to yourself and continue. This is a long journey, so do not expect to do everything well, especially at the beginning. Please continue to unpack what you are feeling, because in your journey through the Exercises, time is on your side and so is God. As you continue, you will become more self-aware and God-aware, and you will have ample material to process with your spiritual director or listener.

Please give yourself the freedom to journal as you are able and not to seek to live up to an idealized sense of what journaling should be. Embrace freedom and grace, choosing to journal as you can and not as you cannot. Continue to remind yourself that it is the process of journaling and not the finished product that is important. And finally, take a day off from journaling every so often.

EXPLORING THE BIBLICAL TEXT

There will be a number of ways you will interact with God during your prayer times each day, but there are two main methods you will be using to interact with God through the Scriptures: *lectio divina* and imaginative prayer.

Lectio divina. The lectio divina (sacred reading) method has been around for centuries and actually incorporates a variety of ways to interact with God as you enter into the Scriptures. This style of interacting with the Word flowed from a Benedictine insight that reading, if it is to be authentic and nourishing, cannot be undertaken simply with the eyes and the mind. It must involve the whole person: mind, heart, body and spirit. It is reading for formation, not information, and for encounter with the living God in such a way that the heart and life are transformed.

Eugene Peterson, author of *The Message*, writes, "Lectio divina is not a methodical technique for reading the Bible. It is a cultivated, developed habit of living the text in Jesus' name. This is the way, the only way that the Holy Scripture becomes formative in the Christian Church and becomes salt and leaven in the world."

Lectio divina has four steps:

1. *Lectio.* This involves slowly and gently reading and rereading the assigned passage or passages of Scripture until a word or phrase draws your attention through either attraction or resistance.

2. *Meditatio.* Once you have landed on a word or phrase, gently repeat that word or phrase to yourself. Receive and reflect on the thoughts, hopes, images and feelings that come to you through this word or words. Strong feelings (positive or negative) are signs of deep inner movements in your heart. Permit the words, which are "living and active" (Heb 4:12), to probe your attitudes, emotions and aspirations. What is being offered to you?

3. *Oratio.* Allow your whole being to become prayer. Honestly express your deepest thoughts, feelings and desires in dialogue with God. Pray yourself empty.

4. *Contemplatio.* Gently let go of all thoughts and feelings. Drop into God's presence beneath thought, beneath emotion. Rest completely in God, grateful for what has been given.

Lectio divina takes you out of the place of being in control as you read the Scripture and turns you into a listener waiting to hear the still small voice of God guide and direct you during your time in the Word. This method will be employed from time to time but will not be the primary method when reading the Gospel narratives. If you are new to this method, it may seem mechanical at first. But stick with it, because once you begin to learn the steps and settle into lectio divina, it will become a seamless experience between you and God, devoid of the initial steps that felt cumbersome or awkward.

During the Exercises, you will conclude your times in lectio divina with journaling and prayer.

Imaginative prayer. As you journey through the Exercises, you will be asked to use your imagination as you reflect on various Bible passages. One of the hallmarks of the Spiritual Exercises of Ignatius is this use of the imagination, which is not surprising, since Ignatius was brought to faith in Christ through his imagination. The turning point in his life came while he was recovering from a broken leg he suffered when hit by a canon ball during a battle.

During the long hours of recovery, Ignatius spent lots of time imagining the future exploits he would have as a soldier once he fully recovered, but after a while he got bored with his daydreams and asked for something to read. The only two books available to him were one on the lives of the saints and the other on the life of Jesus. As he read these two books, Ignatius began to imagine what it would be like to live like the saints and to walk with Jesus. As he did this, he noticed the excitement and inner transformation that took place within his heart and soul, leaving him at peace and satisfied. God used Ignatius's imagination to get ahold of him and transform him from a soldier into a follower of Christ.

So in his writings Ignatius instructed people to imaginatively enter the Gospel stories, to be present to see, smell, taste, touch and hear what was unfolding around them. He saw imagination as the place where we can experience, embrace and internalize spiritual truth. We do not just read about the manger, the garden and the cross. Instead we are present to hear the cries of the newborn king, to feel a Son's pain as he pleads with his Father and struggles within himself, and to see the nails driven into the tender flesh of our Savior.

For Ignatius, imagination unites past with present and brings us face to face with the living God. For him, the use of imagination is essential to prayer and transformation.

Now, that is all well and good for Ignatius, but you may have concerns about the use of your imagination with Scripture. First know this: when I speak of the imagination I am referring to what C. S. Lewis called the baptized imagination and what Bruce Demarest refers to as the "sanctified" use of imagination. The imagination is a God-given gift that is not frivolous, evil or childish.

When I refer to imaginative prayer, I am speaking of a Spirit-infused, God-directed use of your imagination that gives you the ability to experientially enter into the stories, symbolism and images of the Bible. It empowers you to hold the now with both the past and future, and to see and embrace the seen (physical) and the unseen (eternal). The Spirit-infused imagination moves you from sterile head knowledge to life-transforming, heart-healing, biblically informed ways of being and of doing life. It is as we embrace and employ the use of our God-given, Spirit-infused imagination that we can enter the wonder and mystery of God and God's Word. As we use this method, we are trusting in God and will be evaluating the images that arise based on God's revealed truths found in the Bible.

Speaking of the imagination. Richard Foster, author of numerous books on spiritual formation, including *Celebration of Discipline,* talks about the benefits of using our imagination when we interact with Scripture: "We begin to enter the story and make it our own. We move from detached observation to active participation. Using the imagination also brings the emotions into the equation so that we can come to God with both mind and heart."

Peterson writes,

> For Christians whose largest investment is in the invisible (eternal), the imagination is indispensable. . . . Right now one of the essential Christian ministries in our ruined world is the recovery and exercise of the imagination. . . . Imagination is the mental tool we have for connecting material and spiritual, visible and invisible, earth and heaven. . . . Imagination catapults us into mystery.

The greatest validation for using imagination as a tool for interacting with the Scriptures is the Bible. In the opening chapters of Genesis, the earth is formless and void, and the Spirit of God moves across its surface. Out of nothing but God's own imagination, light, sky, mountains, valleys and all of life are created. The final book of Revelation is bursting with dramatic images and descriptions of Jesus, heaven, the turmoil of the world and the birth of a new heaven and new earth. From the first page of Scripture to the last, our fully engaged imagination is needed to enter into and embrace this amazing story of creation and redemption, of good versus evil, of power, love, grace and hope.

The Bible is written imaginatively because we are imaginative. Dramatic biblical imagery exists to help us enter into the living Word of God, to gaze upon the Lord, to look beyond the seen to the unseen (2 Cor 4:18) and to fully embrace the truth that in God we live, move and have our being. Imagination gives us wings to soar into the wonder, mystery and truth of God and God's Word.

Imaginative prayer helps us experience the story and personally hear, see and touch Jesus. In imaginative prayer, God speaks personally and powerfully. It involves using our God-given imagination to hear from and experience God and truth in a deeply forming way. It helps us move from external head knowledge of God to an internalized, deeper knowing of God.

Try these five steps of imaginative prayer:

Step 1. Choose a story from the Bible. It is probably best to begin with an account from the Gospels when you are first learning this way of prayer. Gospel stories are familiar to many of us, they connect with our issues, and they are brief. As such, they are easy to grasp and easy to imagine.

Step 2. Read the story several times. As you do, pay attention to the details of the passage. Notice the setting, the characters and the situation. Who is the central figure? What is the problem? What is the outcome? What is unusual about this story? How does it connect with your life situation? Read the account enough times to understand its main point and to be familiar with its details.

Step 3. Get quiet in yourself and focus on openness to God. Find a place and a posture that will allow you to meditate. Relax your body. Slow your breathing. At the same time, be in prayer, asking God for guidance.

Step 4. Imagine yourself as a participant in the story. You may be an onlooker or you may be involved in the action, but put yourself in that place and time. Begin by noticing the details in the story. What do you see? Smell? Feel? Hear? Taste? Think? Watch the situation as it unfolds. Listen to what is said. What is said to you? If Jesus is in the story, go to him. Tell him about your concerns. Listen to his response. Reply to him.

Step 5. Let your mind move slowly from the past to the present. Take with you the "feel" of the whole experience. Present that to God. Be open to God. Thank God. Listen to God.

Using your imagination. Use your imagination to picture a scene or event from Scripture. Let your senses come into play: sight, hearing, smell, touch and taste. Place yourself in the scene as an onlooker or as a participant in the action, allowing the drama of the story to make its impact on you. Be open to what the Lord wants to show you or say to you. Be open to any revelation or insight that may come through your imaginative contemplation.

Some people are especially adept at such use of the imagination (a right-brain activity) and can see a biblical story clearly, even in vivid colors. If you are not that way, do not get discouraged because of what you may perceive to be a deficiency in your ability to make use of imagination. Just do it to the degree you are able to, and trust that God will honor your efforts. The use of the imagination is a powerful tool of illumination and formation that Ignatius has incorporated into the Exercises.

If this type of prayer is new to you, be patient and gracious with yourself. This is a long journey, and you will have plenty of time to hone this skill. For now, have fun with it. Enter into the Gospel narratives with abandon and the playfulness of a child.

As you journey through the Exercises, you will be encouraged to use lectio divina or imaginative prayer to enter into that day's material.

Once you are fully comfortable with each of these methods, do not be afraid to tweak them each or design your own hybrid, combining what you find helpful in each. Remember, these are tools to be used as God leads. Experiment with each method and see if you find one more helpful than another. The goal is to encounter God through his living Word rather than merely to learn about God.

2

THE BENEFITS OF A SPIRITUAL

DIRECTOR OR LISTENER

IGNATIUS CREATED THE SPIRITUAL EXERCISES with the intention that a spiritual director would be involved in the process. As stated earlier, the Spiritual Exercises of Ignatius were designed to be a manual that was never actually given to the retreatant, but was used as a tool by a spiritual director accompanying that individual. The first twenty paragraphs Ignatius included in the Exercises, known as the "Annotations," are not truly a part of the Exercises but are notes written for the benefit of those who would take someone through the Exercises. Thus, for Ignatius, it would be unthinkable for someone to journey through the Exercises alone. He would see this as unwise. Yet there will be the temptation not to find a listener or spiritual director and to travel this journey through the Exercise alone.

A spiritual director or listener gives you an extra set of ears to better help you to hear the still small voice of God. He gives you an extra set of eyes to help you see what God may be up to and to help you recognize traps you may be falling into and themes that may be emerging. She gives you another brain to think through how you might be able to enter more deeply into your experience through the Exercises. A spiritual director or listener is a critical component for your journey through the Exercises that will bring a depth and breadth to your experience that is not possible without one.

Most spiritual direction sessions are approximately one hour. Some of your times with your spiritual director or listener can be in a group setting (see "Using the Exercises with a Group," p. 288). It is best to meet with a director at least twice a month—once a week is ideal—for about an hour each time when you are going through the Exercises.

FINDING A SPIRITUAL DIRECTOR

A spiritual director is someone trained in the art of spiritual direction. These individuals usually charge a fee for meeting with them. There is a list of questions on the Metamorpha website (www.meta morpha.com) that are good to ask a spiritual director when you first meet with her or him. The bottom line is that you need a spiritual director whom you are able to be open and honest with, someone you trust, who is safe for you and who may be a little ahead of you on the journey. Not all spiritual directors are familiar with the Exercises, so in this book is a special section designed as a resource for spiritual directors or listeners (see "For Spiritual Directors and Listeners," p. 280). It is vitally important to make sure your spiritual director is willing to do the extra work needed to adequately journey with you through the Exercises.

Two websites that can help you find a spiritual director who can walk you through the Exercises are Metamorpha (www.metamorpha .com) and Spiritual Directors International (www.sdiworld.org). Additionally there will be a portion of the Metamorpha site dedicated to those going through the Exercises using this book.

Most retreat houses have someone on site trained in the art of spiritual direction. These will typically be Catholic. My first director was a nun, whom I went to for about eight years; I was truly blessed by her wisdom and insight. The important thing when choosing a spiritual director is not gender or denominational affiliation, but that you feel safe, at ease and understood by your director. Take time to interview potential directors, asking them questions that will help you discover if you could trust them, if they would understand you and if you would be able to be open and honest with them in your times together.

CHOOSING A LISTENER

Please resist the temptation to choose a listener rather than seeking to first find a spiritual director. Spiritual directors have gone through extensive training to companion people who are seeking a deeper relationship with God, so it is worth the time and effort to find a spiritual director.

But if you are not able to find a spiritual director, search for a listener. Do not choose a close friend as your listener, because your friend is not detached from you and may tend to protect you, rescue you or even discount your experience. I have encountered this firsthand: when I first started giving spiritual direction to those I knew, it did not work well.

The listener needs to be a person you trust and with whom you will feel comfortable sharing, a person who is spiritually mature, has a growing relationship with God and knowledge of the Scriptures, and is caring, gracious and loving. Consider asking your pastor for a couple of recommendations for a listener. This person also must be willing to prepare ahead of your meeting time by going to the Metamorpha website and/or "For Spiritual Directors and Listeners" (p. 280) to read the questions for the section through which you are currently journeying. Or you can purchase an additional copy of this book for the listener who has agreed to journey with you.

Tips on How to
Approach the Exercises

Below are a number of tips that will help make your experience with the Exercises fuller and richer. These tips have been birthed through the experiences of others I have taken through the Exercises. *Do not expect that you will have all these in place by the end of the first week or even the first month.*

PREPARATORY EXERCISES

You may be tempted not to enter into part 2, "Preparatory Exercises," thinking that you are a mature Christian who knows God and follows Jesus pretty consistently, so you do not need special preparation for entering the Exercises. Fight against such thinking. The Preparatory Exercises will help you to form a foundation on which the rest of the Exercises are built; they were added because so many who journeyed through the Exercises were having difficult struggles. The time you spend in the Preparatory Exercises will pay dividends as you continue your journey. So, begin at the beginning.

COMMITMENT

You may need to recommit yourself to your journey through the Exercises more than once over the next several months. This is not surprising, but normal. You are beginning a long journey, a journey that will have its ups and downs. There may be times you will feel like giving up or like you are just going through the motions. During these times, remember why you began the Exercises and how God has used them in so many lives over the centuries. Do not get discouraged by these feelings or pretend they are not there. Take time to acknowledge them and bring them to God, as well as to your spiritual director or listener, and to recommit yourself to this process of spiritual formation. It is also helpful to journal about these feelings.

EXPECTATIONS

Beware of your expectations. The expectations you bring to the Exercises can blind you to what God is actually doing, cause you to get discouraged or make you feel like giving up. Your expectations can become an inner voice of judgment of you, your experiences, God and the Exercises—a loud, demanding and cruel voice. It is not the voice of God and needs to be silenced or at the very least ignored.

Your expectations may be based on the experience of others. I ran up against this many times as I led people through the Exercises in a seminary setting. The first year was great; everyone entered them without expectations. However, every year after that, a new group of people came with a whole variety of expectations based on what they had heard about the experience of others who had gone through the Exercises. These expectations became a hurdle individuals had to get over, a hindrance hampering their ability to be fully present to what was really happening. They were looking for something in particular, and the narrowness of their focus blinded them to all else. The beauty of the Exercises is that each person's experience is different. God will meet you as you need to be met.

Another source of expectations is your own desires—desires that are good and God-honoring. Your desire might be to become more like Christ or to do the Exercises well or not to miss a day. These desires then get subtly turned into self-imposed expectations: I will become like Christ (and you will have your own unique definition of what it means to become like Christ). I will do the Exercises perfectly. I will do the morning time, the afternoon examen, the evening examen, the journaling—I will do it all; I will *not* miss a day. Expectations soon become a master who evaluates you. This will drain the life out of you and your experience as you journey through the Exercises.

So, you will come to the Exercises with expectations. That is not the issue. The issue is when these expectations become the voice to which you listen. Each day, as you come before God, name your expectations and let them go. Then seek to be open to God, prepared to enter into whatever God has for you that day.

SPIRITUAL DIRECTOR OR LISTENER

The true benefit of having a spiritual director or listener is proportionate with the level of your honesty and openness with that person. Do not try to look spiritual or good, but purpose to be real and truthful with your spiritual director or listener. It is when you are authentic in these encounters that you will reap the value that they are able to bring to you and your journey.

NOONTIME AND EVENING EXAMEN

Because the prayer of examen is such an important component and because so many people find it difficult to make the examen a part of their daily journey through the Exercises, find creative ways to remind yourself to do the prayer of examen. It may be easy to remember at lunchtime, but evening can be more difficult. I have found it helpful to write *examen* in big letters with a bright marker on the front of a 3-by-5 card and to write the examen questions on the back. I then place the card on my pillow or nightstand each day, so I remember my evening prayer of examen.

One suggestion that has been helpful to many is to put a sticky note on the mirror where you brush your teeth. Or set the alarm on your cell phone before you go to bed, or put a reminder on the refrigerator or on your computer screen saver. Another way is to pick an activity you do most nights and link the examen to the beginning or completion of that activity. For example, plan to do examen after you change out of your work clothes, finish dinner or clear the table, or before you watch television in the evening.

BABY STEPS

When a baby begins to walk, we celebrate each step and overlook each fall. With small children, we understand that beginnings are difficult and seek to encourage rather than condemn. This is the attitude I suggest you bring to the Exercises: start small and build on those initial small successes. I am a big fan of "something is better than nothing." For example, doing the noontime and evening examen once a week is better than doing it no times a week. One of my favorite G. K. Chesterton quotes is, "Anything worth doing is worth doing poorly."

Give yourself grace; be patient with yourself as you journey through the Exercises. Celebrate the baby steps of improvement. The journey on which you are embarking is not easy, so do not expect yourself to do it perfectly. Give yourself permission to start small and grow. This baby-step mindset helps you to enter into the Exercises freely and lightly, and helps you to escape the stress to perform and do it right (whatever "do it right" means). The stress to do it right works against you, while the baby-step attitude promotes ongoing excitement, joy and desire.

RESISTANCE

Pay attention to the resistance that arises within as you journey through the Exercises. It can be experienced as a feeling of not wanting to do the Exercises, as not liking the passage that will be the focus for that day, as a fear that surfaces around a theme or even as a sense that you are not able to believe or enter into a component of the Exercises. This resistance may arise within you for a variety of reasons. When it does, your tendency may be to want to run from it or ignore it, which is the way most people deal with resistance. The tip is this: when you sense resistance during the Exercises, pay attention to it and explore where it is coming from or what is giving birth to it. Resistance is not something to run from or ignore.

Your resistance will likely generate feelings of inadequacy—"I can't do this right"—or insecurity—"I am not ready to do these Exercises." These feelings are not helpful, so when you notice resistance, welcome it as a friend and sit down with it, exploring it rather than getting sucked into your negative and unhelpful feelings. Ask yourself questions such as, What am I feeling? Where is this coming from? What does this tell me about my belief and feelings about God and myself? You see, resistance is the doorway that will lead you to greater freedom and to new discoveries of yourself and the Divine.

Resistance is a gift from God, a gift to embrace, be open to and to explore. Resistance is a friend to welcome in, sit and talk with and learn from. Do not fear resistance. Do not let resistance get you down. Resistance is a good and powerful tool used by God for your transformation, so please choose to embrace it and explore it.

DISCIPLINE

Many people who are attracted to the Spiritual Exercises of Ignatius believe it will help bring discipline to their time with God, a discipline that they have not had before or had in some form at one time and wish to regain. If that is you, beware. You see, there is a reason you do not have a disciplined time with God, and although the Exercises will provide structure, they will also be a struggle for you and possibly even a source of frustration. Just know this and be ready to extend grace to yourself and to resist the temptation to condemn yourself or give up.

UPS AND DOWNS

Here's another tip—a heads-up, really: your experience in the Exercises will be an up-and-down affair. You will have good and wonderful times; God's presence at times will seem close and intimate, and the hour will pass in what seems like a moment. And you will have times when God will feel distant; the clock will seem as if it is not moving at all, and you will wonder how you will make it through the exercise for that day. This is normal. In fact, if these ups and downs are not happening, something is wrong.

EMOTIONS

Be aware of what you are feeling about God, yourself and the exercise of the day. We are often taught to ignore our emotions, but Ignatius found that our emotions are an aid to us in our spiritual formation. As you pay attention to your emotions and unpack them, you will learn more about yourself and your image of God in the process. Your emotions will prove to be an excellent source of material for journaling.

PROCESS, NOT EVENT

I liken the Spiritual Exercises experience to the gestation process. Something is always happening in the womb; growth and transformation are taking place; the baby is, and yet is also becoming. During the Exercises, God is deeply at work within the depths of your being. There may be times when you experience the movement of life within or the discomfort of internal growth as it develops and takes shape, but for the most part, it will be hard to gauge or ascertain what is actually taking place until the process has reached completion. And that will take some time. My tip: do not be tempted to evaluate the value of the Exercises based on your daily experience, good or bad. Your daily experience in the Exercises is not an accurate picture of the work God is doing within you and the transformation that is taking place.

DAILY JOURNEY, NOT DESTINATION

This emphasis on the daily journey may seem to conflict with the above tip, but I assure you it does not. The focus is not on evaluation but on the journey itself. This journey you are on is a long and at times arduous one. It is a marathon, not a sprint. Because of this, it can be discouraging, even overwhelming. When I rode my bicycle across the United States, I found that after a hard day it was easy to get discouraged and be tempted to give up, especially when I focused on how much farther I had to go. But when I could be thankful for the completion of another day of riding, no matter whether it had been easy or hard, it put me into a better mindset for the next day. It helped me to enter each day into the "now" of the journey and to enjoy the beauty and meet the challenges of that day.

The words of Jesus, "Therefore do not worry about tomorrow. . . . Each day has enough trouble of its own" (Mt 6:34), are apt for our topic. Do not get ahead of yourself and do not focus on how much further you still need to travel on this spiritual journey through the Exercises. Instead, enter fully into each day of the Exercises, paying special attention to the invitations and challenges God may bring your way. A focus on the finish line can cause you to become blind to the reality of the now, the presence of God, and what God may be inviting you into or challenging you with in this moment.

JOURNALING

Journaling is a powerful tool for helping you to capture, explore and deepen your experience with God through the Exercises. Your journaling does not have to be confined to words and sentences. (Please take a look at p. 32, where you will find journaling discussed in depth.)

BE PREPARED

This is a good motto not just for Boy Scouts but also for you as you begin and continue your journey through the Exercises. There are a number of ways to "be prepared."

1. Gather your materials (Bible, journal, pens, book) beforehand. Keeping all this together in a box or on a table can be helpful. This may seem unnecessary, but it will help you to jump in and get started if you don't have to gather your things.

2. Have the space in which you are going to do the Exercises free from things that tend to distract you, such as letters, bills, books, music or people. Also remove and silence all phones. This will help you to focus throughout your time in the Exercises.

3. As you arrive in your "space," prepare yourself spiritually, mentally and emotionally to enter into the Exercises. Prayerfully quiet yourself before God.

4. Read tomorrow's passages the night before, as you are getting ready to go to sleep. This puts the passages in your mind and gives God a chance to stir up thoughts and feelings as you sleep. This is an especially good practice to employ if you are choosing to do the Exercises in the morning.

5. If you are seeking to get up early to do the Exercises each morning, be intentional about getting to bed early. For me, staying up late

makes it extra difficult to get up early and do the Exercises, especially when the air is chilly.

BIBLE TRANSLATION

This can be a touchy tip: do not use your regular Bible for your time in the Exercises. Your regular Bible tends to be full of you: your underlining, your handwritten notes in the margin, and your papers—old church bulletins, sermon outlines, notes—stuffed throughout its pages. These can distract you from the daily focus or offer you a way of escape when you encounter difficulties during your time in the Exercises.

Now I will take this one step further: consider using a different translation than the one you are accustomed to. Some people know the words and vocabulary of their translation so well and are so familiar with the wording of the narratives, especially the narratives of Jesus' life, that they no longer read the words but go through the passage in autopilot. When you use a translation you are not familiar with, you may be surprised, caught off-guard and even made uncomfortable with the new wording you come across. These are all good things.

If you really like your current translation and are not willing to give it up, I suggest that you get a second Bible of a different translation. Each time you read a passage, do so in both your preferred and the new translation. The bottom line is this: I urge you *not* to use your current Bible exclusively.

FAITHFULNESS AND TIME

Each day you are asked to spend fifty to seventy-five minutes in the Exercises. Please purpose to spend that entire time. Some days will be easy, while others may be extremely difficult, but either way, put in the time. If you are having trouble, change it up: take a walk as you spend your time in the morning, or put your head down and even allow yourself to doze off. By your presence, you are saying to God, "I am here. I desire to be with you and to hear from you." What you are doing each day as you enter the Exercises is exactly what Paul encouraged believers: present ourselves as a living and holy sacrifice, or gift, to God (Rom 12:1). That is *always* a good thing.

I have been writing a lot about putting in the time even when it is difficult to do so, but another tip: stop at the end of the allotted time. Without this time limit, the Exercises can be twisted to work against your other commitments. Ignatius suffered through this experience when his times with God began to take time from the very things God had called him to do. So be aware that this could happen, and stop after the allotted fifty to seventy-five minutes.

When you faithfully present yourself to God as a gift, each of your times with God will be "successful." You will have honored God and by your presence will have declared to God, "I want to know you, hear from you and be with you." When you come into God's presence that way, day after day after day, you will be transformed. Put in the time and be faithful, and the God who is faithful will work within you in ways beyond anything you could ever think, ask or imagine.

REPETITION OR REVIEW DAYS

These days are not days off. Rather, these days, which will occur once or twice each week, afford you the opportunity to revisit and go deeper with God in an area of your choosing. These can be powerful times of revelation and discovery.

OPTIONAL EXERCISES

The optional exercises are just that: optional. It is entirely up to you to choose if you will do them or not. They are usually a bit different from the regular exercises and are designed to stretch and challenge you in terms of your definition of prayer and what it means to spend time with God. I encourage you to give one a try from time to time. You may be surprised how God will use these optional times, especially when they take you outside your comfort zone. If you do choose to do an optional exercise, have fun with it. Do not get stressed over doing it right; simply enter into it with an attitude of openness and playfulness.

WEBSITE

You may want to make use of the Metamorpha website (www.meta

morpha.com), which has an area set aside to assist those journeying through the Spiritual Exercises using this book.

FINAL TIP

The tips in this chapter are provided to aid you rather than to act as a bag of clubs with which to beat yourself. This is a list you can return to from time to time as you internalize the rhythm of the Exercises. You may even reach the end of your journey and realize you have not incorporated a number of these tips. That's okay! God will still have used the Exercises to mold, shape and transform you into the image of Jesus.

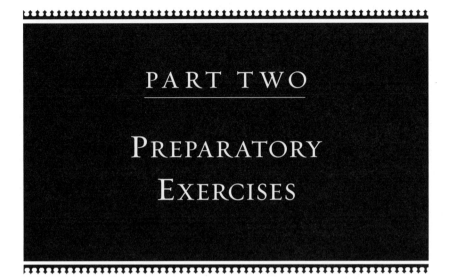

PART TWO

PREPARATORY
EXERCISES

THE HISTORY OF
PREPARATORY EXERCISES

THE PREPARATORY EXERCISES ARE DESIGNED TO prepare you to enter into the formal Exercises from a place of greater spiritual health and wholeness. Because Ignatius experienced how arduous this journey can be and witnessed the same in many of those he led through the Exercises, he felt strongly that individuals must be adequately prepared to enter into the Exercises. Ignatius did not allow one of his earliest followers, Pierre Favre, to enter the Exercises until four years after Pierre first requested to do so, because he did not feel Pierre was ready.

These Preparatory Exercises are a time for your own personal and spiritual preparation, a time for making sure you can enter into the formal Exercises in a way that will lead to health and wholeness. If this groundwork is not laid, your practice of the Exercises can become a time of morbid introspection that can stir up a whirlpool of self-doubt and condemnation. This can lead to shame and self-condemnation rather than spiritual health, wholeness and freedom, which are hallmarks of the Ignatian experience. These Preparatory Exercises are extremely important for those who struggle with shame, self-doubt, self-condemnation and perfectionism, which we all do to some degree. As you begin your journey through the Exercises, you must have a positive sense of whom God is, especially before beginning what is commonly referred to as Week 1.

I cannot state emphatically enough that the Preparatory Exercises are not an added hoop to jump through to earn the right to enter into the Exercises. The Preparatory Exercises are a critical component, grounding you in the essential, heartfelt understanding and experience needed. Do not skip these or skirt over them.

There are two pieces that together form the Preparatory Exercises. The first piece, God's love, focuses on the internalization of God's love by transforming it from a theological construct you mentally assent to into a heart-felt reality that pulsates through the veins of your being. The second piece of the Preparatory Exercises, the Principle and Foundation, exposes you to the theological realities that form the foundation of the Exercises.

This first part of the Preparatory Exercises, focusing on God's love, arose out of a desire to better prepare you for entry into the entirety of the Exercises in general, but specifically into the rigors of Week 1. In Week 1, you will be invited to come face to face with your own sin and brokenness, which can be devastating apart from an internalized sense of God's unconditional, one-of-a-kind love for you. This section on God's love is also a result of Ignatius's emphasis on the need for those who enter into the Exercises to have great courage and generosity toward their Creator and Lord. These attitudes of courage and generosity naturally arise from an internalized belief in the never-ending, unconditional love of God; therefore it is important that you have truly internalized this belief.

Finally, these first exercises were included because as I have taken individuals through the Exercises, I have found that many people truly believe God loves everyone, but in their heart of hearts they doubt that God could truly love them just as they are. Though prevalent, this inability to internally embrace God's love while journeying through the Exercises multiplies the likelihood of shipwreck on the rocks of shame, guilt and self-condemnation. The goal of these next few weeks is to help you to internally know in a deeper and more profound way—heart-know, not just head-know—the height, depth, width and breadth of God's love for you.

Spending a few weeks sitting in God's love may seem like a wonderfully desirable opportunity, but I forewarn you that this may not be your experience. I have found that, for many, these daily prayer sessions can be very trying. You see, it is one thing to believe "God loves me" and quite another to spend twenty-one days pondering, reflecting on and exploring this truth. When some individuals journey through this time, anger begins to arise within them as they recall critical times when they did not experience God's love or caring presence. These individuals begin to wrestle with questions: Does God really love me? If God loves me, why don't I feel God's love? If God loves me, why did _____ happen to me?

If you are one of those who feels these questions arising within you, along with emotions that often accompany these kinds of questions, such as anger, sadness and frustration, do not be afraid to bring all this before God. In fact, read the verses and/or quotes for each day, and then share your feelings and questions with God. Do not try to force yourself to feel a certain way, but instead allow yourself to feel what you are feeling and to bring that to God, because that will be the place where God meets you. God is not afraid of your questions or emotions. God wants to meet you in the midst of them. Remember, God desires honesty, so be honest and be real with God.

The following daily prayer sessions on God's love are very important, not only as you continue through the Exercises but also as you seek to know and follow God all the days of your life. During the next couple of weeks, you will be sitting in, soaking in and pondering God's love so that you will know it, rely on it and live in it (1 Jn 4:16). Before moving on to the second installment of the Exercises (Principle and Foundation), make sure you have come to an internalized sense of God's love for you. There is nothing wrong with going through this preparatory section more than once before moving on. It is also not a problem to return to this section later as you continue through the Exercises.

This section on God's love will help to surface issues you may have with God concerning your ability to trust God and internally embrace God's love for you. It will also help develop some of the disciplines necessary to help make the Exercises the life-shaping and life-transforming experience it was designed to be and has been for almost five hundred years.

You are about to begin an incredible journey with God, with Jesus and with the Holy Spirit. The goal is not to get through the Exercises but to enter into the Exercises, to be open and honest with God and yourself, to be willing to embrace the good times and the difficult times, to purpose to explore the times of inner harmony and internal resistance, welcoming both as a friend and as a doorway to personal and Divine discovery. Let the journey begin.

"RULES OF DISCERNMENT" INSIGHTS

Before you begin your time in the Exercises, familiarize yourself with the Rules of Discernment for Week 1 (see p. 109). Ignatius provided these rules to help people deal with the inner movements that arise as they journey through the Exercises. The first set of Rules of Discernment was designed by Ignatius for those who are just beginning the Exercises. He refers to this section as "rules for perceiving and knowing in some manner the different movements which are caused in the soul."

Ignatius provides definitions on the inner movements of consolation and desolation:

> Consolations are interior movements in the soul generated by an in-flamed love for God. A consolation can result from sorrow for one's sins, passion for Christ, increases in hope, faith, love or joy. In short, a consolation is anything that causes your intention to be focused on God.
>
> Desolations involve all that is contrary to consolations, such as darkness of the soul, internal uneasiness, agitations and temptations, feeling hopeless, and so on. In short, a desolation is anything that takes away from your attention and focus on God.

As you continue through your daily times of meditation, be aware of your internal movements, seeking to determine if they are consolations (leading you to God) or desolations (leading you away from God). Make note of your internal movements in your journal. Remember, the determining factor in discerning consolation from desolation is not your emotions or feelings, but rather the direction in which your heart is pointed (toward God or away from God).

OPTIONAL EXERCISE

The blanket exercise is designed to give you a tangible reminder of how God's love surrounds and embraces you every moment of every day. Use this optional exercise in conjunction with any of the exercises during the preparatory prayer sessions.

The only thing you will need for this optional exercise is a warm, cozy blanket. As you sit down to do your daily preparatory exercise, imagine that your blanket is God's love. Simply wrap yourself up in the blanket as you imagine it to be God's love wrapping around you. Take time after you have completed the preparatory exercise for that day to simply sit with the blanket wrapped around you, focusing on always being surrounded by God's love. When you finish, journal about your experience of sitting in the awareness of God's love surrounding and embracing you.

Another way to use this optional exercise is to wrap the blanket around you and take a walk, once again reminding yourself that God's love surrounds you. As you walk around with this awareness, be sensitive to the feelings arising within you and pay attention to how you see the world around you. This is a great exercise for a cold, windy day or early in the morning around a lake, near the ocean or in a park. Feel free to use this once or twice during the preparatory section. You could also use it on a review day. When you are done with your walk, journal about your experience.

~~~

The information above could feel overwhelming, but do not worry; you will be prompted when to make use of components listed above. I have provided them so you are not caught off-guard when they make their appearance during the daily exercises and to provide additional information regarding these components, without interrupting the flow of the Exercises.

As you enter into and journey through the following exercises, my prayer for you is this:

I pray that God in God's glorious grace would strengthen you with power, so that you who are rooted and established in love may be able to internally grasp and hold onto the width, the length, the height and the depth of Jesus' love for you—not only to know this love but to live a life informed, shaped and sustained by the magnificent love that Jesus has for you. (adapted from Eph 3:16-19)

GOD'S LOVE

The grace you are seeking is *a deeper awareness of God's love for you.*

Examen Questions
(the examen questions for the entire preparatory section)

- When and how did I experience God's love for me today?
- How did my awareness of God's love for me affect the way I interacted with others, my circumstances and myself today?

Process

☐ Opening   ☐ Closing

☐ Daily exercise   ☐ Noontime examen

☐ Journaling   ☐ Evening examen

Day 1. 1 John 3:1; 1 John 4:19

Remember, before you begin your time in the exercise for today, take time to slow down and be present to God. Come before God, letting go of your worries, concerns and expectations, seeking to be open to the moving and invitations of God this day. Do not rush through this time; take as much time as you need to ready yourself for your encounter with

God and God's Word. (See the three slowdown methods in "Slowing Down" on p. 26.)

Neither knowing God nor knowing self can progress very far unless it begins with a knowledge of how deeply we are loved by God. Until we dare to believe that nothing can separate us from God's love—nothing that we could do or fail to do, nor anything that could be done (has been done) by anyone else to us (Romans 8:31-39)—we remain in the elementary grades of the school of Christian spiritual transformation.

Genuine transformation requires vulnerability. It is *not* the fact of being loved unconditionally that is life changing. It is the risky experience of allowing myself to be loved unconditionally.
—*David Benner*

Exercise

Journal about your feelings and thoughts regarding the above passages and quotes. To what are you drawn? Why? Spend time sitting in the truth of God's love for you. After you sit in the thoughts of God's love, consider these questions:

- How does this make you feel about God?

- About yourself?

- Do you truly *feel* that God loves you (as opposed to just *knowing* the truth of God's love)? Why, or why not? Spend some time talking this through with God.

Day 2. Psalm 107:43; Ephesians 3:17-19

Exercise

Below are words various writers have used to describe God's love. Read through the list, sitting with and reflecting on each word. Come up with words of your own. Using these words, write a psalm or poem that celebrates and declares God's wondrous love for you.

Unfailing

Lavish

Extravagant

‡‡‡

Love, Anger,
Frustration and Sadness

Some who journey through this portion of the Exercises do not feel God's love but instead feel emotions such as anger, frustration and sadness. Do not try to force yourself to feel a certain way; instead allow yourself to feel what you are feeling and bring those feelings, as well as the issues that may birth these emotions, to God, because God will meet you in that place. God is not afraid of your questions or emotions. Remember, God desires honesty, so be honest and be real with God.

‡‡‡

Wastefully abundant
Wondrous
Indiscriminate
Boundless
Unconditional

You are the chosen one, the beloved of God!

- What is your reaction to this statement?
- Can you embrace these realities? If yes, how does this make you feel? If no, why is this difficult for you? Allow this to lead you into a time of prayer.

Spend time pondering the fact that you are *rooted* and *established* (grounded) in *love*. What does this stir within you?

Day 3. Romans 5:6-8

Exercise

- What does the above passage from Romans remind you of about the nature of God's love for you?

- What does this tell you about the unconditional nature of God's love for you?

- How do the truths of this passage make you feel about God and about how God loves you?

- What feelings are stirred within you as you reflect on the truth that God chose to demonstrate God's love to you while you were still a sinner?

- What does all this tell you about God's ability to love you and God's desire to love you no matter what?

Day 4. Review the past three days

- In the past three days, which passages were you drawn to or resistant toward? Why?

- How are these passages shaping your image of God and your sense of God's love?

- How has your awareness of God's love been changing?

You may want to use one of the optional blanket exercises today (see p. 61).

Day 5. Ephesians 2:1-5

Exercise

Spend time considering the spiritual reality of your life before and after God made you alive in Christ, as expressed in the passage above.

- What does this passage tell you about God's love, mercy and grace?

- How do the truths of these passages make you feel about who God is and God's love for you?

Day 6. Psalm 103:1-14

Exercise

Quickly compile a list enumerating at least ten of the benefits God

▲▲

"I *Believe,*
Help Me in My Unbelief"

As you spend time pondering the marvelous love God has for you, you may begin to realize that you "know" this, but at a deeper level you do not fully believe it. Do not let this trouble you, but instead repeat the prayer "I believe, help me in my unbelief." This is a prayer Jesus heard and answered. The love of God is a one-of-a-kind, nothing-can-separate-you-from-it love that is hard if not impossible to fully embrace, so give yourself time and grace as your ability to hold on to God's love for you grows. The good news is that God's love is always embracing you, wooing you and indwelling you.

▼▼

has bestowed on you as a result of God choosing and redeeming you. Once you complete your list, go back over it and choose the three benefits that mean the most to you. When you have chosen your three, sit in the reality of these truths, considering how they impact you emotionally. Then reflect on how these truths make you feel about God and yourself. Why did you choose these specific three from your list? Consider why each is so important to you. Spend time remembering "all God's benefits" bestowed on you.

Day 7. *Review this past week*

- Which passages were you drawn to or resistant toward? Why?

- How are these passages shaping your image of God and your sense of God's love?

- How has your awareness of God's love been changing?

Keeping in mind that baby steps are okay, ask yourself how many times you did the prayer of examen this week. If you struggled with the examen, what might you do differently next week to help you have more success with this component of the Exercises (see "Noontime and Evening Examen" on p. 46)?

Trying Too Hard

If you have been feeling yourself pressing to make something happen during your time in the Exercises, go out and buy a bubble bottle with a wand, and keep them near your journal. The next time you feel yourself pressing to make something happen, pressing to do each exercise "right," take out the wand and gently start blowing bubbles. As you blow your bubbles, watch them dance on the currents, and ask God to help you to enter these exercises freely and lightly, dancing on the unforced rhythms of God's grace.

SECTION 2 OF 3:
◠ GOD REALLY LOVES YOU ◠

There is an optional exercise for day 1. To do it, you will need at least one can of whipped cream. Please feel free to do this optional exercise on another day if you would like.

The grace you are seeking is *a deeper awareness of God's love for you.*

Examen Questions

• When or how did I experience God's love for me today?

• How did my awareness of God's love for me affect the way I interacted with others, my circumstances and myself today?

Process

☐ Opening   ☐ Closing

☐ Daily exercise   ☐ Noontime examen

☐ Journaling   ☐ Evening examen

Day 1. 1 John 3:1-2

I am convinced that God loves each and every one of us with depth, persistence and intensity beyond imagination.
—*David Benner*

Exercise

God's love is beyond our ability to fully comprehend. In the passage above, John uses a word translated *lavished;* God's love has been lavished upon you. The word *lavish* can mean "superabundance," "generous," "plentiful," "over the top" and even "wasteful." Spend time pondering the magnitude of God's love for you.

Optional Exercise

For this optional exercise, you will need at least one can of whipped cream, a coffee mug and a saucer. Imagine that the cup represents you, and the whipped cream represents God's love for you. Place the cup on the saucer and begin to fill the cup with the whipped cream. Continue to fill the cup until the can of whipped cream is empty. As you empty the can, remember that the cup represents you and the whipped cream is God's love for you. Be aware of what feelings arise within you as you empty the can and fill the cup.

- What were your feelings as you emptied the can and as you looked at the mountain of whipped cream and reflected on God's love being lavished upon you?

- How does this make you feel about God's love for you?

Day 2. Romans 8:38-39

> We have the formula of the spiritual life: a *confident reliance* on the immense fact of His Presence.
> —*Evelyn Underhill*

ↄↄↄ

Examen Review

How are you doing at making the noontime and evening examen a part of your daily rhythm? Ask yourself what steps you could take to make this a more regular practice as you go through the Exercises. (For tips regarding this, refer back to "Noontime and Evening Examen" on p. 46.)

ↂↂↂ

Exercise

Lie down and rest in the loving presence of the triune God. Close your eyes, and if you are outside, listen to the sounds of nature and feel the warmth of the sun or the cool of the breeze. Be still and know God, and know yourself as one loved by God.

Day 3. Psalm 32:1-5

Exercise

Spend time focusing on God's forgiveness of you. Let this lead into a time of thanksgiving. How does God's forgiveness of you make you feel toward God? Conclude your time confessing to God any sins of omission and commission.

Are you able to receive and internalize God's forgiveness of you? Why, or why not?

Day 4. Review the past three days

- Which passages were you drawn to or resistant toward? Why?

- How are these passages shaping your image of God and your sense of God's love?

- How has your awareness of God's love been changing?

  You may want to use one of the optional blanket exercises today.

Day 5. Mark 1:40-41

Divine love is absolutely unconditional, unlimited and unimaginably extravagant.
—David Benner

Exercise

Reread the above passage, and put yourself in the story as the leper. Imagine that you have been viewed with disdain and disgust all your life, that you have been and are an outcast. People turn away from you and keep their kids from you. You are viewed as one cursed by God. Now you come face to face with Jesus.

- What do you see in Jesus' eyes as he looks into yours?

- What does it feel like to be touched by Jesus, touched for the first time in years, touched by the One who can heal you?

- What does this touch mean to you, communicate to you?

- What does it mean to you that, while you are still a leper, Jesus feels compassion for you?

- How does this make you feel toward Jesus' love for you?

- What does this tell you about how God sees you?

- How does that make you feel about God, about yourself?

Conclude your time by talking with Jesus about the feelings that arose within you toward him as you imagined your encounter with him as the leper. Now stop imagining you are a leper, and go back to being you.

Is it more difficult for you to internalize Jesus' love for you as yourself than it is when you imagined yourself as a leper? Why, or why not?

Day 6. Isaiah 43:1-7

Exercise

Read the above passage as if it was written to you.

- What is God's message to you in this passage?

- What feelings arise within you as you read through it and hear to what lengths God is willing to go in order to be your God?

- How does this make you feel toward God?

Day 7. Review this past week

- Which passages were you drawn to or resistant toward? Why?

- How are these passages shaping your image of God and your sense of God's love?

- How has your awareness of God's love been changing?

Perfectionism

If you are a perfectionist or a recovering perfectionist, please be on guard. The structure of the daily exercises can tap into your strong desire to "do it right" and then stir up negative messages of self-condemnation when you feel you are not "doing it right." If you feel yourself stressing about this or you begin hearing internal voices that birth shame or condemnation within you, stop and ask God to help you be gracious and patient with yourself. These voices are not coming from God but are lies that will distract you and keep you from the journey.

SECTION 3 OF 3:
GOD REALLY, REALLY LOVES YOU

There is an optional exercise for day 5. There are no materials or preparation needed for this optional exercise. Please feel free to do this optional exercise on another day if you would like.

The grace you are seeking is *a deeper awareness of God's love for you.*

Examen Questions:

- When or how did I experience God's love for me today?

- How did my awareness of God's love for me affect the way I interacted with others, my circumstances and myself today?

Process

☐ Opening   ☐ Closing

☐ Daily exercise   ☐ Noontime examen

☐ Journaling   ☐ Evening examen

Day 1. Romans 8:1

Exercise

"There is no condemnation." Pause and let these words sink deep within you.

- What do these words mean to you?
- Are you able to believe these words? Why, or why not?

Make a list of the things that tend to birth condemnation within you. Read through your list line by line and after each entry, say out loud, "There is no condemnation for me in Christ." If you have trouble internalizing the truth of there being no condemnation for you, add the phrase "I believe, help me in my unbelief."

Which of the entries on your list are the easiest or hardest for you to internalize as the truth of there being "no condemnation" for you in Christ?

Day 2. Matthew 20:1-16

Exercise

As you read this passage, imagine you are one of the workers that were hired first.

What are your reactions to the day-end payments made by the owner? Why?

Now read through the passage imagining you are one of the final group of workers hired.

- What are your reactions regarding the payments made to the workers from the groups who were hired prior to you?
- What are your reactions regarding the payment you receive at the end of the day?
- What are your feelings toward the owner regarding the payments made to the other workers and to you?
- What is the difference between your reactions? Why?
- As a Christian, with which group of workers do you identify? Why?
- How does this impact your view of God and God's grace?

✚✚

Your Space

The space you use for your prayer times can be a help or a hindrance to your time with God. Choose a space that has a minimum of distractions. Keep all the materials you use together and, if possible, in the area where you enter into these exercises each day. These simple tips can make a dramatic difference in your ability to be present to God during your prayer time each day.

✚✚

Day 3. John 10:14-15

Exercise

Jesus chose to die for you. Spend your time sitting with and pondering this truth: *Jesus died for you.*

How does that make you feel about Jesus?

Reflect on what it meant for Jesus to come and die for you. Write a letter to Jesus, thanking him for taking your sins upon himself and dying for you. Read your letter while imagining Jesus is sitting across from you.

- What is Jesus' reaction to your letter?
- What, if anything, does he say or do?

Day 4. Review the past three days

- Which passages were you drawn to or resistant toward? Why?
- How are these passages shaping your image of God and your sense of God's love?
- How has your awareness of God's love been changing?

You may want to use one of the optional blanket exercises today (see p. 61).

Day 5. 1 Corinthians 13:3-5

Exercise

Since God is love (1 Jn 4:19), read the above passage, replacing the word *love* with the word *God, Jesus* or a title of God you especially like.

- What does this passage tell you about God's love for you?
- How does this make you feel toward God?

Share your feelings with God.

Optional Exercise

You are invited to come before God and express to God, through dance as prayer, your thanks for God's forever love and caring involvement in your life. I have found it helpful to wrap my "God loves me blanket" around me as I do this. It helps calm my insecurities (I am not a great dancer) and brings me greater freedom to express myself to God through dance.

Day 6. 1 John 4:16

> And so we *know* and *rely* on the love God has for us. God is love. Whoever *lives* in love lives in God, and God in him. (1 Jn 4:16, emphasis added)
>
> In order for our knowing of God's love to be truly transformational, it must become the basis of our identity. Our identity is who we experience ourselves to be—the "I" each of us carry within. An identity grounded in God would mean that when we think of who we are, the first thing that would come to mind is our status as someone who is deeply loved by God.
>
> —*David Benner*

Exercise

- What would it mean for you to rely on and live in God's love for you?
- How would your life be different if you were able to rely on and live out of a place of having internalized God's love for you?
- What keeps you from embracing your identity as one deeply and unconditionally loved by God?

Day 7. Review this past week

- Which passages were you drawn to or resistant toward this week?
- How are these passages shaping your image of God and your sense of God's love?

Review the past twenty-one prayer sessions.

- How has your image of God and your internalized sense of God's love developed during these sessions?

- How is your awareness of God's love now shaping your sense of self, God and your daily circumstances?

- How has your awareness of God's love been changing as you have journeyed through these prayer sessions? If you feel it has not changed or you are having difficulty embracing God's unconditional love for you, see the closing comments below.

Keeping in mind that baby steps are okay, ask yourself the following questions:

- How many times did I do the prayer of examen this week?

- How does that compare to last week and the week before that? Why was this week different?

- How has my experience of the prayer of examen changed over the past three weeks?

If you are still struggling with the examen, ask yourself why.

- What is making it difficult for you to make the examen a part of your day?

- Is it more of an external or an internal reality?

- How might you deal with the issues that have surfaced as you have explored this?

- What might help you have success with this important component of the Exercises?

CLOSING COMMENTS

If you are still having difficulty internally embracing God's unconditional, nothing-can-separate-you-from, one-of-a-kind love, I would suggest three things:

1. Choose to go through one or all of the preparatory sections again. I cannot stress enough the importance and life-transforming power of coming to a place where you know deep within the recesses of

your being that you are uniquely loved, valued and delighted in by God and that nothing—no thing—can ever change that. If all you do is spend an entire nine months seeking to internalize God's love for you, it will be time well spent. That may be the very thing God would be inviting you to do for those nine months.

2. Read two excellent books that will help you to internalize God's love for you, both of which are written by David Benner: *The Gift of Being Yourself* and *Surrender to Love*. I have read them each more than once and have been immensely helped by them. In fact, I give away *The Gift of Being Yourself* more than any book.

3. Talk with your spiritual director or listener about your difficulty embracing God's unconditional love.

Please do not feel that you have to move on to the next section. There is no rush to get through the Exercises. Remember, it is about the journey. Be open to the invitation of God to pitch your tent in the preparatory section for a while longer, sitting along the cool stream and in the spacious meadows of God's love for you.

Before moving on, this might be a good time to reread part 1, "Getting the Most Out of the Exercises." You might want to incorporate additional ideas from page 44: "Tips on How to Approach the Exercises," to help your experience in the Exercises flow more smoothly and to help you get the most out of your daily experience.

3

PRINCIPLE AND FOUNDATION

THE PRINCIPLE AND FOUNDATION IS THE second phase of your preparation for entry into the Spiritual Exercises of Ignatius. If you are tempted to skip the Principle and Foundation, don't. This section is the nuts and bolts of your preparation and, though not as initially attractive as focusing on God's love, it has a rugged beauty all its own that will serve you well, not only as you continue your journey through the Exercises but also as you continue your journey through life.

The Principle and Foundation provides the opportunity to expand your image of God while also affording you the chance to surface some of the issues you have in regard to your image of God. The first phase of your preparation was focused on God's loving involvement in your life and the truth that nothing can ever change that. With that groundwork in place, you are free to sit with and explore your image of God without fear and with abandonment.

In the Principle and Foundation, Ignatius brings you face to face with the fullness of God. You will look at God as creator and explore your own place in God's creation. You will spend time focusing on God as powerful, transcendent and worthy of praise, reverence, honor and service. God is a God of love, but that is not the whole story. The immanence of God that was stressed in the first phase of the Preparatory Exercises now gives way to God as transcendent creator and wholly Other, involved yet separate from creation. You will be challenged in your view of God and your role as one created by God to serve God, praise God and honor God.

The Principle and Foundation centers the Exercises within God's plan for those whom God created. The focus on God as creator is an apt reminder of God's initial and ongoing involvement in the world in general and in you in particular. This phase of the Preparatory Exercises serves to remind you that you are a creation of God "fearfully and wonderfully made" (Ps 139:14) and God's masterpiece "created in Christ Jesus" (Eph 2:10), while putting the twin attributes of God's transcendence (God beyond us) and immanence (God with us) on display. Your image of God will be dealt with implicitly from a variety of vantage points, as will the purpose for which you were created.

Finally, you will spend the entire last part of this section exploring the essential topic of indifference. The word *indifference*, when used in relationship to interaction with God, life and the world, seems out of place within a Christian context because it brings to mind callousness, an uncaring apathy that is not concerned about much of anything. To mitigate against the negative connotations, some writers have translated *indifference* in the Principle and Foundation as *balance*. Though understandable, I think this translation softens the term without bringing clarity to what it means in terms of the Exercises and life. You will ponder and explore indifference in section 5, but first I want to plant some seeds regarding indifference, trusting God to cause them to germinate and even begin to sprout near the time you actually get to that section.

Indifference, as used by Ignatius and other mystic writers, is not a lack of desire but a freeing of desire, and the developing of your ability to say yes to God and the expressed purposes of God. Indifference is about freedom to be and to live in a way that honors and affirms who God created you to be. A helpful way to think about indifference is that it involves a twofold freedom: freedom from those things that would hold you back from saying yes to God (disordered attachments) and freedom to say a more robust and resounding yes to God.

The indifference piece is a much misunderstood and maligned but significant component of spiritual formation and one worthy of taking the time provided in this section to fully understand and personally embrace. Many have commented on the invaluable benefits of spending seven prayer sessions unpacking and processing the concept of indifference. Their ability to understand and embrace God-honoring indifference was a life-changer.

As I have led people through the Principle and Foundation, I have found it to be a valuable time for allowing issues regarding their image of God to surface. Many were initially surprised by what they discovered but were able to process through it and left this portion of the Exercises at a better place with God and ready to enter into Week 1.

The Principle and Foundation is as follows:

> Human Beings are *created* to *praise*, *reverence*, and *serve* God our Lord,
> . . . for this it is necessary to make ourselves *indifferent* to all created things
> in all that is allowed to the choice of our free will and is not prohibited to
> it; so that, on our part, we want not health rather than sickness, riches
> rather than poverty, honor rather than dishonor, long rather than short
> life, and so in all the rest; desiring and choosing only what is most condu-
> cive for us to the end for which we are created. (emphasis added)

You will spend the next thirty-five prayer sessions exploring five key concepts found in the Principle and Foundation, which serve as final preparation for entry into the Weeks section of the Exercises. In the Principle and Foundation, Ignatius shares his answer to these questions: How did we get here (created by God)? Why are we here (praise, reverence and serve God)? What is a key attitude to cultivate to help us order our lives in such a way as to say yes to God in all situations (indifference)?

Summary of Principle and Foundation:

1. There is an original purpose (praise, reverence, service) established by the creator God.

2. Every created thing exists to help us to live into the original purpose(s).

3. We are to embrace that which furthers the original purpose(s) for which we were created and turn away from those things that hinder us from embracing the original purpose(s).

4. We are to keep ourselves free from a preference for the temporal

world so we are free to choose what enables and empowers us to say yes to God.

GETTING STARTED

Note that the "grace" will change with each new week, relating to the theme for that week. Make sure that each week you familiarize yourself with the new grace for that week.

The examen questions will also be changing almost weekly. They are crafted to reflect the theme for each section of the Principle and Foundation. Please take time at the beginning of each week to familiarize yourself with the new examen questions so you can make use of them during your noontime and evening examen.

Each time you get to a new section while making your way through the Exercises, there will be new pieces ("additions") incorporated into that section. These will be found under the heading "Additions to Exercises." It is important that you read these, because they are designed to help you more fully partner with what God is doing in and through the Exercises as you journey through them.

For this section, you will be incorporating the use of your senses. Ignatius strongly believes that you are to bring all of who you are to the Exercises, including your five senses. There will be more on this when you reach Week 2, but for now please seek to incorporate your senses as promoted in the exercises below. Do so while keeping in mind that you cannot force something to happen or "do it right." Instead, enter into the use of your senses freely, lightly and openly, recalling that all is a gift.

The Principle and Foundation is the last piece of your preparation before you enter the Weeks. As you enter into these meditations, earnestly seek to be open to God and the invitations of God's Spirit. Purpose to look at areas of resistance that arise within you (see "Resistance" on p. 47) as well as areas that resonate with you.

As you enter into and journey through the Principle and Foundation, my prayer for you is this:

God help this one to know beyond knowing and understand beyond understanding something of the depths of your riches, the incomprehensibility of your knowledge and wisdom, and the impenetrability of your judgments. In accordance with your grace help this one to be moved to praise, honor and service as he or she begins to glimpse your creative power, magnificent splendor and awe-inspiring holiness. (adapted from Rom 11:33-36)

⤞ SECTION 1 OF 5: CREATED ⤝

Earth's crammed with heaven
And every common bush afire with God;
But only he who sees, takes off his shoes;
The rest sit around it and pluck blackberries.
—*Elizabeth Barrett Browning, poet*

Let us leave the surface and without leaving the world, plunge into God.
—*Teilhard de Chardin, Jesuit priest*

The world is charged with the grandeur of God.
—*Gerard Manley Hopkins, poet and Jesuit priest*

The grace you are seeking this week is *the ability to internalize the great love, power, wisdom and faithfulness of God as revealed in creation in general and God's creation and re-creation of you in Christ in particular.*

Examen Questions

- When were you aware of the love, power, wisdom and faithfulness of God as revealed in creation today, and how did that impact how you lived (the choices you made) and interacted with others?

- What did you purpose to carry with you throughout the day?

- How successful were you in bringing it to mind from time to time?

- What impact did this prayer of recollection have on you?

Process

☐ Opening   ☐ Closing

☐ Daily exercise   ☐ Noontime examen

☐ Journaling   ☐ Evening examen

Special instructions: During your time this week, begin each day by pondering the passage for the day using lectio divina (see "Lectio divina" on p. 35). When you are finished, move into a time of using your senses as a means of connecting with and learning about God. You may want to know a day ahead what sense you will be exploring so you can be somewhat prepared to more fully enter into the experience.

Art Time

This could be a great week to get your art supplies out and have some fun during your journaling time using paints, markers, construction paper or other supplies to communicate your feelings, record the meaningful images that may arise or just to see what happens when you get artsy. Let go of the need to do it well or right. Jump in with both feet and see what emerges.

Day 1. Genesis 1:1-3; John 1:1-5

Use your ears to listen to the sounds around you.

- As you are quiet, what do you hear?

- Now listen to some music, to the chirps of a bird, a water fountain, children playing.

- How do your ears help you to discover God and draw close to God?

- How does hearing impact your heart and mind?

Day 2. Psalm 19:1-4

Use your eyes to take in creation. Take a walk and give yourself permission to stop and look along the way as things grab your attention.

- How does seeing impact your heart and mind?

- How do these things you are seeing speak without words to you about God and God's love and care?

Day 3. Genesis 1:27; Psalm 139:1-16

Look at your body, your hand, your foot, your eyes, and ponder how they work.

What do these tell you about God?

Day 4

There is no Scripture to read today. Instead, explore your sense of taste. Choose some things sweet, sour and spicy to taste and savor.

- How does taste impact your heart and mind?

- What does your ability to taste tell you about God and about God's love and care?

Review your past three days.

- Which verses touched you? Why?

- How are these passages shaping and strengthening your image of God?

- What has been your experience of your senses as a vehicle for connecting with God?

Day 5. 2 Corinthians 5:17

Initially spend time reflecting on being a "new creation in Christ."

What do these words mean to you? What feelings do these words stir within you? Why?

Spend a few moments leaning into your identity as a "new creation in Christ."

When you are finished, use the remaining time to explore your sense of touch. Touch a variety of surfaces. Explore how water makes you feel when it is cold, then warm. Go outside and pick up various things, exploring them with your hands. Take off your shoes and walk around, becoming aware of what you feel with your feet.

- How does touch impact your heart and mind?

- What does your ability to touch and feel tell you about God and about God's love and care?

Day 6. Ephesians 2:10

Initially spend time reflecting on being God's workmanship created in Christ Jesus, but instead of *workmanship*, use the word *masterpiece*.

As you think of yourself as God's one-of-a-kind masterpiece, what feelings arise within you? Why?

Spend a few moments soaking in the truth of you being a one-of-a-kind "masterpiece of God created in Christ Jesus."

When you are finished use the remaining time to explore your sense of smell. You might want to go to a coffee shop, bakery or garden to just enjoy the smells. Grab some things around your house, such as garlic, an orange, coffee or perfume, and spend time taking in the scents of each.

- How does smell impact your heart and mind?

- What does your ability to smell tell you about God and about God's love and care?

Day 7. Review this past week

- Which verses really touched you? Why?

- How are these passages shaping and strengthening your image of God, your image of yourself, your image of others?

- What has been your experience of your senses as a vehicle for connecting with God?

- How has focusing your attention on the creative power of God changed your awareness of God's transcendent power, immediate presence, love and care?

- How have your feelings about God begun to change this week?

✘✘✘✘✘✘✘✘✘✘✘✘✘✘✘✘✘✘✘✘✘✘✘✘✘✘✘✘✘✘✘✘

Resistance

Whenever you become aware of resistance, respond to it as a warning light and seek to discover the source of the resistance. Resistance is a gift from God that invites you to a deeper discovery concerning God and yourself, so internally pause and ponder when you become aware of resistance. Ask God to help you discern where the resistance is coming from. What does it reveal about your image, level of belief, love and trust of God? What does it tell you about your sense of self, your identity? Take the time to reflect and unpack your resistance, for over time the results can be life-changing. (See "Resistance" on p. 47.)

~~~ SECTION 2 OF 5: PRAISE ~~~

Looking ahead: On day 5 you will be invited to take a walk with God. Please plan ahead so you do not feel rushed. Also, feel free to switch day 5 with another day if that would work better for you (for example, do the walk on day 2 and then do day 2 on day 5). If you are able, take your walk at a time and place you enjoy (a park, the beach, a lake shore, on city streets).

There is an optional exercise for one or both of your review days. If you choose to do it, you will need a bottle of bubbles.

The grace you are seeking this week is *the ability to more fully and freely enter into the sacrifice of praise as you become aware of the character of God.*

Examen Questions

- When were you moved to praise God today?
- What prompted you to praise God today?
- What hindered you from praising God today?
- What did you purpose to carry with you throughout the day?

- How successful were you in bringing it to mind from time to time?
- What impact did this prayer of recollection have on you?

Process

☐ Opening ☐ Closing

☐ Daily exercise ☐ Noontime examen

☐ Journaling ☐ Evening examen

Use the lectio divina method as you read through the passage for each day (see "Lectio divina" on p. 35). Some days do not have written exercises (prompt questions), so on those days, sit with whatever God brings forth for you during time in the passage using the lectio divina method of reading.

Day 1. Psalm 96

Spend time praising God for who God is and for what God has done for you—past, present and future.

Day 2. Psalm 103:1-14

Spend time praising God for the benefits that have flowed into your life as a result of the death and resurrection of Christ.

Day 3. Psalm 136

Drawing from your life experience, write your own Psalm 136 by replacing the first line of each verse with an event from your own life. When you finish, share your psalm with God.

Day 4. Review your past three days

- Which verses really touched you? Why?
- How are these passages shaping or strengthening your image of God?
- What themes in these passages most easily move you to praise God? Why?

Optional Exercise

This exercise, which can be used today and/or on day 7, seeks to provide a reminder that God is your creator and that you are called merely to be in harmony with the winds of God's Spirit in your life.

Using a bubble bottle and wand, begin to blow bubbles. As you blow the bubbles, imagine the breath of God creating those bubbles and that those bubbles are you—God is breathing life into you. The wand is Christ, reminding you that all things were made in and through Christ. Now pay attention to your bubbles, watch them float and dance, and experiment with how you blow to create the bubbles.

- How are the bubbles like you?

- What do these bubbles teach you about yourself, about God and about you and God?

  Watch as the wind takes them.

- How is your life like the bubbles on the wind?

- What keeps you from floating on the wind of God's Spirit?

- How is indifference modeled by the bubble?

- How much responsibility does a bubble have in terms of its flight?

Day 5

Take a walk today, seeking to make use of all five senses together and individually. Allow creation and your senses to move you into times of praising God as you walk.

Day 6. Romans 11:33-36

Spend your time pondering the greatness of God. How does pondering God's greatness make you feel about God? Yourself? Why?

Day 7. Review this past week

- Which verses really touched you? Why?

- How are these passages shaping or strengthening your image of God and your love for God?

- How has focusing on praising God impacted your life and how you view and interact with your world?

Optional Exercise: See day 4 above.

Reminder

Remember to make use of your examen questions each day at noontime and evening. The consistent use of the examen questions will dramatically increase the transforming power of your life.

SECTION 3 OF 5: REVERENCE

The grace you are seeking this week *is the ability to be in awe of God.*

Examen Questions

- When were you wowed by the person of God today? What were the circumstances?
- What was your response? Why?
- How did that moment make you feel about God?
- If there was not a moment of being wowed by God, why do you think that was?
- What did you purpose to carry with you throughout the day?
- How successful were you in bringing it to mind from time to time?
- What impact did this prayer of recollection have on you?

Process

☐ Opening ☐ Closing

☐ Daily exercise ☐ Noontime examen

☐ Journaling ☐ Evening examen

Use the lectio divina method as you read through the passage for each day. Some days do not have written exercises (prompt questions), so on those days, sit with whatever God brings forth for you during time in the passage using the lectio divina method.

Day 1. 1 Chronicles 16:23-35

Day 2. Revelation 1:12-18

Day 3. Proverbs 1:7; 9:10; Hebrews 10:31

Day 4. 1 John 4:18

Day 5. Review your past four days

• Which verses really touched you? Why?

• How are these passages shaping or strengthening your image of God?

Day 6. Revelation 4:6-11

Imagine the scene and enter into it.

What are you feeling or experiencing?

Day 7. Review this past week

• Which verses really touched you? Why?

• How are these passages shaping or strengthening your image of God?

• How has focusing your attention on the greatness of God changed how you view and interact with your world?

⟫⟫ SECTION 4 OF 5: SERVICE ⟪⟪

The grace you are seeking is *the ability to own your role as one who serves others.*

Examen Questions

• When did you proactively serve others today?

- How did you feel when you decided to serve someone, as you served him or her, and after you were finished?

- Was there a time that you chose not to serve someone today? Why?

- As you reflect back on your choice not to serve someone, how does it make you feel? Why?

Process

☐ Opening   ☐ Closing

☐ Daily exercise   ☐ Noontime examen

☐ Journaling   ☐ Evening examen

Use the lectio divina method as you read through the passage for each day. Some days do not have written exercises (prompt questions), so on those days, sit with whatever God brings forth for you during time in the passage.

Day 1. Matthew 20:28

Day 2. John 13:12-17

After you have spent time in lectio divina with the above passage, meditate on the ancient prayer below that focuses on serving Jesus.

> Teach us, good Lord, to serve thee as thou deservest;
> to give, and not to count the cost,
> to fight, and not to heed the wounds,
> to toil, and not to seek for rest,
> to labor, and not to ask for any reward,
> save that of knowing that we do thy will.
> —*St. Ignatius of Loyola*

- To what are you drawn? Why?

- What are you resistant toward? Why?

- What might be God's invitations and challenges to you in this prayer?

- Do you have the desire to pray this prayer? Why, or why not?

Day 3. Romans 12:1-2

Day 4. Review your past three days

- Which verses really touched you? Why?

- Around which verses did you feel resistance? Why?

- How are these passages shaping or strengthening your image of Jesus?

- How are these verses shaping your awareness of Jesus' role, and in turn your role, in the lives of others?

- Does Jesus' role as a servant empower you to serve others? Why, or why not?

Day 5. Philippians 2:3-8

After you have spent time in lectio divina with the above passage, meditate again on the ancient prayer below that focuses on serving Jesus.

> Teach us, good Lord, to serve thee as thou deservest;
> to give, and not to count the cost,
> to fight, and not to heed the wounds,
> to toil, and not to seek for rest,
> to labor, and not to ask for any reward,
> save that of knowing that we do thy will.
> —*St. Ignatius of Loyola*

- To what are you drawn? Why?

- What are you resistant toward? Why?

- What might be God's invitations and challenges to you in this prayer?

- Do you have the desire to pray this prayer? Why, or why not?

Day 6. Ephesians 2:10

What might be the good works, which God has uniquely created you in Christ to accomplish?

Day 7. Review this past week

- Which verses really touched you? Why?

🛉🛉

Putting in the Time

One of the greatest and most consistent of the temptations that will come your way as you journey through the Exercises is that of cutting your prayer time short. In the Exercises, Ignatius emphasizes on two occasions the importance of spending the full time in prayer. This temptation to cut the prayer time short will be especially strong during times of desolation. But endeavor to spend the time, for it is of great value for your heart and soul.

- Around which verses did you feel resistance? Why?

- How are these passages shaping or strengthening your image of Jesus?

- How are these verses shaping your awareness of Jesus' role, and in turn your role, in the lives of others?

- Does Jesus' role as a servant empower you to serve others? Why, or why not?

Meditate another time on the ancient prayer below that focuses on serving Jesus.

> Teach us, good Lord, to serve thee as thou deservest;
> to give, and not to count the cost,
> to fight, and not to heed the wounds,
> to toil, and not to seek for rest,
> to labor, and not to ask for any reward,
> save that of knowing that we do thy will.
> —*St. Ignatius of Loyola*

- To what are you drawn? Why?

- What are you resistant toward? Why?

- What might be God's invitations and challenges to you in this prayer?

- Do you have the desire to pray this prayer? Why, or why not?

⋙ SECTION 5 OF 5: INDIFFERENCE ⋘

It is necessary to make ourselves *indifferent* to all created things in all that is allowed to the choice of our free will and is not prohibited to it; so that, on our part, *we want not* health rather than sickness, riches rather than poverty, honor rather than dishonor, long rather than short life, and so in all the rest; *desiring and choosing only what is most conducive for us to the end for which we are created.* (emphasis added)

The term *indifference* was an important term for Ignatius. Often *indifference* is used to speak of not caring about something or having a lack of passion. But for Ignatius, this word was a critical component that, when properly understood and embraced, led to freedom—a freedom to say yes to God and the invitations of God, and to say no to the those things that would draw us away from God. This freedom birthed from indifference is a desired outcome expressed by Ignatius. In his exercises he states the goal as the ability to order one's life in such a way that no decision is made resulting from a disordered attachment.

Reflecting on indifference, or as he refers to it, "detachment," Gerald May writes,

Detachment is the word used in spiritual traditions to describe freedom of desire. Not freedom from desire, but freedom of desire. . . . An authentic spiritual understanding of detachment devalues neither desire nor the objects of desire. Instead, it "aims at correcting one's own anxious grasping in order to free one's self for committed relationship to God."

According to Meister Eckhart, detachment "enkindles the heart, awakens the spirit, stimulates our longings, and shows us where God is." This freedom from attachment leads to a freedom of desire that is characterized by "great unbounded love, endless creative energy and deep pervasive joy," according to May.

For Ignatius, indifference (detachment) was for the purpose of spiritual freedom. The opposite of indifference for him would be a disordered love that would exert authority over an individual to such a degree that he would be incapable of choosing to say yes to God and to God's purpose for his life. Ignatius's Exercises are "structured for the purpose of leading a person to a true spiritual freedom. To grow into a freedom by gradually bringing an order of values into the lives of individuals so that they may find at a moment of choice or decision that they are not swayed by any disordered love."

As you spend this week reflecting on the concept of indifference, remember it is not saying no to desires but rather seeking a healthy balance where no thing has power over you. Indifference is about freedom to live the kind of life that at any moment can say yes to the invitations and person of God.

The grace you are seeking is the ability to identify those areas and desires in your life that hinder you from freely being able to choose God's purpose for you (praise, honor, service of God).

Examen Questions

- Look back over your day, seeking to identify the areas and desires that made it difficult for you to say yes to God. What were they?
- What is the source of their power over you?

Share your insights with God, asking for God's help and wisdom.

Process

☐ Opening ☐ Closing

☐ Daily exercise ☐ Noontime examen

☐ Journaling ☐ Evening examen

Use the lectio divina method as you read through the passage for each day.

Day 1. Philippians 4:11-13; Psalm 23:1

Spend time thinking through how Paul's contentment helped him to be able to embrace the strength of Christ in his life.

- What do these verses teach about the place and power of contentment (indifference, detachment)?
- Look at your own life. Can you say with Paul, "I have learned to be content whatever the circumstances," or with the psalmist, "The

LORD is my shepherd I shall not want"? Why, or why not?

Ask God to show you areas in which you need to learn contentment and embrace indifference.

Day 2. 1 John 2:15-17

Meditate on the following phrases, asking God to speak to you regarding struggles you may be having in any of these areas. Journal insights God gives you. Conclude this time with a prayer of commitment to respond to the insight(s) God has given you during this time.

- Do not love the world or anything in the world.
- If anyone loves the world, the love of the Father is not in him.
- the cravings of sinful man
- the lust of his eyes
- the boasting of what he has and does
- comes not from the Father but from the world
- The world and its desires pass away.

Day 3. Matthew 6:19-25

> We cannot see things in perspective until we cease to hug them to our own bosom.
> —*Thomas Merton*

Read the passage for today and consider these questions:

- What do you treasure?
- How do these treasures lead you to God or away from God?
- Who or what is your master? Explain your answer.

Spend time sitting before God, asking God what are you treasuring, depending on or trusting in that is taking your attention and your heart away from God and lessening your desire for God.

Read Matthew 6:25 and consider these questions:

- What are the things you worry about?
- Why are you concerned about those things?

- Why are they important to you, that is, what do they represent to you (such as security, significance, power, love)?
- What does this show you about your level of trust in God?

Spend time prayerfully processing your responses with God.

Day 4. Review your past three days

- What have you discovered regarding the link between indifference and freedom to say yes to God?
- What have you learned about inordinate attachment and enslavement to the world? To self?
- What might it mean for you to "seek first the kingdom of God"?

Day 5. Psalm 63:1; Psalm 42:1-2; Philippians 3:8

Spend time pondering the level of your desire for God. Share your thoughts and feelings with God. Ask God if there is anything in your life that is quenching your desire for God.

Day 6. John 21:15-17

Imagine you are standing before Jesus, and he looks you in the eye and asks you, "Do you love me more than these?"

- What might *these* refer to in your life?
- Do you love Jesus more than these?

Julian of Norwich prayed that she would let God be enough for her. This notion is extremely challenging. Reflect on the following two questions, and journal your response.

- Is God enough for you?
- Can you be satisfied with just having God and not having whoever or whatever is being emptied out of your life?

Day 7. Review this past week

- Which verses really challenged you? Why?
- Around which verses did you feel some resistance? Why?

- What have you discovered regarding the link between indifference and freedom to say yes to God?

- What have you learned about inordinate attachment and enslavement to the world? To self?

- What might it mean for you to "seek first the kingdom of God"?

CONCLUDING COMMENTS AND REFLECTIONS

You have now completed the preparatory section of the Exercises. You have spent the past several weeks soaking in God's love and working through the Principle and Foundation. This section was designed to help you develop an *internalized sense of God as one involved and as one whose interaction with you is characterized by love, care and grace.* This awareness of God, which may not be fully developed, is nonetheless a critical internalized awareness for those continuing on into Week 1 of the Exercises.

Before choosing to enter Week 1, it is extremely important that you determine if you are in a spiritually healthy place in terms of your sense of God and self. You also need to be in a place where you have an internalized sense of faith and hope. Week 1 is one of the most difficult sections of the Exercises, and if you do not feel ready to proceed, feel free to go back and revisit the previous exercises.

Remember, the goal is not to reach the end of the Exercises, but to experience God in the midst of them. Therefore, it does not matter if you now move to Week 1 or if you spend more time in the Preparatory Exercises. What is important is entering into the exercises each day with openness to the invitations and promptings of God.

Take a day or two to work through the following reflection and questions before making your choice to enter or not enter Week 1. I strongly suggest that you work through this with your spiritual director or listener.

- Take time to think about God. What images of God come to mind? Come up with three to five images of God, and write them down. Now explore each of these images. Do they seem to have a predominantly positive or negative sense to them? Why?

- What is your internalized sense of God's love for you? Do you believe (not just give theological assent) that God loves you and accepts you just as you are in this moment? Why, or why not?

- Where would you place yourself on the following continuums?

positive sense of self   negative sense of self

|————————————————————————————————|

positive sense of God   negative sense of God

|————————————————————————————————|

strong faith   weak faith

|————————————————————————————————|

strong sense of God in life   weak sense of God in life

|————————————————————————————————|

strong hope   weak hope

|————————————————————————————————|

indifference   disordered attachments

|————————————————————————————————|

As you have interacted with the questions and worked through each continuum, what has been your sense concerning your view of God? Is it a more positive: God is there for me, loving and caring sense? Or is it more negative: God is against me, judging and demanding? Also, what is your level of faith and hope? Would you characterize the level of your faith and hope more toward the strong or weak end of the continuum? Finally, where are you on the indifference/disordered attachment continuum? Do you sense your desire to be free from disordered attachments in order to say yes to God is growing? Why?

As you honestly look at where you are in terms of God as well as your levels of faith and hope, *it is important that you are brutally honest with yourself.* If you do not have a positive internalized sense of God and a level of faith and hope that is on the strong end of the continuum, I encourage you to spend more time in the preparatory sessions.

Before making your final decision regarding moving on to Week 1, reentering the Principle and Foundation, or concluding your journey through the Exercises, speak with your spiritual director or listener, sharing your insights from the questions and continuums above.

If you are feeling like you are in a good place internally for moving forward, do one more thing: take time to recommit to your journey through the Exercises, pledging to give yourself wholly to God (as you are able). Seek to gain nothing from God, but rather purpose each day to present yourself to God as "your spiritual act of worship," which is "holy and pleasing to God" (Rom 12:1).

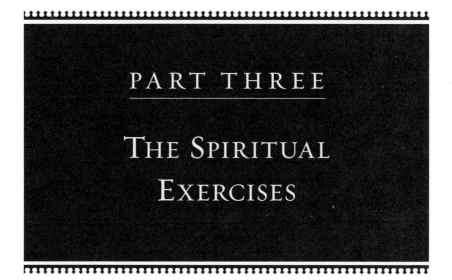

PART THREE

THE SPIRITUAL
EXERCISES

WEEK 1

SIN, ME AND GOD'S LOVE

You have now reached what is officially known as Week 1 of the Spiritual Exercises of Ignatius. The preparatory section was designed to equip you to enter this Week. *It is critically important before beginning this section that you have internalized the truths of the prior weeks.* You need to have come to a place that you know in your heart at an experiential level, not just a knowledge level, that God loves you, cares for you and stands with you. If this is not the case, return to the preparatory weeks, and work through those exercises again and/or read one of the books suggested at the end of chapter 2 before moving on (see "Closing Comments," p. 76).

If you feel that you have been able to internalize God's love for you, I welcome you to Week 1. As you enter this Week, you may be taken by surprise by its subject matter: sin. You will be spending time pondering the sin of the angels and the sin of Adam and Eve, and then you will be invited to take a look at your own sin. You will also be asked to ponder hell.

Much of the material in Week 1 is reminiscent of Ignatius's experience in Manresa, Spain. Manresa was the place Ignatius traveled to after making his profession of faith. He journeyed there to spend a couple of days praying and fasting before continuing on to secure passage to Jerusalem. These couple of days turned into an eleven-month period that God used to mold and shape Ignatius in incredibly profound and transforming ways—heart, soul and spirit. Later he would refer to this as a time when God taught him "like a little school boy." It was during these eleven months that he became deeply aware of and wrestled with his sin and brokenness.

It was a time of deep personal anguish, self-loathing and torment that ultimately led to great spiritual freedom. During that time he learned the power of detachment, humility and absolute trust in God. Because of his experience at Manresa, Ignatius had a strong conviction that *without a deep sense of your own sinfulness and your absolute need for the salvation rendered in Christ,* you will not truly be able to know and appreciate in a transformative way the cost God expended on your behalf.

So during this section, Ignatius takes you to a preconversion mindset in which you once again feel confusion and sorrow regarding the sins that led you to make the decision to turn away from those sinful choices and actions and turn toward God. These twin experiences of repentance (becoming aware of your condition as a sinner) and conversion (embracing anew your experience of salvation) will be entered into throughout this week. As you go through this section, you will be asking God for confusion (why did I and do I choose to sin?), intense sorrow and even tears because of your sins.

This remembering, examining and detailing of your sins and sinfulness can easily lead to desolation and despair. The exercises of Week 1 are designed in part to bring you to a place of feeling naked, vulnerable and sorrowful in your own sin, but you are not left there. Ignatius built into this week four particular prayer practices, referred to as colloquies (Latin for "little conversations"). These colloquies take you into the presence of God, Jesus and the Holy Spirit, seeking to tether you to their love for you and forgiveness of you even as you look at your own sin and sinfulness. You are invited to move into a consideration of the wondrous gifts of God's grace and mercy, which God offers to you as a sinner. For while you were still a sinner, God demonstrated God's love for you.

A series of meditations based on the Ten Commandments is provided to aid you in unpacking and naming your sins. These are given to help you get to a place of sorrow for your sins. The type of sorrow you are expected to experience is a godly sorrow, which brings repentance and leads to salvation while leaving no regret; not the worldly sorrow, which leads to death (2 Cor 7:10).

Please pay attention to yourself, asking yourself if these exercises are ultimately leading you to God or if you are getting stuck in feelings of shame and worthlessness that are sending you into a downward spiral of self-loathing and condemnation. If the latter is the case, step away from these exercises for a few days and make use of the alternate passages at the end of this section (p. 140).

The goal of this section is that you will be enabled to acknowledge and embrace the destructive nature of sin globally and personally as you also realize and embrace the transforming power of God's love, grace and mercy. As you reflect on your sin, you may come to realize that it wasn't your sin that drove Jesus to the cross, but Jesus' love for you that led him to the cross and kept him on the cross. Ultimately this section helps you fix your eyes on Jesus, the author and perfecter of your faith, "who for the joy set before him endured the cross" for you (Heb 12:2).

It is extremely important to be aware of your internal movements during this Week. Take time to ask yourself, *Where is my sorrow taking me?* If your sorrow is taking you into places of self-loathing, condemnation, darkness of the soul, internal uneasiness and feelings of hopelessness, this is not what God desires for you. It is a worldly self-preoccupied sorrow that leads you away from God and toward internal destruction. If your feelings of self-loathing, condemnation and hopelessness persist, talk to your listener or spiritual director.

If your sorrow for your sins takes you to the cross of Christ and ultimately to the assurance of God's love, grace, mercy and faithfulness, which is what the Exercises were designed to do, continue on through Week 1. But as you continue, be vigilantly aware of your internal movements. Ignatius himself got caught in the downward spiral of self-loathing, condemnation and hopelessness as he wrestled with his own sin.

Remember, the goal of this section is to purge from your life the lie that because of your sin you are unlovable. There is no need for you to continually try to prove you are lovable by doing things for God, by parading around as one without struggles, doubts and sin, to save yourself. You are a forgiven and beloved sinner. Keep yourself tethered to the truth of the unconditional, nothing-can-separate-you-from-it love that God has for you. This is the same truth you have been soaking in throughout out the preparatory section leading up to Week 1.

SUMMARY OF WEEK 1

1. Sin has historical roots (angels, Adam and Eve) and universal consequences.

2. Sin has had a grip on your life and has caused you and others pain and suffering.

3. Jesus loves you and died for you while you were a sinner and offers you forgiveness, grace, mercy and love.

4. Your sin can lead you to God/Jesus or away from God/Jesus.

5. Sin brings confusion and is an indication that you have turned from God to disordered attachments.

The grace you will be seeking throughout Week 1 is *the gift of a growing sorrow, even to the depth of tears (if grace so moves you) for all your sins, as well as confusion over your choices to sin in light of God's limitless love, grace, mercy and faithfulness.*

Resist the temptation to judge or evaluate your experience of Week 1 based on the amount of tears you shed or do not shed. Many people who journey through Week 1 do not experience the shedding of tears for their sins. There are a number of reasons for this, such as the personal history with sin, personality or theological upbringing. The bottom line is for you to enter into Week 1 as you are able, trusting God to guide and direct as God sees fit. Seek to trust God and trust the process.

EXAMEN QUESTIONS

The questions for noontime and evening examen remain the same throughout Week 1.

- How did your meditation on the destructive nature of sin impact how you lived your life today (choices you made, interaction with others, and so on)?

- When were you aware of the love, grace and forgiveness of God in your life?

OPENING TIME

This Week you will add an additional component to the beginning of your time in the exercises. This addition flows out of the Principle and Foundation section you have just completed. You are encouraged to come to prayer, conscious of the reverence God deserves while asking God that everything in your day may lead you to divine praise and service. This will be added to the initial activities leading you into your time in the daily exercises. Please feel free to place it where you feel it fits best. For the purpose of the book, it will be placed right before the slowdown.

COLLOQUY

As you begin this first Week of the Exercises, you will discover another addition: the colloquy. There are four colloquies for this section. The term *colloquy* is derived from the Latin word for "conversation." Ignatius describes the practice of it as speaking as one friend speaks to another, or as a servant to his master—now speaking, now asking for some grace, now confessing some misdeed, now communicating thoughts and feelings, and asking for wisdom.

Reciting the Lord's Prayer often follows the colloquy. As you proceed through Week 1, you will be instructed on certain days to conduct a colloquy as part of your prayer time. You will receive instructions regarding the what, how and to whom of your colloquy on the days it is part of your time in the daily exercises.

LORD'S PRAYER (OUR FATHER)

Do not rush through the Lord's Prayer; let yourself linger with each phrase. If you practice this way of saying this prayer, you will be able to make use of the Lord's Prayer in other areas of your life as a tool to center you and reconnect you with God, no matter your circumstances. Do not rush through your recitation of the Lord's Prayer, but give God the freedom to stop you along your way through the prayer. Just as with the Exercises, the goal is not to get through the prayer but to open yourself up to God through the Lord's Prayer.

SUGGESTIONS FOR PRAYER

In the course of giving instructions to the director, Ignatius provides seven helps for prayer. These are found in his Exercises 73-79. Please read through the following summary of the tips for prayer, and make use of them as you see fit.

1. As you go to bed at night, briefly call to mind what you will be meditating on during the following day.

2. When you awake, focus your thoughts on the subject of your meditation for that day.

3. As you enter into your prayer time, remind yourself that you are entering the presence of God. Do so with reverence and humility.

4. Experiment with different postures while praying, such as kneeling, sitting, standing or lying prostrate. Seek to choose positions that seem to be helpful in reinforcing your internal mood or capturing the feeling of the prescribed meditation.

5. After finishing your prayer time, take a few moments to review what happened during that time, such as consolations, desolations, fear, drowsiness, anxiety or boredom.

6. Seek to remain in the feelings that surface during the time of meditation.

7. As you are able, create an environment that helps to reinforce the focus of your meditation. Since the heart of your prayer times during the next few weeks will be sin and hell, keeping the room dark and avoiding the pleasantness of sunlight and the beauties of nature during your prayer time will be in keeping with the mood.

Once again, the above tips are given as possible aids to your daily times of prayer. They are not a list of things you are required to make use of, but I would suggest you experiment with these tips from time to time and see if they are at all helpful to you.

Use of the Anima Christi (Soul of Christ) Prayer.

Soul of Christ, sanctify me.
Body of Christ, save me.
Blood of Christ, inebriate me.
Water from the side of Christ, wash me.
Passion (suffering) of Christ, strengthen me.
O good Jesus, hear me;
Within thy wounds hide me;
Suffer me not to be separated from thee;
From the malignant enemy defend me;
In the hour of my death call me,
And bid me come to thee,
That with thy saints I may praise thee
Forever and ever. Amen

Although this prayer has been a part of the Exercises for centuries (first appearing in the 1576 edition of the Exercises) and is attributed by many to Ignatius, it actually dates back to the fourteenth century. This was most likely a prayer with which Ignatius had become familiar and which he found helpful during his spiritual journey, and thus eventually incorporated it into the Exercises.

RULES OF DISCERNMENT

Ignatius provided key insights for discernment for those journeying through the Exercises. He refered to this section as "rules for perceiving and knowing in some manner the different movements which are caused in the soul." Hopefully you have already familiarized yourself with these rules during your time in the Preparatory Exercises and the Principle and Foundation.

Even if you have already read over the rules for Week 1, as you were encouraged to do before entering into the Preparatory Exercises, I would invite you to do so again.

The material in Week 1 is capable of stirring up desolation, and so it is extremely important to have a keen awareness of Ignatius's insights regarding dealing with desolation and using consolation.

Overview of the Rules of Discernment. The Rules of Discernment resulted from Ignatius's experiences during his time convalescing at Loyola and his eleven-month sojourn in Manresa. The incident leading to Ignatius's need to convalesce at his brother's castle in Loyola resulted from his involvement in a battle at Pamplona, Spain (May 1521). It was in the midst of this battle that his leg was shattered by a cannonball. Eventually he was transported to Loyola where he recuperated from June 1521 to February 1522. During this time Ignatius began to turn his thoughts from being an earthly knight to imagining what following Jesus and the saints might entail. The following rules are a byproduct of when Ignatius alternated times of meditating on being an earthly knight, seeking personal honor and glory, and meditating on the lives of Jesus, St. Francis and St. Dominic. As he meditated he became aware of the impact that consolations and desolations had on him, and he formulated the insights he gleaned into rules of discernment.

The rules, which are probably best understood as principles, are divided into two sections. The first is for those just entering the Exercises. Its overarching focus is desolation—defining it as well as giving reasons for it and aids to combat it. The second section is designed for those entering Week 2 and beyond. Its focus is on the subtlety of spiritual attacks and the uncertainty that experiences of consolation are a trustworthy indicator of God's presence.

Timothy Gallagher came up with an excellent paradigm for understanding the role played by the Rules of Discernment in the life of the retreatant. He writes that these rules help the retreatant to "be aware" (noticing what is going on within), "understand" (whether this is from God or not) and "take action" (accept or reject what you have noticed and understood). This threefold paradigm succinctly conveys the goal to which both sections of the Rules of Discernment were designed by Ignatius to accomplish.

In these Rules of Discernment, Ignatius stressed the importance of paying attention to the emotional affect (inner movement) that arises as you journey through the Exercises. Ignatius's concern was not with the thoughts of the retreatant but rather with the affect beneath the thoughts. This emphasis on feelings is evident from the feeling terms in the rules that Ignatius used to describe consolation (joy, love, peace) and desolation (darkness, dryness, disturbance, lack of peace, absence of God). It is your feelings that will help to reveal where your thoughts originated, namely, the "good spirit" or the "evil spirit."

"Good spirit" and "evil spirit." There has been much written concerning what is actually represented by the good spirit and the evil spirit as employed by Ignatius in the Exercises. Those who write concerning this identify the good spirit as referring to God, the Holy Spirit and angels. This designation is generally agreed on.

The identity of the evil spirit has been much more problematic. Ignatius referred to the evil spirit as "the evil one" and "the enemy" or "our enemy." From this it would seem clear that Ignatius meant the devil. However, the question is, does this represent the entire scope of the term "evil spirit," or is there more to it? Did Ignatius's understanding allow for other factors to be included under the umbrella of the term "evil spirit"? The simple answer would be no; Ignatius did not see a broader scope to the term "evil spirit." This is not surprising, because Ignatius was a person fully entrenched in his own time and place. But if we change the above question slightly to *Would Ignatius allow his definition of evil spirit to be expanded based on the further knowledge of the inner workings of the human psyche?* I believe the answer would then be an emphatic yes! This yes reflects the elements of flexibility, adaptation and accommodation that are characteristic of the Exercises in particular and Ignatian spirituality in general.

In response to this, Gallagher writes, "The word further signifies the weakness of our humanity." In "the weakness of our humanity" Gallagher includes the flesh, with its desire against the Spirit, as well as the world around us (society, culture). I would add to this list the false self, "the lust of the flesh and the lust of the eyes and the boastful pride of life" (1 Jn 2:16 NASB).

Thomas Green, who would be in agreement with what has been written above regarding the expanded scope of the term "evil spirit," writes, "From the point of view of discernment we can take the 'evil spirit' of the 'devil' to mean whatever forces are working against God, whether they be 'natural' or strictly diabolical." For the purposes of this book, the evil spirit, the evil one and so on will refer to anything that seeks to take people away from following God's call or invitation in their life.

With the above background laid, it is time to focus on the Rules of Discernment for Week 1.

Rules of Discernment: Week 1. These rules are given to help you during encounters with the evil spirits during your initial time in the Exercises. Before diving into the Rules of Discernment, it is helpful to make some general observations. The major focus of the Rules of Discernment in this section is desolation. There are fourteen rules, of which six deal solely with desolation, two deal solely with consolation, three deal with consolation and desolation, and three deal with temptation.

Based on my experience with those making their way through the Exercises, the first few weeks in the Exercises can be a time of significant desolation and temptation. This may or may not be the case for you, but it would behoove you to be ready for this possible eventuality. Week 1 is a time of purgation, which can be very demanding. Taking the time to become familiar with the insights from the Rules of Discernment below can be very helpful as you begin your journey.

Note that Ignatius was not so concerned with the surface manifestation of a feeling or emotion but would encourage you to explore what is beneath that feeling to determine if it is from the good spirits or the bad. This is much more involved than a superficial inventory of what you may or may not be feeling.

The Rules

1. If the flow or focus of your life is away from God, you will experience the evil spirit as something positive, bringing you pleasures and delight, and you will experience God as harsh and stinging.

2. If the flow or focus of your life is toward God, you will experience God as positive, bringing you pleasures and delight, and will experience the evil spirit as harsh and stinging.

The key discernment insight found in rules 1 and 2 does not concern feelings but rather the flow of your life. Your feelings, though important, are not to be judged solely on face value but need to be interpreted in light of inner movements of your heart—toward God or away from God. Only when you are aware of this inner reality can you accurately discern what is happening. Because the easiest person to fool is always yourself, it is important to have a trusted spiritual director or listener to journey with you and help you discern.

3. Consolation is characterized by being inflamed with the love of God, growing in faith, love and hope, being strengthened and encouraged, interior joy and a desire to serve God and connect with God in all things. Ignatius also wrote that pain and tears may also be a consolation if these take you to the feet of Jesus, praising and worshiping God.

4. The affects for desolation are darkness, emptiness, slothful complacency, inner turmoil, sadness, despair, selfishness, rebelliousness, discouragement and feeling distant from God.

On the surface it would appear that when you are feeling good, it is consolation, and when you are feeling bad, it is desolation. But such a reading of these two rules is not congruent with what was stated in them regarding taking into account the flow of your life as an aid to deciding if your affect is pointing to consolation or desolation. Consolation is an outflow of your interior movement toward God, while desolation has to do with interior movement away from God, regardless of your feelings of pain or peace, comfort or confusion. Think of the focus of your life as being a computer screen. A simple way to remember the difference between consolation and desolation is this: consolation means that God is on the computer screen, while desolation means God is not on the computer screen. The critical question becomes not "what am I feeling?" but "who is on my screen?"

Rules 5 through 9 deal with desolation.

5. When in desolation (your life flow is away from God), do not change a decision that was made during a time of consolation (God was on your screen).

6. When in desolation, continue in prayer, meditation and the examen with more resolve.

7. Though you will feel alone and separated from God during your time of desolation, remember that God is with you.

8. Be patient in the midst of your desolation, knowing that this is not the end. God is faithful, and consolation will come in time. Also seek to determine the possible reason for your desolation. (See rule 9.)

9. Reason for desolation:

   a. You are lazy, careless, lukewarm or caught up in sin.

   b. It is allowed by God to show you how closely your faithfulness is tied to your experiences of consolation and greater graces.

   c. It is a gift from God to demonstrate to you that yours is not a causal, tit-for-tat spirituality. All is gift. Everything that comes your way as you pray is because of God's grace. This gift of dryness can be used to purge you of pride (I am making myself grow and experience God) and vainglory (I am great because of my experiences of God).

These last two reasons for desolation (9a, b) serve to remind you that desolation can be a gift from God that can become fodder for your continuing spiritual development and will equip you so you can continue on through the Exercises. It is important to determine the why behind your experience of desolation so you can respond accordingly.

Next Ignatius provided insight regarding what to do when you are experiencing consolation:

10. Garner strength from your consolation for your continuing journey, preparing for the time when desolation will come. Journaling about periods of consolation can help you during times of desolation.

11. Receive your consolation as a gift from God and not as a result of your spiritual striving or accomplishment. Endeavor to humbly accept the consolation while fighting the urge to think it was your own doing.

Ignatius concluded this section by delineating three ways that the evil spirits attack:

12. The first is the spoiled child. The evil spirit will whine, scream,

beg, make promises and pursue you relentlessly to give in to its demands. You need to stand firm in your resolve, employing courage and determination.

13. Second, the evil spirit will be like a secret lover: something is going on that only you know about. You need to bring your sin into the light of day; share it with your spiritual director, listener, pastor or a trusted friend. The power of that sin is linked to its secrecy and, when revealed, the power will be greatly lessened.

14. Third, the evil spirit is a brilliant military commander who will attack you again and again at two points: your personal weakness and places of internal complacency and spiritual pride. To withstand these attacks, you need a degree of self-knowledge and self-awareness, which can be cultivated through the daily use of the General Examen of Conscience, accompanied with the commitment to be absolutely honest and open with God and yourself.

The three lines of attack by the enemy outlined above can provide you with insights of how to combat them if you are willing to take an honest look at your own life to discern how you tend to be attacked. Take time to consider which of these ways you are primarily attacked, bearing in mind that there are often multiple modes of attack.

As you continue through the Exercises, you will struggle with desolation, times of dryness in prayer and attacks by the enemy. The above rules will help you to fight the good fight. Remember from these rules that, first, consolation and desolation have little to do with what you are feeling and much more to do with the direction of your mind, heart and spirit—if toward God, consolation, if toward the enemy and the deeds of the flesh, desolation. The key question remains: who is on your screen? Second, when in desolation, use the tools God has given you—the prayer of examen and prior consolations—and continue the course you have set by presenting yourself to God daily through the material found in the Exercises.

CONFESSION

At the end of this section, you are encouraged to make a confession.

The purpose of the confession is to acknowledge to another your grief and sorrow for your sins and revulsion over its consequences in your life and the lives of others. Please take time to carefully and prayerfully consider making a formal confession, in accordance with James 5:16 and 1 John 1:9. If you decide to make a confession, choose wisely the person to whom you will confess. Ask God to show you someone you can trust, someone who truly cares about you and will not judge or condemn you. Although this is scary, I strongly encourage you to step out in this way. Remember, confessing your sins is about acknowledging before God that you have done wrong and agreeing with God that, indeed, it was wrong.

OPTIONAL EXERCISE: THE JESUS PRAYER

Although the Jesus Prayer was not part of the original Exercises, I believe it fits well into this section. It can help you to maintain the tension between your own sins and God's love, while also helping deepen your ability to find God in all things. The Jesus Prayer is part of a larger category of prayers called breath prayers.

Breath prayer arose out of a desire to pray without ceasing. It is a short, simple prayer of petition that would be spoken in one breath, thus the name "breath prayer." Breath prayers are brief, seldom more than seven or eight syllables. They express love, dependency, meekness and trust. This type of prayer is a very helpful tool in refocusing your entire being back to God in a single moment.

The most famous breath prayer is the Jesus Prayer: "Lord Jesus Christ, have mercy on me." Later it was lengthened to "Lord Jesus Christ, Son of God, have mercy on me, a sinner." This prayer was derived from Jesus' parable on self-righteousness, in which the tax collector beat his chest and prayed, "God, have mercy on me, a sinner!" (Lk 18:13). It was used extensively in the sixth century, and in the fourteenth century it was revived in the Eastern church.

The Jesus Prayer involves turning aside from images and concentrating your attention on, or rather within, the words. It is not a hypnotic incantation but a heartfelt cry seeking a living connection with God.

The optional exercise over the next thirty-five days is to make the

Jesus Prayer a part of your experience. If you choose to participate in this, please endeavor to practice the prayer from time to time throughout your day. The Jesus Prayer will be an aid, reminding you of your need for Jesus and his mercy. Here are three forms of the Jesus Prayer:

- Jesus Christ, Son of God, have mercy on me.
- Jesus Christ, Son of God, have mercy on me, a sinner.
- Lord Jesus Christ, Son of God, have mercy on me, a sinner.

Remember, optional means optional. It is up to you if you make this a part of your experience during Week 1 or not. This practice has been found helpful for many with whom I have journeyed through the Exercises.

A final word of wisdom: Be on guard as you work your way through Week 1. As you seek to hold onto the seemingly contradictory realities of your sinfulness and God's love, and you sense you are landing on the side of your sinfulness, and feelings of self-condemnation are gaining a foothold within you, stop and refocus on God's unconditional love and forgiveness while reciting this prayer: "I believe; help me overcome my unbelief" (Mk 9:23-25). Jesus heard and answered this prayer.

The above section containing all the additions for Week 1 could be overwhelming to you, but do not worry; you will be prompted when to make use of the components listed above. I have discussed them first so you are not caught off-guard when they make their appearance and to provide additional information regarding these components without interrupting the flow of the Exercises.

As you enter into and journey through Week 1, my prayer for you is this:

> God, as this precious chosen one of yours walks through Week 1, coming face to face with sin, help him or her to remember your grace, bathe your beloved in your love and free her or him from the prison of guilt and shame, from which you have delivered this one by the shedding of your blood. (adapted from Eph 1:3; Rom 3:23; 5:12; Eph 1:7; Rom 8:1)

Exercises for Week 1

➤ SECTION 1 OF 5 ➤

The grace you are seeking this week is *the ability to experience sorrow, tears and confusion over your choices to sin in light of God's limitless love, grace, mercy and faithfulness.*

Examen Question

- How did your meditation on the destructive nature of sin impact how you lived your life today (choices you made, interaction with others and so on)?

- When were you aware of the love, grace and forgiveness of God in your life?

  Come to prayer, conscious of the reverence God deserves, while asking God that everything in your day may more and more lead you to divine praise and service.

Process

☐ Opening   ☐ Closing

☐ Daily exercise   ☐ Noontime examen

☐ Journaling   ☐ Evening examen

Day 1. Jude 6

Angels: the sin of the angels (led by Satan) involved a radical choice of self before God, a rejection of the very source of all life and love, a turning from God.

Spend time pondering the sin of the angels, letting its decisiveness and consequences strike deep within your heart.

†††

Be Aware

One of the struggles of Week 1 will be the tendency to enter the exercises intellectually rather than with your heart. This is understandable but not helpful. It is important for you to enter into these exercises emotionally so you can feel sorrow and confusion arise within you as you explore the pervasive reality of sin in the world and in your own life. It will be hard not to want to protect yourself from the pain this week may surface within you, but it is this pain that will take you to God and to freedom, and it will lead you to experience God's love in a deeper way.

†††

Consider how you have turned from God, rejecting the life and love God offers you.

Conclude by slowly reciting the Anima Christi (Soul of Christ) Prayer:

> Soul of Christ, sanctify me.
> Body of Christ, save me.
> Blood of Christ, inebriate me.
> Water from the side of Christ, wash me.
> Passion (suffering) of Christ, strengthen me.
> O good Jesus, hear me;
> Within thy wounds hide me;
> Suffer me not to be separated from thee;
> From the malignant enemy defend me;
> In the hour of my death call me,
> And bid me come to thee,
> That with thy saints I may praise thee
> Forever and ever. Amen

Day 2. Genesis 3:1-13

Adam and Eve: their sin is a direct rejection of God's love. They seek to escape the responsibility of their choice by blaming someone or something. Through their sin, we see the personal and cosmic consequences of sin.

Spend time pondering the sin of Adam and Eve, letting its pervasive and destructive consequences become fully present to your mind and heart.

Consider this: if one sin can wreak so much havoc, what about your own sins?

Day 3. Romans 6:23

Sin: an act that leads to separation from God, from life, from love, bringing destruction and death to all of creation.

Spend time thinking through the results of sin in the world, your country, your city, your family and your life. Glance through the newspaper or surf the Internet, and see the results of the destructive, corrupting power of sin.

Remember, the purpose of Week 1 is not self-loathing, condemnation or hopelessness but a deep awareness of sin in yourself and the world, along with a deeper appreciation and realization of God's love for you.

Day 4. Review your past three days

- How has meditating on the sins of the angels, Adam and Eve, and your own sin impacted your heart and your appreciation of God's love and grace?

- Have you felt sorrow, confusion, been moved to tears? Why, or why not?

Colloquy. Approach Jesus, and ask him for three favors:

1. A deep realization of the sin in your life and a sorrow for your sinful acts

2. An understanding of and feeling for the havoc in your life due to your sin and sinful tendencies, as well as wisdom regarding how to bring order into your life

3. An awareness of the ways in which the world actively and passively stands in opposition to Christ, so that you may distance yourself from all that is worldly and vain

Conclude this time by slowly reciting the Lord's Prayer.

Day 5. *Ephesians 2:1-3*

Your own sin: see yourself as a sinner, helpless and alienated before a loving and holy God. Let the sins (of commission and omission) and sinful tendencies of your life float through your mind.

Let the weight of your sins be felt throughout your entire being.

Reflect on the evil that has flowed from you, one among billions of people living on the earth. Feel the combined weight and horror of your sinful acts multiplied by billions.

Day 6. *Luke 12:4-5*

Hell: choosing to say no to God's love, turning away from God to self and rejecting the life and love God offers through Jesus is to condemn oneself to hell for all eternity.

Consider the number of times you have said no to God up to this point in your life. Spend time talking to God about those choices.

Colloquy. Spend time thanking Jesus for the love and mercy he has shown you throughout your life.

Conclude this time by slowly reciting the Lord's Prayer.

Day 7. *Review this past week*

- Which day's meditations touched you? Why?
- How did these meditations impact your heart and your appreciation of God's love and grace?
- Have you felt sorrow, confusion, been moved to tears? Why, or why not?
- Did these meditations increase your ability to make more God-honoring choices? Why, or why not?

You Are Loved

As you focus on your own sin and brokenness, remember that your sin does not define you. You are forgiven. You are a saint uniquely loved by God. If you struggle with this, pray this prayer: Jesus, I believe, help me overcome my unbelief.

⤙ SECTION 2 OF 5 ⤚

The grace you are seeking this week is *the ability to experience sorrow, tears and confusion over your choices to sin in light of God's limitless love, grace, mercy and faithfulness.*

Examen Questions

- How did your meditation on the destructive nature of sin impact how you lived your life today (choices you made, interaction with others and so on)?

- When were you aware of the love, grace and forgiveness of God in your life?

Come to prayer, conscious of the reverence God deserves, while asking God that everything in your day may more and more lead you to divine praise and service.

Process

☐ Opening   ☐ Closing

☐ Daily exercise   ☐ Noontime examen

☐ Journaling   ☐ Evening examen

Day 1. Joshua 7

The sin of Achan: Achan chose to disobey the commands of God and follow the inner voices of his own desires.

Spend some time pondering Achan's sin, letting its pervasive and destructive consequences become fully present to your mind and heart.

Pay special attention to Joshua 7:20-21, looking at the sequence of Achan's sin, then exploring your own heart. Are there things you are coveting, are there sins that you are hiding from God? If so, take some time to be open and honest with God.

Conclude by slowly reciting the Anima Christi (Soul of Christ) Prayer:

> Soul of Christ, sanctify me.
> Body of Christ, save me.

Blood of Christ, inebriate me.

Water from the side of Christ, wash me.

Passion (suffering) of Christ, strengthen me.

O good Jesus, hear me;

Within thy wounds hide me;

Suffer me not to be separated from thee;

From the malignant enemy defend me;

In the hour of my death call me,

And bid me come to thee,

That with thy saints I may praise thee

Forever and ever. Amen

Desolation

There is probably an up-and-down dynamic to your experience as you travel through the Exercises. Seek to continue your journey, spending your allotted time in the prayer times, giving special attention to praying the examen while seeking to discern what is the cause of your desolation (see rule 9 in the "Rules of Discernment" list above). When in the grip of desolation, it will be hard to continue moving through the Exercises, but that is exactly what you need to do, recalling to mind that this is just a season and God is faithful and ever-present, no matter what you are feeling.

Day 2. Genesis 3:17-19

Spend your time pondering the consequences of Adam's sin, letting its pervasive and destructive consequences become fully present to your mind and heart.

Consider this: if one sin can wreak so much havoc, what about your own sins?

Special instructions for journeying through the Ten Commandments: As you journey through the Ten Commandments over the next few days, ask God for the grace to know how you have failed to keep them and for a deeper understanding of what they most truly convey, so that you are better able to live in internal harmony with them. As you ponder each commandment, reflect both on how you have been faithful in living out the commandment and on how you have failed to live out the commandment. As you become aware of your failings, ask God for forgiveness. Conclude your time in the commandment by speaking intimately with God (colloquy), sharing with God whatever arises within you.

Conclude this time by slowly reciting the Lord's Prayer.

Day 3

Spend your time reviewing your life using the commandments listed below.

"You shall have no other gods before me.

"You shall not make for yourself an idol in the form of anything in heaven above or on the earth beneath or in the waters below. You shall not bow down to them or worship them; for I, the LORD your God, am a jealous God, punishing the children for the sin of the fathers to the third and fourth generation of those who hate me, but showing love to a thousand {generations} of those who love me and keep my commandments.

"You shall not misuse the name of the LORD your God, for the LORD will not hold anyone guiltless who misuses his name.

"Remember the Sabbath day by keeping it holy. Six days you shall labor and do all your work, but the seventh day is a Sabbath to the LORD your God. On it you shall not do any work, neither you, nor your son or daughter, nor your manservant or maidservant, nor your animals, nor the alien within your gates. For in six days the LORD made the heavens and the earth, the sea, and all that is in them, but he rested on the seventh day. Therefore the LORD blessed the Sabbath day and made it holy.

"Honor your father and your mother, so that you may live long in the land the LORD your God is giving you." (Ex 20:3-12)

- How have you lived them out?
- How have you gone astray?
- What has lured you away from God? What have you desired more than God? Why?

Colloquy. Approach Jesus, and ask him for three favors:

- A deep realization of the sin in your life and a sorrow for your sinful acts
- An understanding of and feeling for the havoc in your life due to your sin and sinful tendencies, as well as wisdom regarding how to bring order into your life
- An awareness of the ways in which the world actively and passively stands in opposition to Christ, so that you may distance yourself from all that is worldly and vain

Conclude this time by slowly reciting the Lord's Prayer.

Prayer Postures

If you have not yet done so, I encourage you to experiment with different prayer postures (kneeling, lying face down or face up, standing, arms raised, head bowed, and so on). Prayer postures can be an aid in helping us move from head to heart as we come before God. Also, with a prayer posture, you may be able to communicate to God what your words fail to convey. Give it a try.

Day 4

Spend your time reviewing your life using the verses listed below.

Honor your father and your mother, so that you may live long in the land the LORD your God is giving you. You shall not murder. You shall not commit adultery. (Ex 20:12-14)

You have heard that it was said to the people long ago, "Do not murder, and anyone who murders will be subject to judgment." But I tell you that anyone who is angry with his brother will be subject to judgment. Again, anyone who says to his brother, "Raca," is answerable to the Sanhedrin. But anyone who says, "You fool!" will be in danger of the fire of hell. (Mt 5:21-22)

You have heard that it was said, "Do not commit adultery." But I tell you that anyone who looks at a woman lustfully has already committed adultery with her in his heart. If your right eye causes you to sin, gouge it out and throw it away. It is better for you to lose one part of your body than for your whole body to be thrown into hell. And if your right hand causes you to sin, cut it off and throw it away. It is better for you to lose one part of your body than for your whole body to go into hell. (Mt 5:27-30)

- How have you lived them out?
- How have you gone astray?
- What has lured you away from God? What have you desired more than God? Why?

Colloquy. Spend time thanking Jesus for the love and mercy he has shown you throughout your life.

Conclude this time by slowly reciting the Lord's Prayer.

Day 5

Spend your time reviewing your life, using the these commandments.

You shall not steal.

You shall not give false testimony against your neighbor.

You shall not covet your neighbor's house. You shall not covet your neighbor's wife, or his manservant or maidservant, his ox or donkey, or anything that belongs to your neighbor. (Ex 20:15-17)

- How have you gone astray? What has lured you away from God?
- What have you desired more than God? Why?

It Is Not Happening

During Week 1 of the Exercises, some people get discouraged because they are not moved to tears because of their sin or do not feel like they are able to fully connect emotionally with their sinfulness. Be patient with yourself and trust God and the process. God is at work!

Day 6. 2 Thessalonians 1:9

Hell: choosing to say no to God's love, turning away from God to self, and rejecting the life and love God offers through Jesus is to condemn oneself to hell for all eternity.

Imagine what it would be like in hell as it is described in the above passage.

Colloquy. Spend time thanking Jesus for the love and mercy he has shown you throughout your life.

Conclude this time by slowly reciting the Lord's Prayer.

Day 7. Review this past week

- How has meditating on the sins of the angels, Adam and Eve, and your own sin impacted your heart and your appreciation of God's love and grace?

- Have you felt sorrow, confusion, been moved to tears? Why, or why not?

Colloquy. Place yourself before Jesus as he hangs on the cross. Talk to him regarding his love for you and his choice to die for your sins. While reflecting on your life, let these questions penetrate your heart and mind:

1. In the past, how have you responded to God's love, to the sacrifice of Jesus?

2. How are you currently responding to God's love, to the sacrifice of Jesus?

3. How might God be asking you to deepen your response to God's love, to the sacrifice of Jesus?

As you look at Jesus hanging on the cross, spend time reflecting on and interacting with Jesus about whatever God may bring to your attention.

Close this time by slowly reciting the Lord's Prayer.

***

Journaling

It is very helpful to journal through these exercises. Journaling helps you to see patterns in your prayer times, to recall what God has spoken to you. Often as you journal, God expands on what you have discovered or been made aware of. Journaling will deepen your experience with the Exercises.

***

✍ SECTION 3 OF 5 ✍

The grace you are seeking this week is *the ability to experience sorrow, tears, and confusion over your choices to sin in light of God's limitless love, grace, mercy and faithfulness.*

Examen Questions

- How did your meditation on the destructive nature of sin impact how you lived your life today (choices you made, interaction with others and so on)?

- When were you aware of the love, grace and forgiveness of God in your life?

Come to prayer, conscious of the reverence God deserves, while asking God that everything in your day may more and more lead you to divine praise and service.

Process

☐ Opening   ☐ Closing

☐ Daily exercise   ☐ Noontime examen

☐ Journaling   ☐ Evening examen

Day 1. James 1:13-15

What is the birthing process of sin conveyed in this passage?

Ask God to show you the desires and disordered attachments in your heart that tend to take you away from God and give birth to sin, death and destruction in your life. Confess to and grieve before God your ongoing sins that are birthed by the counterfeit fulfillment of the desires of your heart.

Forgiven and Loved by God

As you are looking at your own sin, recall to mind that nothing can separate you from the love of God and that there is no condemnation for those who are in Christ Jesus. If you are feeling condemnation during Week 1, it is not coming from God.

Colloquy. Spend time thanking and praising God the Father, Jesus the Son, and the Holy Spirit for the grace, mercy, love and forgiveness you have been given.

Close this time by slowly reciting the Lord's Prayer.

Day 2. 1 Corinthians 10:13; James 4:17

What do these passages reveal about temptation, sin and God?

Take a look at some of the past times of sin in your life, and ask God to help you to see how God was faithful in those times to provide you with a way of escape. Why did you not avail yourself of God's provision in those instances?

Ask God for help in the future to take the ways of escape that God graciously provides for you.

Think back over your life in the past few months, and ask God to show you when you knew the "good thing" to do and did not do it. What led to your decision to not do the "good"? Share your insights with God.

Day 3. Romans 8:19-22

Spend time thinking through the results of sin in the world, your country, your city, your family and your life. Glance through the newspaper or surf the Internet, and see the results of the destructive, corrupting power of sin in the world.

Day 4. Review your past three days

- How has meditating on your own sin and temptation impacted your heart and your appreciation of God's love, grace and faithfulness?

- Have you felt sorrow, confusion, been moved to tears? Why, or why not?

Close this time by slowly reciting the Lord's Prayer.

Colloquy. Approach Jesus, and ask him for three favors:

1. A deep realization of the sin in your life and a sorrow for your sinful acts

2. An understanding of and feeling for the havoc in your life due to your sin and sinful tendencies, as well as wisdom regarding how to bring order into your life

3. An awareness of the ways in which the world actively and passively stands in opposition to Christ, so that you may distance yourself from all that is worldly and vain

Close this time by slowly reciting the Lord's Prayer.

Day 5

Spend your time reviewing your life using this passage:

The acts of the sinful nature are obvious: sexual immorality, impurity, and debauchery; idolatry and witchcraft; hatred, discord, jealousy, fits of rage, selfish ambition, dissensions, factions and envy; drunkenness, orgies, and the like. (Gal 5:19-21)

- How have you gone astray? What has lured you away from God?

- What have you desired more than God? Why?

Day 6

Confession: Drawing from your reflections on the Ten Commandments and the Galatians 5 passage above, write out a confession.

Conclude by slowing reciting the Anima Christi (Soul of Christ) Prayer:

Soul of Christ, sanctify me.
Body of Christ, save me.

Blood of Christ, inebriate me.

Water from the side of Christ, wash me.

Passion (suffering) of Christ, strengthen me.

O good Jesus, hear me;

Within thy wounds hide me;

Suffer me not to be separated from thee;

From the malignant enemy defend me;

In the hour of my death call me,

And bid me come to thee,

That with thy saints I may praise thee

Forever and ever. Amen

Day 7. Review this past week

- Which day's meditations touched you? Why?

- How did these meditations impact your heart and your appreciation of God's love and grace?

- Have you felt sorrow, confusion, been moved to tears? Why, or why not?

- Did these meditations increase your ability to make more God-honoring choices? Why, or why not?

Colloquy. Spend time thanking and praising God the Father, Jesus the Son, and the Holy Spirit for the grace, mercy, love and forgiveness you have been given.

Spiritual Director or Listener

If you haven't, please meet with your spiritual director or listener soon. This can be a difficult time for some, a time that may become destructive and not life-giving, especially if experienced alone.

ᗢ SECTION 4 OF 5 ᗢ

The grace you are seeking this week is *the ability to experience sorrow, tears and confusion over your choices to sin in light of God's limitless love, grace, mercy and faithfulness.*

Examen Questions

- How did your meditation on the destructive nature of sin impact how you lived your life today (choices you made, interaction with others and so on)?

- When were you aware of the love, grace and forgiveness of God in your life?

Come to prayer, conscious of the reverence God deserves, while asking God that everything in your day may more and more lead you to divine praise and service.

Process

☐ Opening   ☐ Closing

☐ Daily exercise   ☐ Noontime examen

☐ Journaling   ☐ Evening examen

Day 1. Psalm 32:1-5

Your own sin: see yourself as a sinner, helpless and alienated before a loving and holy God. Let the sin (sins of commission and omission) and sinful tendencies of your life float through your mind.

Colloquy. Spend time thanking and praising God the Father, Jesus the Son, and the Holy Spirit for the grace, mercy, love and forgiveness you have been given.

Day 2. Matthew 15:10-11, 17-20

Spend time thinking through the root of sin in your life.

What internal desires lead you away from God rather than toward God? Why?

Day 3. Mark 9:43-48

What does this passage communicate concerning the seriousness of sin?

Do you take the destructive nature of your own sin seriously? Why or why not?

Are there sins in your own life that need to be cut out? If yes, ask God to help you discover the desires within that are giving birth to those sins.

Colloquy. Spend time thanking and praising God the Father, Jesus the Son, and the Holy Spirit for the grace, mercy, love and forgiveness you have been given.

Close this time by slowly reciting the Lord's Prayer.

Day 4. Review your past three days

- How have these times of meditation touched your heart?

- Have you felt sorrow, confusion, been moved to tears? Why, or why not?

Colloquy. Today use your time thanking and praising God the Father, Jesus the Son, and the Holy Spirit for the grace, mercy, love and forgiveness you have been given.

Close this time by slowly reciting the Lord's Prayer.

Day 5. Luke 18:9-14

Your own sin: see yourself as a sinner, helpless and alienated before a loving and holy God. Using imaginative reading, place yourself into this Gospel story.

Spend time repeating the famous breath prayer taken from the one in this passage: "Lord Jesus, have mercy on me, a sinner." Say the prayer two to three times, letting the words find a home in your soul. Now say the prayer slowly, lingering before God with each separate word.

What is the invitation or challenge for you in this prayer?

Make use of this breath prayer, praying it again and again as you go through your day.

Day 6. Psalm 51:1-10

Your own sin: see yourself as a sinner, helpless and alienated before a loving and holy God. Let the sin (sins of commission and omission) and sinful tendencies of your life float through your mind.

Colloquy. Spend time thanking and praising God the Father, Jesus the Son, and the Holy Spirit for the grace, mercy, love and forgiveness you have been given.

Day 7. Review this past week

- Which day's meditations touched you? Why?

- How did these meditations impact your heart and your appreciation of God's love and grace?

- Have you felt sorrow, confusion, been moved to tears? Why, or why not?

- Did these meditations increase your ability to make more God-honoring choices? Why, or why not?

Conclude by slowing reciting the Anima Christi (Soul of Christ) Prayer:

> Soul of Christ, sanctify me.
> Body of Christ, save me.
> Blood of Christ, inebriate me.
> Water from the side of Christ, wash me.
> Passion (suffering) of Christ, strengthen me.
> O good Jesus, hear me;
> Within thy wounds hide me;
> Suffer me not to be separated from thee;
> From the malignant enemy defend me;
> In the hour of my death call me,
> And bid me come to thee,
> That with thy saints I may praise thee
> Forever and ever. Amen

⌇ SECTION 5 OF 5 ⌇

Looking ahead: Day 3 and day 4 are a little different here in section 5. Take a look ahead so you can come up with a plan. Please feel free to switch these days to another time during this week if doing so would make it easier for you to enter into these exercises.

The grace you are seeking this week is *the ability to experience sorrow, tears and confusion over your choices to sin in light of God's limitless love, grace, mercy and faithfulness.*

Examen Questions

- How did your meditation on the destructive nature of sin impact how you lived your life today (choices you made, interaction with others and so on)?
- When were you aware of the love, grace and forgiveness of God in your life?

Come to prayer, conscious of the reverence God deserves, while asking God that everything in your day may more and more lead you to divine praise and service.

Process

☐ Opening   ☐ Closing

☐ Daily exercise   ☐ Noontime examen

☐ Journaling   ☐ Evening examen

Day 1

Take your confession from section 3, day 6, and share it with someone and/or with God.

Please take time to carefully and prayerfully consider making a formal confession. If you decide to make a confession to another, choose the person to whom you will confess carefully. Ask God to show you someone you can trust, someone who truly cares about you and will not judge or condemn you. Although this is scary, I strongly encourage you to step out in this way. Remember, confessing your sins is about acknowledging before God that you have done wrong and agreeing with God that indeed these things were wrong.

You can also make your confession before God. After you are finished, I suggest burning or shredding your confession as an indication that these are forgiven and God has removed them as far as the east is from the west.

Colloquy. Spend time thanking and praising God the Father, Jesus the Son, and the Holy Spirit for the grace, mercy, love and forgiveness you have been given.

Day 2. Romans 8:1, 38-39

Imagine yourself underneath a giant waterfall of God's love. God's love is rushing over you, drenching you. Imagine that instead of hearing the roaring of the water as it cascades down on you, you hear the gentle whisper of God saying to you, "There is no condemnation in Christ; nothing can or will ever separate you from my love for you." Spend time soaking in God's love, being caressed by God's loving touch, and hearing God whisper to you, "There is no condemnation in Christ; nothing can ever separate you from my love."

What feelings does this stir within you? Share your feelings with God.

Use all or part of the sentence "There is no condemnation in Christ; nothing can separate you from my love" as a breath prayer throughout your day.

Day 3

Take a walk, sit outside, lie down on your couch, get something to eat or grab a cup of coffee, and spend your time being open to God. This time is about intentionally being with God. Share with God any feelings that arise.

Day 4

Have a play day with God doing something you enjoy, and share your experience with Jesus.

Days 5-6. Review these past thirty-five prayer sessions

- What meditations really touched you? Why?

- How have these meditations impacted your heart and your appreciation of God's love and grace?

- Have you felt sorrow or confusion, or been moved to tears? Why, or why not?

- Did these meditations increase your ability to make more God-honoring choices? Why, or why not?

Colloquy. Spend time thanking and praising God the Father, Jesus the Son, and the Holy Spirit for the grace, mercy, love and forgiveness you have been given.

Day 7

Spend time recalling those who have shown you God's love, carried you to Jesus, prayed for you and chosen to journey with you during certain legs on your adventure of faith—those whom God has used to help grow, sustain and deepen your faith. Ponder their involvement in your life even as you were broken, struggling and messy.

- What feelings arise as you recall these individuals?

- What are the gifts they gave you through their presence with you?

- What does their love, care and involvement reveal to you about God?

Give thanks to God for these individuals. Pray for them and be open to God leading you to write one or more of these instruments of God a note of thanks and appreciation.

CONCLUDING COMMENTS AND REFLECTIONS

You have completed Week 1 of the Exercises. They were designed to help you to cultivate a deep conviction of your sinfulness while reminding you of your absolute need for the salvation rendered in Christ and God's eagerness to forgive you, love you and be gracious toward you. Hopefully you have been able to move through this section without trivializing your sin or feeling overwhelmed by the immensity of it. It is important that you were able to sit with the seemingly paradoxical realities of your sin and God's love, your absolute poverty and God's immeasurable riches provided to you in Christ, your brokenness and God's transformation of you into a one-of-a-kind masterpiece. When all is said and done, the above twin realities are to be embraced and internalized before you continue your journey through the Exercises.

Now is the point when you begin to discern with God if it is time for you to move on to Week 2. As you are making your decision, please remember that the point is not to get through the Exercises but to interact with God and yourself through them. During the almost five hundred years of the Spiritual Exercises of Ignatius, there are many who did not continue beyond Week 1. That is okay. So, as you begin your discernment process, let go of internal pressure to move on to Week 2. Instead, open yourself to God's leading regarding moving on.

Begin by pondering where you find yourself on the continuums below. These are designed to help you explore how you have been able to internalize God's love and forgiveness, even as you have been focused on your sin. As you work through the continuums, endeavor to answer from your heart and not merely your head. Seek to embrace indifference.

Where would you place yourself on the following continuums?

naked, broken, alienated   loved, forgiven, accepted

|———————————————————————————————————|

SIN/grace   GRACE/sin

|———————————————————————————————————|

sinner   sinner radically loved by God

|———————————————————————————————————|

intellectual sense of   strong heartfelt sense of
need for God   need for God

|———————————————————————————————————|

my abject poverty   God's radical love

|———————————————————————————————————|

self-condemnation   no condemnation in Christ

|———————————————————————————————————|

conditional love of God   unconditional love of God

├──┤

preoccupied with my sin   eyes fixed on Jesus

├──┤

- As you look at each continuum, what do you think changed in your view of God and of yourself during Week 1?
- Have you seen your ability to internalize God's love, grace, mercy and forgiveness through Jesus deepen during Week 1? Why, or why not?
- Are you able and comfortable living in the tension of being a forgiven sinner who is also the one-of-a-kind masterpiece of God created in Christ Jesus and dearly loved by God? Why, or why not?

If you feel that you are predominately on the left side on the above continuums, consider taking six days to do the exercise below, under "Additional Exercises." If you find yourself predominately on the right side of the continuums, please move on to the exercises in the following "Important" section.

Important: Take a moment to consider with head and heart the reality of sin (commission/omission) in your life—your past sins, your present sins and the fact that you will sin again.

Now add to your pondering of the pervasive reality of sin in your life the idea of your brokenness.

What are the overriding feelings that well up in your heart as you consider these two realities of your life? Why?

However, if your overriding feelings were of love and not condemnation, skip past the following "Additional Exercises" to the paragraph marked "Moving On."

If your overriding feeling was self-condemnation, shame or hopelessness—or any combination of these—I would encourage you to spend an additional week in the additional exercises below. These exercises will provide additional time and opportunity for you to sit with God's forgiveness, unconditional love, acceptance and embrace of you just as you are in this moment, even as God knows all that you have done and will do in terms of sin.

The rhythm for these six days is this: on days 1, 3 and 5, you will be involved in working through a normal formatted exercise with slow-down, and so on. On days 2, 4 and 6, you will spend time soaking in the love, grace, mercy and forgiveness of God.

ADDITIONAL EXERCISES

Day 1. Ephesians 2:1-3

Your sin: see yourself as a sinner, helpless and alienated before a loving and holy God. Let the sins (of commission and omission) and sinful tendencies of your life float through your mind.

Now read and focus all your attention on Ephesians 2:4-5. Allow the truths found in these verses to speak to you concerning who you are now as a result of God's great love and mercy.

- How does this make you feel?

- Which verses have more power in your heart: 2:1-3 or 2:4-5? Why?

Colloquy. Spend time thanking and praising God the Father, Jesus the Son, and the Holy Spirit for the grace, mercy, love and forgiveness you have been given.

Day 2

Spend your time soaking in the love, grace, mercy and forgiveness of God.

Day 3. Romans 5:6-11

Spend time with this passage, considering when Jesus died for you. It was not when you had your act together but when you were powerless, un-godly, a sinner and an enemy of God. That is when Jesus died for you.

- What does this passage reveal to you regarding the nature of God's love for you?

- How does that make you feel?

- Are you able to hang on to the extraordinary love God has for you? Why, or why not?

Colloquy. Spend some time thanking and praising God the Father, Jesus the Son, and the Holy Spirit for the grace, mercy, love and forgiveness you have been given.

Day 4
Spend your time soaking in the love, grace, mercy and forgiveness of God.

Day 5. Romans 8:1, 38-39
Imagine yourself underneath a giant waterfall of God's love. God's love is rushing over you, drenching you. Imagine that instead of hearing the roaring of the water as it cascades down on you, you hear the gentle whisper of God saying to you, "There is no condemnation in Christ; nothing can or will ever separate you from my love for you." Spend time soaking in God's love, being caressed by God's loving touch, and hearing God whisper to you, "There is no condemnation in Christ; nothing can ever separate you from my love."

What feelings does this stir within you? Share your feelings with God.

Use all or part of the sentence "There is no condemnation in Christ; nothing can separate you from my love" as a breath prayer throughout your day.

Day 6
Spend your time soaking in the love, grace, mercy and forgiveness of God.

Day 7
Read through and interact with the material contained in the section above beginning with "Important."

MOVING ON
If you have not talked to your spiritual director or listener about moving on to Week 2, please do so now. Walk through the above continuums together, and make sure you have truly internalized the love and

forgiveness of God as provided for through the death and resurrection of Christ.

If you are feeling that you are in a good internal place for moving forward, do one more thing: take time to recommit to your journey through the Exercises, pledging to give yourself wholly to God (as you are able) and to seek to gain nothing from God. Purpose to each day present yourself to God as "your spiritual act of worship," which is "holy and pleasing to God" (Rom 12:1).

FINAL REMARKS

These past few sections (the Preparatory Exercises, the Principle and Foundation, and Week 1) have all been building up to the rest of the Exercises. This has been bringing you to a place of deep realization and internalization of the greatness and love of God.

In Week 1, as you pondered the global and personal realties of sin, spending significant time naming and exploring your own sins, the goal was to realize the unlimited, unreserved and unconditional love of God in spite of your own sin and brokenness. This love of God is not some kind of warm fuzzy feeling that God has toward you but an engulfing love that propelled Jesus from the freedom of heaven to the confines of a human body and a cross on your behalf. This is a transforming love that meets you right where you are and yet also transforms and reshapes you even as your sin seeks to deform and destroy you.

It is only with this love of God in mind that you can fully and honestly enter into the next phase of the Exercises, known as Week 2. Week 2 plunges you squarely in the life of Jesus and confronts you with questions concerning your willingness to follow Jesus and the depth of your commitment to him. As you enter Week 2, it is critically important for you to experience yourself as one uniquely and unconditionally loved by God so that you are able to honestly explore where you currently are in regard to your heartfelt desire to follow Jesus.

When you are ready to enter Week 2, read Mark 1–10 in one sitting as your final preparation.

WEEK 2

WALKING WITH JESUS

You HAVE NOW REACHED WHAT is traditionally known as Week 2 of the Spiritual Exercises of Ignatius. This marks the beginning of your time in the Gospel narratives. This section's focus—the life of Jesus up to the Passion Week—is the heart and soul of the Exercises and constitutes the largest single section. This emphasis on the life of Jesus as the focal point for the Exercises is not at all surprising given Ignatius's spiritual journey, for the seeds of his conversion experience were planted as he spent time reading the *Life of Christ* by Ludolph of Saxony, while recuperating from the damage suffered when a cannon ball hit his leg during the battle at Pamplona.

And that was just the beginning. In his autobiography Ignatius spoke of special encounters with Jesus, his long and arduous journey to Jerusalem to walk where Jesus walked and his strong desire to return with his followers to Jerusalem before pledging his allegiance to the church. For Ignatius and those with him who founded the Society of Jesus, Jesus was the nucleus that everything else revolved around.

As you move into Week 2, your focus shifts from the sins of the world, Adam and Eve, the angels and your own sin and brokenness to the life of Jesus. Your prayer time each day will involve walking with Jesus, listening to Jesus and interacting with Jesus as you enter into the Gospel narratives. Your desire will now be focused on deepening your knowledge of Jesus and your love for him as well as on walking more closely with him.

To put this week within the framework of the classical stages of spiritual development, you have moved from the Purgative Way of Week 1 and entered into the Illuminative Way of Week 2. The Purgative Way in the Exercises has been concerned with naming, resisting and overcoming disordered passions globally and personally and at the same time seeking to nourish and strengthen your awareness of God's love for you and your trust of God for your salvation while stimulating your love for God. In Week 2, the Illuminative Way is focused on enlightening you to spiritual things and fostering a life orientated to the person and teachings of Jesus while continuing to realize a deepening love for God/Jesus.

In Week 2 you will be seeking to know and embrace Jesus, his values and his mission. From this week through the rest of the "19th Annotation," you will be setting your eyes, heart and mind on Jesus, the author and perfecter of your faith. You will be invited into life with Christ, and Christ will become the prototype and inspiration for your ongoing journey through the Exercises and through life itself.

This Week and those that follow (Weeks 3 and 4) help you to move toward a more Christ-centered life. It is the living out of the apostle Paul's words found in Galatians 2:20: "I no longer live, but Christ lives in me." As you work through the daily exercises, you will be fixing your attention on Jesus, which, according to Paul, brings transformation: "We all, with unveiled face, beholding as in a mirror the glory of the Lord, are being transformed into the same image from glory to glory, just as from the Lord, the Spirit" (2 Cor 3:18 NASB).

In Week 2, you will see and experience the Gospel narratives as never before. You will discover things about yourself, about Jesus, about your faith and about your level of commitment that you did not know. You will be walking, talking and being with Jesus. The method for interacting with the narratives will primarily involve the imaginative reading of Scripture. You will be encouraged to implement the "application of the senses," which involves using your senses along with your imagination to be more fully present and involved in the Gospel narratives.

This section leads to a deepened awareness regarding who Jesus is for you and who you are as a follower of Jesus. As you journey through

Week 2, you will explicitly and implicitly be confronted by a few questions from Jesus: Who do you say that I am? What is the level of your desire and willingness to follow me? Will you follow me?

Ignatius designed four different meditations with the purpose of helping you discover and gauge the level of your desire to be involved with Christ and to gauge your commitment to him. You will be spending time in three of these meditations: the "Call of the King," the "Two Standards" and the "Three Classes of Persons." The subject matter of the first two is taken from the life of Ignatius and thus reflects the political system (kings) and violent reality of his times (war). Therefore, these two meditations have been recast to keep intact the original intention of helping you explore your willingness to follow Jesus. The third meditation, "Three Classes of Persons," remains much the same as it appears in the original Exercises.

The purpose of these three meditations is not to make you choose but rather to help you to discern where you currently are in regard to whom you are following and your level of commitment. As you make your way through these meditations, you may become aware of how the desire for honor, security, possessions, health, wealth, peace, happiness and so on blind you to the invitations of Jesus or render you powerless to say yes to him. A key question in these meditations is, "What will it cost me to follow (say yes to) Jesus, and am I willing to pay that price?"

Although the three meditations can be powerful and challenging, they play only a small role in your overall experience of Week 2. The majority of your time will be spent entering into the Gospel narratives in a holistic way that encourages you to use your imagination and the application of your senses. Incorporating the imagination and the senses as a means to enter into the Gospel narratives is the genius of the Exercises and once again flows out of Ignatius's own conversion experience, which resulted from hours spent imaginatively journeying with Jesus through the Gospel narratives as he recuperated. Ignatius came to realize that employing the imagination and senses helps people to involve their feelings and creativity as well as the cognitive aspects of their being, while opening themselves to God in deeper and more profound ways.

If you have concerns about using your imagination, I encourage you to revisit the biblical rationale for the use of your God-given imagination (under "Imaginative prayer" on p. 36). Also remember that as you enter the Gospel narratives, you are not trusting your imagination but you are ultimately trusting God, the one who created your imagination. God will be the one you are depending on to guide, lead and teach you through the daily exercises as you utilize your God-given imagination.

Please remember as you enter into these Gospel narratives using your God-given imagination to resist the inner voices that pressure you to do it "right" or "well." Instead, just have fun with it and let your ability grow and develop over time. As you enter the text in this way, your time will be transformed from knowing *about* Jesus to experiencing Jesus and yourself in life-giving and transforming ways. Since it is children who readily use their imaginations, it would make sense that when we use our God-given imagination to walk through the Gospels with Jesus, we find freedom and playfulness.

REMINDER AND ENCOURAGEMENT

Journaling. Journaling through these exercises will help you to see patterns in your prayer times and to recall what God has spoken to you. Often as you journal, God expands on what you have discovered or been made aware of. I *strongly* encourage you to journal. It will deepen your experience with the daily exercises.

Prayer of examen. Please continue to strive to make the daily examen part of your time in the Exercises. This is a very important part of the Exercises. If you are still struggling with incorporating this practice into your life, go back and review the section "Prayer of Examen" on page 28.

The Lord's Prayer. Once again, the Lord's Prayer will play a part in this section. When you pray the Lord's Prayer, please do so slowly, lingering with each of the words or phrases. Do not feel compelled to complete the prayer, but rather be open to the inner prompting of the Holy Spirit, seeking to be sensitive to God's invitations and challenges as you pray this prayer. You may find yourself camping on a single phrase for your entire time. Just as with the Exercises, the goal is not to get through the Lord's Prayer but to be open to God as you pray the prayer.

ADDITIONS TO EXERCISES

As you enter into Week 2 of the Exercises, there are a number of additions besides the imaginative reading of Scripture, the employing of your senses and the three meditations Ignatius designed for use during this Week. These additions are briefly described below to help you be better prepared as you enter Week 2, so you can fully enter into the experience of it.

Bowing. Bowing will become a part of your opening sessions during this entire Week. The practice of bowing builds on the use of the body in prayer that was mentioned during Week 1. You will bow to begin your time with God. It is a physical declaration of respect, honor, even humility. For centuries, bowing has also been used in religious practices as a sign of submission, adoration, gratitude, reverence and trust. It demonstrates trust when we bow before another, because we render ourselves helpless and fully vulnerable to their attack.

Two new graces. The second addition to this Week is two new graces. The first grace will be used only in conjunction with the three meditations mentioned above. You will be asking *to not be deaf to Jesus' call and to be ready and willing to do what Jesus asks.* This will be the grace for section 1 and 6 of this Week. The rest of the time you will be asking *to know Jesus intimately, to love him more intensely and to follow him more closely.* Remember to ask God for the suggested grace each day as you begin your time in the exercise for that day. It can also be helpful to recall the grace to your mind as you rise in the morning and to make it a prayer throughout your day.

New colloquies. The third addition during Week 2 is occasionally ending prayer time with a couple of new colloquies (little conversations). These colloquies will transition you from activity to quiet presence, from striving to being still and being with God. In Week 2 there is a definite move to a time of resting in God as a part of your daily experience. During those times, seek to just be.

Two prayers. On a number of days, you will be invited to sit with the words of two prayers, seeking to discern whether they express your heartfelt desires. Be honest with yourself and God as you ponder the words of the prayers, seeking to discover why the prayers do or do not truly express your inner desires regarding following Jesus. These two prayers take the place of the Anima Christi (Soul of Christ) Prayer of Week 1.

> Eternal Lord and King of all creation, humbly I come before you. . . . I am moved by your grace to offer myself to you and your work. I deeply desire to be with you in accepting all wrongs and all rejections and all poverty, both actual and spiritual—and I deliberately choose this, if it is for your greater service and praise.

> Lord Jesus,
> Help me to know you, to love you, to follow you
> Help alleviate my fears
> and fan the embers of trust within me
> Give me the strength to say yes to your invitations
> the courage to continue my journey with you
> Remind me that you are
> the Way
> the Truth
> and the Life
> and apart from you there is no life
> but with you
> and you alone
> is fullness of life,
> life everlasting.

Ignatius also suggests, if you are so inclined, to do some spiritual reading. A book that he recommended for this very purpose is *The Imitation of Christ* by Thomas à Kempis. Ignatius used this book devotionally throughout his life. If you have the desire to make it a part of your Week 2 experience, consider downloading the entire book and listening to it as you drive or exercise.

Recalling the focus. The final new addition involves recalling to your mind the focus of your morning meditation throughout your day. This simple practice can radically impact your experience through this section of the Exercises. It helps you to be more open and aware of your desires and of what God may be up to in and through you. It is a way of continually presenting yourself to God throughout the day and reminding yourself that you are living with God, in God, and that God is living in you.

THREE CAUTIONS

First, please keep in mind that this may not be an easy section to make your way through. You will be challenged interiorly in terms of your own "stuff," but also exteriorly. It seems that during this section of the Exercises, distractions more readily arise, such as the temptation to say no to the exercises and yes to something else, something that is not bad but is not the focus of your time with God.

As I have journeyed with others, I have seen many abandon their journey during this Week of the Exercises, even though they were initially very excited about focusing on the life of Jesus. I believe a spiritual battle intensifies in Week 2 because of the transforming power that flows from time spent with Jesus in the ways incorporated in this section.

As you enter into this Week, you more fully enter into a spiritual battle between the flesh and the spirit and the principalities and powers of this world. Be on guard, for there is often a level of spiritual warfare that arises as you intentionally focus on the person of Jesus, seeking to love him more dearly and follow him more closely, which is exactly the grace you will be seeking this Week. This is a good time to come before God and recommit yourself to the journey, not just now, but weekly and even daily.

Second, as you work your way through Week 2, you will soon discover that you know, or are at least familiar with, most if not all of the Gospel narratives that will make up your daily experiences through this Week. Please be aware that you may be tempted not to enter fully into the narratives or prepare yourself to enter into them because you may assume you know how God will meet you in the story or teach you from the story. Let go of all expectations, and endeavor to truly use your imagination and senses as you enter into the story and let the Spirit guide and direct your time.

Finally, beware of the expectations and feelings that may spontaneously arise within you as you enter Week 2, knowing you are going to spend your prayer times walking with Jesus through the Gospel narratives. You may anticipate powerful emotional times, or you may be anticipating some jaw-dropping experiences and mind-blowing insights. But you need to embrace indifference, endeavoring to be present to and trusting of God and the process. Seek to enter each prayer experience expectation-free and desiring simply to "show up," presenting yourself as a living sacrifice, "holy and pleasing to God—this is your spiritual act of worship" (Rom 12:1). Resist the temptation to evaluate your daily times on the basis of your felt experience or what you feel you "got out of" your prayer time.

If the new additions seem overwhelming, do not worry. You will be prompted when to make use of them, so you are not caught off-guard and to provide additional information regarding these components without interrupting the flow of the Exercises. Please also seek to incorporate journaling and the prayer of examen into your day. And do take heed of the cautions above, even rereading them from time to time.

RULES OF DISCERNMENT: WEEK 2

Ignatius provides key discernment insights for those entering into Week 2. These new Rules of Discernment deal with the subtleties of spiritual attacks—the danger of taking consolations at face value and the tendency of the enemy to appear disguised as "an angel of light" (2 Cor 11:14). The tactics of the evil spirit may become much more subtle as you continue to journey through the Exercises. It is important to have a keen awareness of Ignatius's insights regarding discerning the source of consolations you experience.

These new Rules of Discernment are for you who are maturing in your faith as you continue your journey through the Exercises. These rules presuppose that you are walking with God, that you are choosing to say yes to God and that praising, worshiping and serving God is the desire of your heart.

Unlike the first set of Rules of Discernment, which dealt primarily with desolation, these rules focus on the ambiguity of consolation.

Consolation, which was the realm of the good spirit in the Rules of Discernment for Week 1, is now portrayed as a likely weapon of the evil spirit. The concern addressed with the Rules of Discernment for Week 2 is the subtlety of the evil spirit's new strategies. These rules, like the first set, help you to "be aware" (noticing what is going on within), and "understand" (whether this is from God or not) your inner movements (feelings) and then prepare you to "take action" (accept or reject what you have noticed and understood).

Just like the first set of rules, these too arose out of Ignatius's experiences. It was during his time in Manresa that Ignatius discovered that the evil spirit not only uses desolation but also makes use of consolation for his own purposes. While in Manresa, Ignatius would go to bed for much-needed sleep and begin to receive great enlightenment and consolation that would rob him of sleep. Over time he came to realize these were not coming from God but from the evil one. Additionally, while he was studying Latin, he received great spiritual delights and insights into spiritual matters that hindered his ability to continue his studies. Once again he realized that these consolations were not from God but from the evil one. Through these two experiences and the help of his spiritual director, Ignatius became convinced that consolations did not always have their source in God but could be used by the evil spirit against those who seek to follow after God.

Because you are changing, the strategies of the enemy are changing too. Now the evil one will not tend to tempt you with something overtly evil, but will come under the appearance of good. The brilliant military commander will now become subtler, cleverer and craftier, making use of Trojan horses and all sorts of evil camouflaged as good to ensnare you. Jesus warned regarding wolves in sheep's clothing (Mt 7:15), and the apostle Paul admonished that Satan himself masquerades as an angel of light (2 Cor 11:14).

The Rules

1. When you are living with Jesus on the screen of your life, you will tend to experience God's presence as supportive, encouraging, even joy filled, and you will tend to experience the presence of the evil

one as bringing dissatisfaction, anxiety, self-doubts, even feelings of pride concerning your walk with God.

2. If you experience the rising of consolation without an external catalyst, this is a consolation you can trust as coming from God. It is called "a consolation without previous cause." This type of consolation is not given because of anything you did but as a gracious gift from God. This is the only type of consolation that can be fully trusted and entered into without reservation. (However, in rule 8 below, Ignatius will even give some cautionary advice about the period immediately following this type of consolation.)

3. When you experience consolation that has an external cause to it (music, Scripture, a sunset, a child's smile, a work of art, a sermon, a passage in a book), its source can be the good or evil spirit. Ignatius advised that the source of consolation, even if it flows from something good, may not be from God but can just as easily be from the evil spirit and used for his ends.

4. In case you did not get the message in rule 3, rule 4 clearly states that the evil one can and does appear as an angel of light and will even use good and holy thoughts to achieve his ends. The days of solely being tempted with something overtly evil are over. Wisdom and discernment are now the order of the day.

This is a tactic experienced by those in Week 2 and beyond. As you go through the Exercises, you may be tempted to use your entire hour in the slowdown or feel the need to ponder something that has arisen within you during that time instead of entering into the Exercises that day. Be careful, this is exactly how the evil one may get you off track. These things are not wrong, but they do take you away from the Exercises.

5. A good, God-honoring beginning that brings consolation does not guarantee a good, God-honoring ending. Here you are cautioned to be self-aware and discerning, not only as you make a decision but as you proceed with that decision. You may make a decision based on wisdom that seems like a good decision, but that does not mean you

will not fall into the snare of the evil one. The angel of light can begin to subtly divert your attention and course from where you began. If at some point you discover that your heart and mind are far from God, the evil spirit has derailed you.

The prayer of examen can be a great tool in this discernment process when used in the prescribed way at noontime and night. A few good questions for use during your examen in order to discern the source of a consolation are, Where is this leading me: God, evil, distraction, less good? Am I currently experiencing harmony, distress, peace or disturbance in my heart? What changes have taken place regarding the beginning trajectory of the consolation and where it is now leading me?

6. When you realize that you have been deceived, retrace your steps. Go back to the beginning, middle and end of your choice, exploring your attitudes to see where the evil spirit got its hooks into you.

7. When you are proceeding from good to better, you will experience God's touch as light and gentle, like a drop of water falling on a sponge, but you will experience the evil spirit like a drop of water hitting a stone. However, if you are proceeding from good to bad, your experience of God and the evil spirit will be the opposite of what is stated above.

8. Beware of the afterglow of consolation without previous cause. Although consolation without previous cause is without a doubt from God, all that follows from that experience is not necessarily from God. Be careful about making heartfelt commitments and vows to God after such a time; this could very well be the evil spirit sidetracking a holy moment for his own ends. These afterglow feelings are not directly connected to the consolation without previous cause and can be used by the evil spirit to lead you to make decisions that appear to be God-honoring but are not what God is inviting you into. So purpose not to make any decision immediately after an experience of consolation without previous cause.

These Rules of Discernment for Week 2 serve to warn you that the strategies of the evil one are becoming more subtle and sophisticated.

It is extremely important for you to be vigilant, evaluating and re-evaluating perceived consolations and good and holy thoughts to discern their origin and determine if they should be embraced and followed or not.

I have seen this twisting of consolations for the enemy's purpose again and again as I have journeyed through the Exercises with others. It can be very subtle and always seems like a good thing, even a God-honoring endeavor, yet it gradually leads the person away from God, away from the very journey into which God invited her to enter. Be on guard! The Rules of Discernment for Week 2 serve to remind you of the perils of your journey and hopefully reinforce the value of having a spiritual director or listener to companion with you. As your journey continues, so the attacks continue to grow in their devious subtlety.

FINAL REMARKS

The above could very well feel overwhelming to you, but do not worry. You will be prompted below when to make use of those components listed above. They are provided so you are not caught off-guard when they make their appearance during the daily exercises and to provide additional information regarding these components without interrupting the flow of the Exercises.

If you have not yet done so, please read Mark 1–10 in one sitting before entering Week 2. This will provide you with a brief overview of much that you will be exploring during this section of the Exercises.

As you enter into and journey through Week 2, my prayer for you is this:

> God grant this one strength in accordance with your incredibly great power at work within him or her to continue the journey; give this precious one your wisdom that she or he would come to know Jesus more intimately, love Jesus more intensely and be emboldened in faith to follow him more closely. (adapted from Eph 1:19; 1:17; 2 Tim 1:7)

Exercises for Week 2

The grace you are seeking is *to not be deaf to Jesus' call and to be ready and willing to do what Jesus asks.*

Examen Questions

When and how did you choose to follow Jesus and embrace his call today?

Start your time with a bow—slowly bending from your waist—as a visible sign of your reverence for and honoring of God, while asking God that everything in your day may more and more lead you to divine praise and service.

Process

☐ Opening   ☐ Closing

☐ Daily exercise   ☐ Noontime examen

☐ Journaling   ☐ Evening examen

Day 1. Will You?

Part 1. In your imagination, stand before a truly good and powerful person who says, "It is my will to rid all lands of injustice and bring them peace, rest, healing, hope and love. I would like you to join me. If you agree to join me, and I hope you do, you would have to be content to eat as I do, and to drink and dress and live as I do. Likewise, you will labor with me in the day and watch with me in the night, being alert and ready at all times to do my bidding. And you will have a place at my table, a part with me in the victory. And I will call you friend."

Consider how you would respond to such a request.

Part 2. In your imagination, stand before Jesus and hear him say to you, "It is my will to bring all the world into the glory of my Father's kingdom, to rid all lands of injustice and bring peace, rest, healing, hope and love. I would like you to join me. If you agree to join me, and I hope you do, you will walk as I walk and live as I live, laboring with me, being alert and ready at all times to do my bidding, following me in the pain so that you may also follow me in the glory. And you shall have a place at my table, a part with me in my victory. And I will call you friend."

Consider how you would respond and how you are currently responding to this call of Christ.

Day 2. Matthew 8:18-22

Imaginatively enter into this passage at least twice. The first time, picture yourself as one who comes to Jesus, moved by Jesus' teaching and pledging to follow him wherever he goes.

- What are your expectations as you approach Jesus?
- What do you feel as you hear Jesus' reply?
- What do you do?

The second time, picture yourself as the disciple who asked Jesus to allow him to travel home "to bury my father."

- What are your expectations as you approach Jesus?
- What do you feel as you hear Jesus' reply?
- What do you do?

Ask God to show you if there are any things in your life that may either hinder your ability to hear Jesus' call to follow or hamper you from actually following Jesus.

Sit with the words of the following prayer.

Eternal Lord and King of all creation, humbly I come before you. . . . I am moved by your grace to offer myself to you and your work. I deeply desire to be with you in accepting all wrongs and all rejections and all poverty, both actual and spiritual—and I deliberately choose this, if it is for your greater service and praise.

- What do these words stir within you?

- Are you willing to pray this prayer in a heartfelt way? Why, or why not?

Day 3. Matthew 10:1-15

Read through this passage a couple of times, being open to verses, words or phrases to which you are drawn. Once you have gathered a number of these, spend the rest of your time pondering them.

- Is there a theme that connects them?

- What feelings do these verses, words or phrases stir within you?

- What are you feeling about saying yes to Jesus and going out with the Twelve?

Share your thoughts and feelings with God.

Day 4. Review part 2 of the Kingdom Meditation from day 1

Consider how you are currently responding to this call of Christ to embrace his life and follow him.

- Has your level of desire and commitment to follow Jesus changed at all? Why, or why not?

Colloquy. Spend time expressing thanksgiving and gratitude to God the Father, Jesus the Son, and the Holy Spirit individually.

Day 5. Matthew 10:16-24

Read through this passage a couple of times, being open to verses, words or phrases to which you are drawn. Once you have gathered a number of these, spend the rest of your time pondering them.

- Is there a theme that connects these words?

- What feelings do they stir within you?

- What are you feeling about saying yes to Jesus and going out with the Twelve?

Share your thoughts and feelings with God.

Recall to Mind

Recall the focus of your morning meditation throughout your day. This simple practice can radically impact your experience through this Week of the Exercises. It can help open you up to God, providing an opportunity for you to present yourself to God throughout your day, and serve to remind you that you are living with God and in God, and that God is living in you.

Day 6. Sit with the words of this prayer.

> Eternal Lord and King of all creation, humbly I come before you. . . . I am moved by your grace to offer myself to you and your work. I deeply desire to be with you in accepting all wrongs and all rejections and all poverty, both actual and spiritual—and I deliberately choose this, if it is for your greater service and praise.

- What do these words stir within you?
- Are you willing to pray this prayer in a heartfelt way? Why, or why not?

If not, take some time to write your own prayer that would communicate your desire to follow Jesus.

Conclude your time by slowly praying the Lord's Prayer.

Day 7. Review

Read your journal entries from this week and part 2 of the Kingdom Meditation from day 1. Consider how you are currently responding to this call of Christ to embrace his life and follow him.

Has your level of desire and commitment to follow Jesus changed at all? Why, or why not?

Slowly pray the Lord's Prayer.

▲▲

Opening Time in Prayer

Make sure you make full use of the slowdown and commitment time at the beginning of your time in prayer each day. Do not rush through the opening time, which is designed to help you slow down and foster respect for God as you come into God's presence. This opening involves a conscious effort to present yourself before God as a living and holy sacrifice (Rom 12:1) and to ready yourself to be present to God. It can be an aid in helping you fully enter into the Exercises and experience God throughout your day.

▼▼

⤜ SECTION 2 OF 15 ⤛

The *new* grace you are seeking today is *to know Jesus intimately, to love him more intensely and to follow him more closely.*

Examen Questions

- How and when did I demonstrate my trust in God today?
- How and when did I demonstrate my lack of trust in God today?

Start your time with a bow—slowly bending from your waist—as a visible sign of your reverence for and honoring of God, while asking God that everything in your day may more and more lead you to divine praise and service.

Process

☐ Opening   ☐ Closing

☐ Daily exercise   ☐ Noontime examen

☐ Journaling   ☐ Evening examen

Day 1. Matthew 1:18-25

Imagine you are Joseph.

- What are you feeling?

- What is your reaction? What would you do?
- What do Joseph's responses reveal about his faith and trust in God?
- What about your responses? What do they reveal about your faith and trust in God?

Day 2. Matthew 1:23

Spend your time today pondering and journaling about the implications of the name Immanuel, which was given to Jesus.

What does this name convey to you and stir within you?

Day 3. Luke 1:26-39

Imagine you are Mary, an unwed but pledged young girl in a male-dominated culture, where you can rightfully be killed for being unfaithful to your husband-to-be. You have been told by an angel that you are with child.

- What are you feeling after the angel leaves you?
- What are your fears, concerns and doubts?
- Will you tell anyone? Why, or why not?

Day 4. Review

Read through your journal entries from the past couple of days, seeking something that resonated deep within you, something that was either drawing you or stirring resistance in you. Spend your prayer time pondering, unpacking and exploring whatever you come up with.

Day 5. Luke 1:37-38

Sit with these words of the angel to Mary (to you).

- Do you believe these words to be true?
- Do you currently live in a way that would confirm or deny your answer? How?
- How might your life be different if you really believed these words?
- What is your level of trust in God (not trust in God doing what you want God to do for you but trust in the person and character of God, come what may)?

Sit with Mary's response to God, a response that springs from a deep place of trust and little understanding.

Would your response be different or the same as Mary's? Why?

Day 6. Luke 2:1-7

Imagine you are Joseph.

- What are you feeling as Mary's labor begins?
- What are you feeling as you hear the baby's first sounds, as you hold Immanuel, God with us, in your arms and you feel his heart beating?
- As you look into the eyes of the Lord your God?
- As you remember the angel's words to you?
- As you watch the Creator of heaven and earth get his first mouthfuls of nourishment at Mary's breast?

Imagine you are Mary.

- What are you feeling as labor begins?
- What are you feeling as you hear the baby's first sounds, as you hold Immanuel, God with us, in your arms and you feel his heart beating?
- As you look into the eyes of the Lord your God?
- As you remember the angel's words to you?
- As you watch the Creator of heaven and earth get his first mouthfuls of nourishment at your breast?

Day 7. Review your week

- Which passages really touched you? Why?
- How are these passages shaping and strengthening your ability to trust God and your appreciation of the gift of Jesus and the faith of Mary, Joseph?

When you are finished, just be with Jesus, resting in his love for you and acknowledging his presence with you. Take a few moments to cease from striving and to be still in the presence of the One who is with you and within you.

I Am Not Doing This Right

If you feel that you are not journeying through the Exercises correctly, please seek to trust God and trust the process. God is at work. The exercises are bringing you into the presence of God with intentionality; the rest is up to God. Do not try to make something happen. Trust God and trust the process, focusing not on what is seen, but on what is unseen and thus eternal (2 Cor 4:18).

SECTION 3 OF 15

The grace you are seeking this week is *to know Jesus intimately, to love him more intensely and to follow him more closely.*

Examen Questions

- How and when did I demonstrate my trust in God today?
- How and when did I demonstrate my lack of trust in God today?

Start your time with a bow—slowly bending from your waist—as a visible sign of your reverence for and honoring of God, while asking God that everything in your day may more and more lead you to divine praise and service.

Process

☐ Opening   ☐ Closing

☐ Daily exercise   ☐ Noontime examen

☐ Journaling   ☐ Evening examen

Day 1. Luke 2:8-14

Imagine you are a shepherd.

- What are you feeling as you see the angels and hear the message they bring?

- What does it feel like to have the angel tell you, a lowly shepherd, this good news? What does this tell you about God?

- What is it that drives you to the manger (such as curiosity, hope, boredom, peer pressure, fear)?

- What are you feeling and thinking as you look up and see the star in the sky?

- What are you feeling and thinking as you run to the manger?

- Why doesn't anything else matter to you except going to see this newborn baby?

- When you arrive at the manger, where do you stand? What do you do, think, feel and say?

- Imagine Mary calling you to come closer, and as you approach, she gently hands Jesus to you. What goes on in your heart? What do you feel?

- What is it like to hold in your arms the Creator and Sustainer of all that is seen and unseen, to see his little hands and feet, to feel him gripping your finger, to feel the warmth of his body against your chest?

- What do you see in his eyes?

- What do you say to the Lord your God as you cradle him in your arms?

Day 2. Luke 2:22-39

Imagine you are Simeon.

- What are you feeling about this child? About God?

- What does this event demonstrate about the character of God?

Day 3. Matthew 2:13-18

Imagine you are Mary, who becomes aware that though she is safe with her child, many mothers in Israel are weeping over the deaths of their children.

- What are you feeling?

- What questions do you have for God?

- What goes through your mind as you hold Jesus, knowing that others no longer have a child to hold?

Day 4. Review

Read through your journal entries from the past couple of days, seeking something that resonated deep within you, something that was either drawing you or stirring resistance in you. Spend your prayer time pondering, unpacking and exploring whatever you come up with.

Slowly pray the Lord's Prayer.

Day 5. Matthew 1:23

Think over all you have pondered about Jesus thus far. In light of all this, spend your time today pondering and journaling about new awareness, insights and implications of the name Immanuel, which was given to Jesus.

- What does this name now convey to you?

- What does it stir within you?

Spend time thanking God the Father for the gift of his Son, and thanking Jesus for his willingness to become a child, to be Immanuel, God with us.

Slowly pray the Lord's Prayer.

Day 6. Luke 2:41-52

Spend time imagining Jesus at the following ages: infant to two years, three to five years, and six to twelve years. Try to appreciate his development, his vulnerability and his challenges at each age.

Conclude your time thanking God for sending Jesus, and thanking Jesus for choosing to come to earth, clothed in the flesh of an infant who had to grow and develop like the rest of us.

Day 7. Review your week

- Which passages really touched you? Why?

- How are these passages shaping or strengthening your ability to trust God and your appreciation of the gift of Jesus?

Spend time thanking God the Father for the gift of the Son, and thanking Jesus for his willingness to become a child, to become Immanuel. When you are finished, just be with Jesus, resting in his love for you, acknowledging his presence with you. Take a few moments to cease from striving and be still in the presence of the One who is with you and within you.

Slowly pray the Lord's Prayer.

You and Jesus

As you meditate on these various passages of Scripture, focusing on the life of Christ, please be aware of what draws you to Christ, challenges you, amazes you or gives you pause. Please take time to journal about and ponder these internal movements.

SECTION 4 OF 15

The grace you are seeking this week is *to know Jesus intimately, to love him more intensely and to follow him more closely.*

Examen Questions

- How and when did you experience Immanuel (God with you) today?
- When were you aware of your love for Jesus today?
- When do you "follow Jesus" in your relationships, circumstances, reactive and proactive responses, and actions?

Start your time with a bow—slowly bending from your waist—as a visible sign of your reverence for and honoring of God, while asking God that everything in your day may more and more lead you to divine praise and service.

Process

☐ Opening   ☐ Closing

☐ Daily exercise   ☐ Noontime examen

☐ Journaling   ☐ Evening examen

Day 1. Matthew 3:13-17

Read through this passage, keeping in mind the circumstances surrounding the birth of Jesus, who as a child grew up as one who was conceived out of wedlock.

- What must it have been like to grow up among the whispers, condemnation and ridicule of others?

- What do you think God's words, "This is my Son, whom I love; with him I am well pleased," meant to Jesus?

- What do you think they made him feel?

- What are the words you long to hear from God? Spend some time listening for the still small voice of God.

Day 2. Matthew 4:1-11

Imagine you are looking on from afar.

- What do you notice about Jesus before Satan comes to tempt him, during the temptation and after the temptation?

  When the temptations are over, go and speak to Jesus. Journal your interaction with Jesus. What do you say, and why? How does Jesus respond to you?

Day 3. John 1:35-42

Imagine you are with John's disciples as they are following Jesus, and Jesus turns around and asks, "What do you want?" Sit before God, before Jesus, and answer that question as if it is addressed to you right now. Spend time pondering, journaling about and unpacking your response. Conclude your time by expressing your desire to God the Father and then to Jesus.

Expectations and Jesus

Be aware of expectation and feelings that may spontaneously arise within you, knowing you are going to keep spending your prayer times walking with Jesus through the Gospel narratives. You may anticipate powerfully emotional times, you may be anticipating some jaw-dropping experience, mind-blowing insights—but you need to come seeking to embrace indifference, endeavoring to be present to and trusting of God and the process. Seek to enter each prayer experience expectation-free and desiring simply to "show up," presenting yourself as a living sacrifice, "holy and pleasing to God—this is your spiritual act of worship" (Rom 12:1).

Day 4. Review

Read through your journal entries from the past couple of days, seeking to find something that resonated deep within you, either drawing you or stirring up resistance in you as you spent time in the daily exercises. Spend your prayer time pondering, unpacking and exploring whatever you come up with.

Slowly pray the Lord's Prayer.

Day 5. Mark 1:16-20

Imagine you are one of those called by Jesus to "follow me."

- What do you feel as you hear his words addressed to you?

- What draws you to follow Jesus?

- What fears arise within you?

Colloquy. Seek to end your time "just being with" Jesus, rather than having a verbal response. Be still and be with God.

░░

Imagination

The use of the imagination enables you to incorporate your mind and heart in your times of contemplation or meditation. Do not get discouraged because of what you perceive to be a deficiency in your ability to make use of imagination. The important thing is to do it to the degree you are able and to trust that God will honor your efforts. The use of the imagination is a powerful tool of illumination and formation that Ignatius incorporated in the Exercises (see "Imaginative Prayer" on p. 36).

░░

Day 6. Luke 5:1-11

Imagine you are Peter.

- What do you think and feel as Jesus tells you to put your net on the other side of the boat?

- What do you learn about Jesus as a result of the extraordinary catch of fish?

- Would this be enough for you to realize who Jesus is? Why, or why not?

- Would this be enough for you to leave behind all and follow Jesus? Why, or why not?

- In what ways could this event with Jesus impact how you live your life?

Day 7. Review your week

- What qualities of Jesus were you drawn to as you journeyed through the past week?

- What surprised or shocked you about Jesus?

- How has this week helped you to know Jesus more intimately, to love Jesus more intensely and to follow him more closely?

- Was there anything that encouraged you or gave you pause or concern regarding following Jesus? If so what, and why?

- Are you becoming more in tune with Jesus' call in your life, and is your willingness increasing to say yes to the invitations of Jesus? Why, or why not?

Share your thoughts and feelings with God/Jesus, and when you are finished, just be with Jesus, resting in his love for you, acknowledging his presence with you. Take a few moments to cease from striving and be still in the presence of the One who is with you and within you.

Showing Up

Your part is to show up and enter into the exercises for each day, as you are able. By doing that, you have offered yourself to God and declared your desire to be with God and hear from God. That is all you can do. What happens beyond that is up to God. Rest assured that to come into God's presence is to be changed. You may or may not feel something, but God is at work.

⟩⟩⟩ SECTION 5 OF 15 ⟨⟨⟨

During part of this week, you will focus on two extrabiblical meditations found in Week 2 of Ignatius's Exercises. The purpose of these meditations is for you to discern where you currently are in your spiritual life. It is not about deciding where you want to be or think you should be, but about honestly assessing where you currently are in terms of following Christ and making choices. You will spend two days on each of the meditations.

The grace you are seeking this week is *to not be deaf to Jesus' call in my life and to be ready and willing to do what he wants.*

Examen Questions

- When were you not able to be indifferent today? Why?

- What were you attracted to today?

- When were you aware of choosing to follow after Jesus? What helped you to make that decision?

Start your time with a bow—slowly bending from your waist—as a visible sign of your reverence for and honoring of God, while asking God that everything in your day may more and more lead you to divine praise and service.

Process

☐ Opening   ☐ Closing

☐ Daily exercise   ☐ Noontime examen

☐ Journaling   ☐ Evening examen

Days 1-2. Who will it be?

Imagine that you are at a beautiful setting of your choosing, and there are two people vying for your attention, desiring an alliance with you. The first catches your eye, and with an alluring smile and self-assured manner begins to flatter you, promising you personal value, riches, fame, power, physical intimacy, the satisfaction of all your desires. The words are intoxicating and seductive. Pay attention to the ways in which you are enticed, seduced, ensnared.

Which is it—flattery, personal value, riches, fame, power, physical intimacy, the satisfaction of all your desires—that entices, seduces or ensnares you? Why?

Spend time asking Jesus to help you fight these battles.

Now imagine Jesus standing in the same setting before you. Hear him calling you away from what has enticed you, and calling you to embrace love, joy, peace, patience, kindness, goodness, faithfulness, gentleness and self-control. Inviting you to embrace an attitude of indifference—not desiring life over death, health over sickness or riches or poverty, but being willing to say yes to God.

Spend time thinking over which of these things might be hard for you to stop seeking after. Explore with Jesus why this might be the case.

Colloquy. Seek to end your time "just being with" Jesus, rather than having a verbal response. Be still and be with God.

Days 3-4. Three Classes of People

Using your imagination, consider the three types of people described below. People in each of these types have great wealth and consider themselves to be a faithful follower of Jesus.

> *Class one.* These individuals desire to be free from their dependence on their possessions because they see their possessions as hindrances to fully following after Jesus. They have good intentions but remain busy with the daily demands of life. They end their lives still thinking about getting rid of their possessions and fully following Jesus, but have not done so. Their lives are characterized by a lot of talk but no action.
>
> *Class two.* These individuals would like to free themselves from all the attachments that get in the way of relating to God. They believe that working harder will bring them freedom. These individuals are willing to do just about anything, but face a block that hinders their ability to fully follow Jesus. They may do any number of good things, all the while avoiding the real issue. Their lives are characterized by doing everything but the one necessary thing.
>
> *Class three.* These individuals desire to be rid of attachments that get in the way of fully following Jesus. Their desire is to be sensitive to the movements of God's Spirit in their lives and to be ready and willing to follow God's lead. These individuals seek to arrive at a place where they want neither to retain their possessions nor to give them away, unless God directs them to do so. Their lives are characterized by a desire to hear and respond to God's invitation.

- As you look at your life, which of these types of people would best characterize how you live your life?
- What can you point to in your life that would confirm your choice?

Share your insights with God the Father, Jesus the Son, and the Holy Spirit.

Colloquy. Seek to end your time "just being with" Jesus, rather than having a verbal response. Be still and be with God.

Emotions

Beware of what you are feeling about God, yourself and the exercise of the day. We are often taught to ignore our emotions, but Ignatius found that our emotions are an aid in our spiritual formation as we become aware and unpack them. As you pay attention to your emotions—such as resistance—and unpack them, you will learn more about yourself and your image of God in the process. Your emotions will prove to be an excellent source of material for journaling.

Day 5. Review the previous four days

What insights have you gained about you and about your desire and commitment to follow Jesus?

Day 6. Luke 14:25-34

Imagine Jesus speaking the words of this passage to you. Spend time thinking through what the cost might be that would hinder you from being able to say unequivocally to Jesus, "*Yes*, I will follow you."

- What might it be difficult for you to part with to follow Jesus? Why?

  Share your thoughts, feelings and concerns with Jesus.

  Sit with the words of the following prayer.

  Eternal Lord and King of all creation, humbly I come before you. . . . I am moved by your grace to offer myself to you and your work. I deeply desire to be with you in accepting all wrongs and all rejections and all poverty, both actual and spiritual—and I deliberately choose this, if it is for your greater service and praise.

- What do these words stir within you?

- Are you willing to pray this prayer in a heartfelt way? Why, or why not?

Day 7. Review your week

- How has this week helped you to know Jesus more intimately, to love Jesus more intensely and to follow him more closely?

- What have you learned about your level of trust in God/Jesus and the impact that it has on your ability to follow Jesus in your daily life?

- Are you becoming more in tune with Jesus' call in your life, and do you desire to say yes to the invitations of Jesus? Why, or why not?

Share your thoughts and feelings with God/Jesus, and when you are finished, just be with Jesus, resting in his love for you, acknowledging his presence with you. Take a few moments to cease from striving, and be still in the presence of the One who is with you and within you.

About Questions and Suggestions

The questions given to ponder and suggestions regarding how to enter into the story are just that: questions and suggestions. These are given to help you get started. In my own journey through the Exercises, I found it helpful to enter the same Gospel narrative from a variety of perspectives: as a bystander, as a disciple, as a person interacting with Jesus and even as Jesus. Each different way of entering into the narrative can bring additional insights and opportunity for connection with Jesus. Putting yourself in Jesus' place also can bring great insight and opportunity to discover some aspects of who he is or how he interacts with others. In short, do not feel constrained by the suggestions and questions. Have fun, explore and experiment, always being open to God.

SECTION 6 OF 15

The grace you are seeking this week is *to know Jesus intimately, to love him more intensely and to follow him more closely.*

Examen Questions

- How and when did you experience Immanuel (God with you) today?

- When were you aware of your love for Jesus today?

- When do you "follow Jesus" in your relationships, circumstances, reactive and proactive responses, and actions?

Start your time with a bow—slowly bending from your waist—as a visible sign of your reverence for and honoring of God, while asking God that everything in your day may more and more lead you to divine praise and service.

Process

☐ Opening   ☐ Closing

☐ Daily exercise   ☐ Noontime examen

☐ Journaling   ☐ Evening examen

Day 1. John 2:1-11

Imagine you are a bystander who knows what is going on.

- What are you feeling as this story unfolds?

- What is your reaction as you realize Jesus has turned the water into wine?

- What does this miracle show you?

- What does this miracle teach you about God?

- About Jesus?

- About what it might mean to follow Jesus?

Colloquy. Freely speak out of your joy, thanks, wonder and praise to the triune God, earnestly beseeching God that God would enable you to know Jesus more closely and follow Jesus more nearly.

Day 2. John 2:13-16

Imagine you are following Jesus up the steps to the temple. People are coming and going in this time of the Passover. Watch Jesus fashion a

Imagine Freely and Lightly

Do not get bogged down trying to perfectly imagine the scene, especially if you, like Ignatius, have traveled to the Holy Land. The composition of the scene is but a small part of what imaginative prayer is about. The purpose of imaginative prayer is encounter with the living God through the living Word.

whip and turn over tables. Hear his words to those selling goods in the temple.

- What are you feeling?
- What are you learning about Jesus?
- How do Jesus' actions and words change how you see him and feel toward him?

Subtlety of Temptations

Be on guard. The tactics of temptations can change drastically during Week 2. The evil one will seek to derail your journey by using even good things: godly thoughts, consolations, spiritual insights. But these will take you away from your time in the Exercises. So be aware. If these things take you from the very thing God has called you to, there is a good chance that they are not from God. (See "Rules of Discernment: Week 2" on p. 150.)

Day 3. Matthew 8:5-13

Imagine you are the centurion.

- Why do you come to Jesus for help?
- What is stirred within you as Jesus says he will come and heal your servant?

- When Jesus praises your faith, what do you feel?
- What do you learn about Jesus through this story?
- What ways could this truth about Jesus impact how you live your life?

  Pray the following prayer, and spend time sitting with its words:

  Lord Jesus,
  Help me to know you, to love you, to follow you
  Help alleviate my fears
  and fan the embers of trust within me
  Give me the strength to say yes to your invitations
  the courage to continue my journey with you
  Remind me that you are
  the Way
  the Truth
  and the Life
  and apart from you there is no life
  but with you,
  and with you alone
  is fullness of life,
  life everlasting.

- What are the truths that resonate with you? Why?
- Does this prayer express your desires? Why, or why not?

Day 4. Review
Read through your journal entries from the past couple of days, seeking something that resonated deep within you, something that was either drawing you or stirring resistance in you. Spend your prayer time pondering, unpacking and exploring whatever you come up with.

Slowly pray the Lord's Prayer.

Day 5. Matthew 8:23-27
Imagine you are in the boat. Allow yourself to feel the force of the storm and the fear rising within you as the waves build and begin to crash over the bow of the boat. Look at the faces of the other disciples.

Look at Jesus fast asleep.

- What do you feel as you see Jesus asleep while you fear for your very life?

- What do you feel as you hear Jesus say, "You of little faith, why are you so afraid?"

- What do you feel as you hear Jesus speak and as you see the wind and waves stop?

- What do you learn about Jesus through this story?

- What ways could this truth about Jesus impact how you live your life?

As you look over your own life in light of this story, can you remember a time when you experienced Jesus as being asleep, seemingly not caring about you and what you were going through? Take time to work through this, looking at and embracing your feelings and bringing all that to Jesus.

Different Roles

Please enter the narratives taking on different roles, not only in terms of bystander, disciple, Jesus or a person being healed or interacted with, but as someone who is poor, a woman (if you are a man), rich, religious, desperate for help but not helped. Going through the same narrative from different perspectives can be very enlightening.

Day 6. Matthew 8:28-34

Imagine you are one of the owners of the pigs.

- What are your feelings as you see Jesus heal?

- What are you feeling as you watch your pigs run off a cliff?

- Why do you ask Jesus to leave?

- What do you learn about Jesus through this story?

- What ways could this truth about Jesus impact how you live your life?

Colloquy. Freely speak out of your joy, thanks, wonder and praise to the triune God, earnestly beseeching God that God would enable you to know Jesus more closely and follow Jesus more nearly.

Day 7. Review

- What qualities of Jesus were you drawn to as you journeyed through the past week?

- What surprised or shocked you about Jesus?

- How has this week helped you to know Jesus more intimately, to love Jesus more intensely and to follow him more closely?

- Was there anything that encouraged you or gave you pause or concern regarding following Jesus? If so what, and why?

- Are you becoming more in tune with Jesus' call in your life, and is your willingness increasing to say yes to the invitations of Jesus? Why, or why not?

Share your thoughts and feelings with God/Jesus, and when you are finished, just be with Jesus, resting in his love for you, acknowledging his presence with you. Take a few moments to cease from striving and be still in the presence of the One who is with you and within you.

⟫⟫ SECTION 7 OF 15 ⟪⟪

On day 5 of this section, you will be invited to take a walk with Jesus. Please feel free to do this on another day if it would help you to enter more fully into the experience.

The grace you are seeking this week is *to know Jesus intimately, to love him more intensely and to follow him more closely.*

Examen Questions

- How and when did you experience Immanuel (God with you) today?

- When were you aware of your love for Jesus today?
- When do you "follow Jesus" in your relationships, circumstances, reactive and proactive responses, and actions?

Process

☐ Opening ☐ Closing

☐ Daily exercise ☐ Noontime examen

☐ Journaling ☐ Evening examen

Day 1. Mark 2:1-12

Imagine you are one of the individuals in this story (the paralytic, the people who carry the paralytic, one of the crowd or a Pharisee).

- What are you thinking and feeling as this unfolds?
- What really captures your attention as you watch what transpires?
- What do you think or feel when you hear the words of Jesus, "Your sins are forgiven," and "Get up, take your mat and go home"?
- How does this impact your view of Jesus and your love for him and desire to follow him?

Spend a few moments asking Jesus if there is someone in your life whom you need to bring to him. If there is, ask Jesus what he would have you do.

Day 2. Mark 2:13-17

Imagine you are one of the Pharisees who is following Jesus from a distance, listening but not trusting or believing in Jesus or his teachings.

- What are you feeling and believing to be true about this Jesus as he invites a tax gatherer (sinner) to be one of his followers?
- As he sits down for a meal with so many sinners, what do you feel?
- As you hear his words directed to you, what do you feel?
- What does all this tell you about Jesus and make you feel toward him?

Resistance

As you journey through the Exercises, pay special attention when you experience internal resistance. Whenever you become aware of resistance, respond to it as a warning light and seek to discover the source of the resistance. Resistance is a gift from God that invites you to a deeper discovery concerning God and/or yourself. So internally pause and ponder when you become aware of resistance. Ask God to help you discern where this resistance is coming from. What does it reveal about your image, level of belief, love and trust of God? What does it tell you about your sense of self, your identity? Take the time to reflect and unpack your resistance because, over time, the results can be life changing.

Day 3. Matthew 9:18-26

Imagine you are the ruler of the synagogue, the sick woman or a follower of Jesus.

- What do you learn about Jesus?
- What ways could this truth about Jesus impact how you live your life?

Colloquy. Seek to end your time "just being with" Jesus, rather than having a verbal response. Be still and be with God.

Day 4. Review

Read through your journal entries from the past couple of days, seeking something that resonated deep within you, something that was either drawing you or stirring resistance in you. Spend your prayer time pondering, unpacking and exploring whatever you come up with.

Day 5

Take a walk with Jesus. Imagine Jesus is with you as you walk, and just talk or be silent. Share a thought or a feeling with Jesus, or point something out and listen as he does the same with you. Do not try to make something happen; just be with Jesus. If you are up to it, continue this practice throughout your day today.

Day 6. Matthew 7:15-23

Listen to these words of Jesus. What strikes you about them?

Take some time to look over your life as a Christian. What does your life fruit reveal concerning who you are?

As you spend time mulling this over, share your feelings with Jesus as they arise, and listen to him.

Using Imagination

Children readily use their imagination, so there should be a playfulness to our endeavor, a freedom to use our imagination. Resist the inner voices that seek to pressure you to do it right or well instead of having fun with it. As you enter into this way of engaging the text, your time will be transformed from knowing about Jesus to experiencing Jesus and yourself in life-giving and transforming ways.

Day 7. Review your week

- What qualities of Jesus were you drawn to as you journeyed through the past week?

- What surprised or shocked you about Jesus?

- How has this week helped you to know Jesus more intimately, to love Jesus more intensely and to follow him more closely?

- Was there anything that encouraged you or gave you pause or concern regarding following Jesus? If so what, and why?

- Are you becoming more in tune with Jesus' call in your life, and is your willingness increasing to say yes to the invitations of Jesus? Why, or why not?

Share your thoughts and feelings with God/Jesus, and when you are finished, just be with Jesus, resting in his love for you, acknowledging his presence with you. Take a few moments to cease from striving and be still in the presence of the One who is with you and within you.

⤙ SECTION 8 OF 15 ⤚

The grace you are seeking this week is *to know Jesus intimately, to love him more intensely and to follow him more closely.*

Examen Questions

- How and when did you experience Immanuel (God with you) today?

- When were you aware of your love for Jesus today?

- When do you "follow Jesus" in your relationships, circumstances, reactive and proactive responses, and actions?

Start your time with a bow—slowly bending from your waist—as a visible sign of your reverence for and honoring of God, while asking God that everything in your day may more and more lead you to divine praise and service.

Process

☐ Opening   ☐ Closing

☐ Daily exercise   ☐ Noontime examen

☐ Journaling   ☐ Evening examen

Day 1. Matthew 12:1-14

Imagine you are the man with the shriveled hand. Watch as Jesus interacts with the Pharisees. Listen to his words, his tone.

- What do you learn about Jesus through this story?

- What ways could this truth about Jesus impact how you live your life?

I Don't Like Jesus

As you spend time with Jesus day after day, you may begin to discover that there are aspects of his dealings with people you do not like. If you discover this, do not fret, but bring this to Jesus even as you continue your journey with him. You will discover that he is much more complicated than we make him out to be. Him rubbing you the wrong way indicates that you are being real and honest with Jesus and with yourself.

Day 2. Luke 7:11-17

Imagine you are the mourning mother.

- What are you feeling about life, about God and about your son?
- How do you feel about Jesus when he says, "Don't cry"?
- When he touches the coffin and tells your son to "get up"?
- When you see your son alive once again?
- What do you learn about Jesus through this story?
- What ways could this truth about Jesus impact how you live your life?

Day 3. Luke 7:36-50

Imagine you are the woman who anoints Jesus' feet.

- What are you feeling as you enter the room and you feel all eyes on you?
- Why are you drawn to Jesus in this way?
- What are you seeking to communicate to Jesus through your actions?
- What do Jesus' words mean to you?
- What do you learn about Jesus through this story?
- What ways could this truth about Jesus impact how you live your life?

Day 4. Review

Read through your journal entries from the past couple of days, seeking something that resonated deep within you, something that was either drawing you or stirring resistance in you. Spend your prayer time pondering, unpacking and exploring whatever you come up with.

Slowly pray the Lord's Prayer.

Day 5. Pray the following prayer

> Lord Jesus,
> Help me to know you, to love you, to follow you
> Help alleviate my fears
> and fan the embers of trust within me
> Give me the strength to say yes to your invitations
> the courage to continue my journey with you
> Remind me that you are
> the Way
> the Truth
> and the Life
> and apart from you there is no life
> but with you,
> and with you alone
> is fullness of life,
> life everlasting.

- Did these words express your heart's desire? Why, or why not?

  Try your hand at writing your own prayer.

  Sit with the words of the following prayer:

  Eternal Lord and King of all creation, humbly I come before you. . . . I am moved by your grace to offer myself to you and your work. I deeply desire to be with you in accepting all wrongs and all rejections and all poverty, both actual and spiritual—and I deliberately choose this, if it is for your greater service and praise.

- What do these words stir within you?

- Are you willing to pray this prayer in a heartfelt way? Why, or why not?

Day 6. *Write a letter to Jesus*

What do you want to tell Jesus, ask Jesus, share with Jesus? Take your time writing your letter, and when you are finished, prayerfully share your letter with Jesus. Imagine yourself reading him the letter.

- How does Jesus respond?

- What is your sense of Jesus as you come to him with your letter and as you read him your letter?

    Pray this prayer if it reflects your desires:

    Lord Jesus,
    Help me to know you, to love you, to follow you
    Help alleviate my fears
    and fan the embers of trust within me
    Give me the strength to say yes to your invitations
    the courage to continue my journey with you
    Remind me that you are
    the Way
    the Truth
    and the Life
    and apart from you there is no life
    but with you,
    and with you alone
    is fullness of life,
    life everlasting.

    Did you pray this prayer? Why, or why not?

Day 7. *Review your week*

- What qualities of Jesus were you drawn to as you journeyed through the past week?

- What surprised or shocked you about Jesus?

- How has this week helped you to know Jesus more intimately, to love Jesus more intensely and to follow him more closely?

- Was there anything that encouraged you or gave you pause or concern regarding following Jesus? If so what, and why?

- Are you becoming more in tune with Jesus' call in your life, and is your willingness increasing to say yes to the invitations of Jesus? Why, or why not?

Share your thoughts and feelings with God/Jesus, and when you are finished, just be with Jesus, resting in his love for you, acknowledging his presence with you. Take a few moments to cease from striving and be still in the presence of the One who is with you and within you.

Beware of Consolations

In Week 2 and beyond, consolations can be used to derail your journey through the Exercises. Be on guard. This often happens during the opening of your prayer time. You will be tempted by insights, worthwhile subjects to ponder or even a desire just to be with God. Though each one of these is good, they can actually take you away from the Exercises. Be alert to this tactic. Remember that the evil one can very well appear as an angel of light using good and godly thought for his own ends. (See "Rules of Discernment: Week 2" on p. 150.)

⤞ SECTION 9 OF 15 ⤝

The grace you are seeking this week is *to know Jesus intimately, to love him more intensely and to follow him more closely.*

Examen Questions

- How and when did you experience Immanuel (God with you) today?

- When were you aware of your love for Jesus today?

- When do you "follow Jesus" in your relationships, circumstances, reactive and proactive responses, and actions?

Start your time with a bow—slowly bending from your waist—as a visible sign of your reverence for and honoring of God, while asking

God that everything in your day may more and more lead you to divine praise and service.

Process

- ☐ Opening
- ☐ Closing
- ☐ Daily exercise
- ☐ Noontime examen
- ☐ Journaling
- ☐ Evening examen

Day 1. Mark 6:30-44

Imagine you are following Jesus.

- What are you feeling as Jesus invites you to come "to a quiet place and get some rest"?

- What are your expectations?

- What excites you about Jesus' plan?

- What do you feel when you notice that the crowd has followed you and that you will not be alone with Jesus and will not be able to rest?

- When Jesus challenges you to feed the crowd, what goes through your mind?

- When you tell Jesus what provisions you have found to feed the crowd (five loaves and two fish) and he responds by telling you to get the people in groups, what are you thinking?

- When you begin to feed the crowd and come back again and again to pick up more food, what is going on within you?

Contemplation

Take time at the end of your prayer time each day just to be with Jesus. Do not seek anything from him; just be still and rest in and with him in silence—knowing that Jesus is with you and is actively loving you in this moment and into the next moment.

- When you notice the huge amount of food that remains after the five thousand have been fed, what do you feel and think?

- What do you learn about Jesus through this story?

- What ways could this truth about Jesus impact how you live life?

Day 2. Mark 6:45-52

Imagine you are following Jesus. After reading the story, sit with these words of Jesus: "Take courage! It is I. Don't be afraid."

- What is it that stirs fear within your heart and mind?

- How does the presence of Immanuel help you escape fear and oppression?

    Colloquy. Freely speak out of your joy, thanks, wonder and praise to the triune God, earnestly beseeching God that God would enable you to know Jesus more closely and follow Jesus more nearly.

Day 3. Mark 7:24-30

Imagine you are the woman in this story, a Gentile, an outsider.

- What are your feelings as you come to Jesus?

- What are you hoping for?

- What are you afraid of?

- What do you feel as you hear Jesus' initial response to your plea? How did you experience Jesus when he responded as he did; what did you see in Jesus' eyes, hear in the tone of his voice?

- Do you believe Jesus when he says your daughter is healed? Why, or why not?

- What was your overall experience with Jesus like? Why?

    If you have time, imagine that you are a disciple or onlooker.

- What do you think of this Gentile woman who dares to approach Jesus?

- What is your response to Jesus' initial words to this woman?

- Do you believe that Jesus actually heals her daughter? Why, or why not?

- What do you learn about Jesus through this interaction?

Day 4. Review

Read through your journal entries from the past couple of days, seeking something that resonated deep within you, something that was either drawing you or stirring resistance in you. Spend your prayer time pondering, unpacking and exploring whatever you come up with.

Slowly pray the Lord's Prayer.

Day 5. John 4:1-26

Imagine you are the woman at the well.

- What are you feeling as Jesus speaks with you?

- What do you feel coming from Jesus as you interact with him?

- What do Jesus' promises regarding the water that quenches thirst forever and produces living water welling up to everlasting life mean to you?

- What do you learn about Jesus through this story?

- What ways could this truth about Jesus impact how you live life?

Day 6. Matthew 14:22-36

Focusing on verses 28-36, imagine you are Peter.

- What are the wind and waves in your life that draw you away from knowing Jesus more intimately, loving him more intensely and following him more closely?

   Colloquy. Seek to end your time "just being with" Jesus, rather than giving a verbal response. Be still and be with God.

Day 7. Review your week

- What qualities of Jesus were you drawn to as you journeyed through the past week?

- What surprised or shocked you about Jesus?

- How has this week helped you to know Jesus more intimately, to love Jesus more intensely and to follow him more closely?

- Was there anything that encouraged you or gave you pause or concern regarding following Jesus? If so what, and why?

- Are you becoming more in tune with Jesus' call in your life, and is your willingness increasing to say yes to the invitations of Jesus? Why, or why not?

Share your thoughts and feelings with God/Jesus, and when you are finished, just be with Jesus, resting in his love for you, acknowledging his presence with you. Take a few moments to cease from striving and be still in the presence of the One who is with you and within you.

ᴙ SECTION 10 OF 15 ᴙ

The grace you are seeking this week is *to know Jesus intimately, to love him more intensely and to follow him more closely.*

Examen Questions

- How and when did you experience Immanuel (God with you) today?

- When were you aware of your love for Jesus today?

- When do you "follow Jesus" in your relationships, circumstances, reactive and proactive responses, and actions?

Start your time with a bow—slowly bending from your waist—as a visible sign of your reverence for and honoring of God, while asking God that everything in your day may more and more lead you to divine praise and service.

Process

☐ Opening   ☐ Closing

☐ Daily exercise   ☐ Noontime examen

☐ Journaling   ☐ Evening examen

Day 1. Mark 9:14-29

Imagine you are following Jesus.

- As you realize your inability to drive the spirit from the boy, what thoughts cross your mind?

- What doubts arise in your heart?

- What goes on inside you as you watch the interchange between Jesus and the boy's father?

- What is stirred within you as you hear Jesus' words, "Everything is possible for him who believes" and "This kind can only come out by prayer"?

- What are your internal reactions to the words of the father, "I do believe; help me overcome my unbelief"?

- What do you learn about Jesus through this story?

- What ways could this truth about Jesus impact how you live?

Day 2. Luke 10:38-42

Read this passage two times using imaginative reading. The first time, imagine you are Martha.

- What are you feeling and thinking as you see Mary?

- As you approach Jesus?

- As Jesus responds to your request?
  The second time through, imagine you are Mary.

- What are you feeling and thinking as you see Martha?

- As you hear Martha's request?

- As you hear Jesus' response?

- Whom do you most easily identify with—Mary or Martha? Why?

- What is Jesus' invitation to you through this story?

Day 3. Luke 17:11-19

Imagine you are an onlooker, watching as ten lepers call out and interact with Jesus. You see them healed as they begin to walk away from Jesus. You see that only one comes back to offer thanks.

- What feelings are stirred within you as you watch this scene unfold?

- How has Jesus brought healing change to you?

- How does this affect how you see and think about Jesus?

- Spend some time thanking Jesus for what he has done, is doing and will do on your behalf.

Day 4. Review

Read through your journal entries from the past couple of days, seeking something that resonated deep within you, something that was either drawing you or stirring resistance in you. Spend your prayer time pondering, unpacking and exploring whatever you come up with.

Slowly pray the Lord's Prayer.

Day 5. Mark 10:46-52

Imagine you are blind Bartimaeus.

- What goes on inside you as you realize Jesus is passing by?

- As others tell you to be quiet?

- As still others tell you that Jesus is calling you?

- What goes through your mind and heart as Jesus asks you what you want? What are the fears, dreams and desires that arise within you?

- What was it like to be able to see; what have you gained and what have you lost?

- How has Bartimaeus's story also been your story?

- What have you learned about Jesus from your story?

- In what ways do these truths about Jesus impact how you live?

As you look at your life, ask yourself these two questions: To what am I currently blind? What do I long to see?

Day 6. Matthew 17:1-9

Imagine you are going up the hill with Jesus.

- As you watch Jesus transfigured right before your eyes, what are you thinking and feeling?

- What are you feeling when you hear Peter's words?

- When you hear the words of God, what do you feel?

- What is going on inside you as you lay face down on the ground?

- When Jesus touches you and says, "Don't be afraid"?

- What do you learn about Jesus through this story?

- What ways could this truth about Jesus impact how you live?

Colloquy. Freely speak out of your joy, thanks, wonder and praise to the triune God, earnestly beseeching God that God would enable you to know Jesus more closely and follow Jesus more nearly.

Day 7. Review your week

- What qualities of Jesus were you drawn to as you journeyed through the past week?

- What surprised or shocked you about Jesus?

- How has this week helped you to know Jesus more intimately, to love Jesus more intensely and to follow him more closely?

- Was there anything that encouraged you or gave you pause or concern regarding following Jesus? If so what, and why?

- Are you becoming more in tune with Jesus' call in your life, and is your willingness increasing to say yes to the invitations of Jesus? Why, or why not?

Share your thoughts and feelings with God/Jesus, and when you are finished, just be with Jesus, resting in his love for you, acknowledging his presence with you. Take a few moments to cease from striving and be still in the presence of the One who is with you and within you.

⤙ SECTION 11 OF 15 ⤚

The grace you are seeking this week is *to know Jesus intimately, to love him more intensely and to follow him more closely.*

Examen Questions

- How and when did you experience Immanuel (God with you) today?

- When were you aware of your love for Jesus today?

- When do you "follow Jesus" in your relationships, circumstances, reactive and proactive responses, and actions?

Start your time with a bow—slowly bending from your waist—as a visible sign of your reverence for and honoring of God, while asking God that everything in your day may more and more lead you to divine praise and service.

Process

☐ Opening ☐ Closing

☐ Daily exercise ☐ Noontime examen

☐ Journaling ☐ Evening examen

Day 1. Matthew 6:19-24

Imagine Jesus speaking these words to you, and ponder them. Before answering the following questions, take a moment to become aware of feelings they raise within you. Share your honest answers with Jesus, and listen for his response.

- What are your treasures?
- Who has your heart?
- Who are your masters?

  Pray this prayer if it reflects your desires:

  Lord Jesus,
  Help me to know you, to love you, to follow you
  Help alleviate my fears
  and fan the embers of trust within me
  Give me the strength to say yes to your invitations
  the courage to continue my journey with you
  Remind me that you are
  the Way
  the Truth
  and the Life
  and apart from you there is no life
  but with you,
  and with you alone

is fullness of life,
life everlasting.

Did you pray this prayer? Why, or why not?

Day 2. Matthew 19:16-30

Imagine you are the rich young man who comes to Jesus.

- Why have you come to Jesus? What are you hoping to receive from your encounter with Jesus?

- When you hear Jesus' initial response, "Do not commit murder, do not commit adultery" and so on, what are you feeling inside?

- What happens inside you when you hear Jesus' request to "sell all you have"?

- What is the promise riches hold for you that gives them so much power over you?

Imagine you are standing before Jesus, and you ask him, "What do I lack?"

- What do you fear will be Jesus' response to you? Why?

Share your fear and seek to unpack it with Jesus.

Pray this prayer if it reflects your desires:

Eternal Lord and King of all creation, humbly I come before you. . . . I am moved by your grace to offer myself to you and your work. I deeply desire to be with you in accepting all wrongs and all rejections and all poverty, both actual and spiritual—and I deliberately choose this, if it is for your greater service and praise.

Did you pray this prayer? Why, or why not?

Day 3. Luke 18:15-17

Imagine you are a child brought by your parent(s) to Jesus.

- When you see Jesus, what do you sense to be true about Jesus? What draws you to Jesus?

- What kind of interaction takes place between you and Jesus?

After a while, imagine you are sitting on Jesus' lap.

- What are you experiencing?
- What does Jesus say to you? What do you say to Jesus? Why?

Finally, imagine Jesus placing his hands on your head and blessing you.

- What does Jesus speak over you and into you?
- Are you able to receive these words of Jesus? Why, or why not?

Colloquy. Seek to end your time "just being with" Jesus rather than giving a verbal response. Be still and be with God.

Day 4. Review

Read through your journal entries from the past couple of days, seeking something that resonated deep within you, something that was either drawing you or stirring resistance in you. Spend your prayer time pondering, unpacking and exploring whatever you come up with.

Slowly pray the Lord's Prayer.

Day 5. John 11:1-44

Imagine you are one of the disciples with Jesus, and you get word that Jesus' friend is dying.

- What do you think Jesus will do?
- What surprises you about how Jesus deals with this situation?
  Pay close attention to his words.
- What do you think or feel about what Jesus said? Or what is your reaction to what Jesus said?
- Are you surprised by how Jesus is initially handling this situation? Why, or why not?
  Now sit with the words of John 11:35: "Jesus wept."
- What do Jesus' tears mean to you?
- What do Jesus' tears tell you regarding who he is?
- Do you think Jesus ever shed tears for you? Why, or why not?
- If you answered yes, when did Jesus shed tears for you?
- How does that impact your relationship with Jesus?

- If your answer was no, how does that feel? How does that impact your relationship with Jesus?

Spend time talking all this over with Jesus.

Day 6. *Matthew 20:20-28*

Imagine you are hearing the words of Jesus regarding what it means to be a leader.

- What is your internal reaction?
- How do those words impact your desire to follow Jesus, to say yes to Jesus?

Now listen to Jesus' self-description.

- What do his words and example convey about being a follower of Jesus?
- What do Jesus' words stir within you?

Let this lead you into a time of thanksgiving and praise.

Day 7. *Review your week*

- What qualities of Jesus were you drawn to as you journeyed through the past week?
- What surprised or shocked you about Jesus?
- How has this week helped you to know Jesus more intimately, to love Jesus more intensely and to follow him more closely?
- Was there anything that encouraged you or gave you pause or concern regarding following Jesus? If so what, and why?
- Are you becoming more in tune with Jesus' call in your life, and is your willingness increasing to say yes to the invitations of Jesus? Why, or why not?

Share your thoughts and feelings with God/Jesus, and when you are finished, just be with Jesus, resting in his love for you, acknowledging his presence with you. Take a few moments to cease from striving and be still in the presence of the One who is with you and within you.

⤳ SECTION 12 OF 15 ⤫

The grace you are seeking this week is *to know Jesus intimately, to love him more intensely and to follow him more closely.*

Examen Questions

- How and when did you experience Immanuel (God with you) today?

- When were you aware of your love for Jesus today?

- When do you "follow Jesus" in your relationships, circumstances, reactive and proactive responses, and actions?

    Start your time with a bow—slowly bending from your waist—as a visible sign of your reverence for and honoring of God, while asking God that everything in your day may more and more lead you to divine praise and service.

Process

☐ Opening   ☐ Closing

☐ Daily exercise   ☐ Noontime examen

☐ Journaling   ☐ Evening examen

Day 1. Matthew 22:34-38

Sit with the words of Jesus, "Love the Lord your God with all your heart and with all your soul and with all your mind."

- How has your love for the triune God changed as you have journeyed through this section of the Exercises?

- Which is more difficult for you to do: to love God in a heartfelt way (all your heart) or in a more intellectual (with all your mind)? Why?

- Do you find it easier to love God the Father, Jesus, or the Holy Spirit with all your heart, soul and mind? Why?

Day 2. Matthew 22:34-40

Sit with the words of Jesus, "Love your neighbor as yourself."

- As you have journeyed with Jesus through the exercises in this section, what have you learned about what it might mean to love your neighbor?

Ask Jesus to reveal to you how you might be able to grow in your ability to love your neighbor. Also ask him to show you "neighbors" currently in your life that God may want you to commit to loving.

Day 3. Review

- What is it from these passages that draws you to Jesus, challenges you, amazes you, gives you pause, causes resistance in you or causes another reaction? Why?

Slowly pray the Lord's Prayer.

During days 4, 5 and 6, you will be encouraged to ask God to reveal areas of struggle in your life that correspond to the woes Jesus pronounces over the Pharisees in Matthew 23. If there is something that God reveals to you as a possible growth area, make note of it, bring it to God during your noontime or evening examen.

Day 4. Matthew 23:1-12

As you listen to Jesus pronounce these "woes," ask God to show you which you are susceptible to and any you may currently need to pay special attention to. Think back over your journey with Jesus through the Gospels, and recall incidents or teachings from his life that demonstrate the opposite of the woes he proclaims.

Day 5. Matthew 23:13-28

As you listen to Jesus pronounce these woes, ask God to show you which you are susceptible to and any you may currently need to pay special attention to. Think back over your journey with Jesus through the Gospels, and recall incidents or teachings from his life that demonstrate the opposite of the woes he proclaims.

Day 6. Matthew 23:29-39

As you listen to Jesus pronounce these woes, ask God to show you which you are susceptible to and any you may currently need to pay special attention to. Think back over your journey with Jesus through

the Gospels, and recall incidents or teachings from his life that demonstrate the opposite of the woes he proclaims.

Day 7. Review your week

- What qualities of Jesus were you drawn to as you journeyed through
  the past week?

- What surprised or shocked you about Jesus?

- How has this week helped you to know Jesus more intimately, to love
  Jesus more intensely and to follow him more closely?

- Was there anything that encouraged you or gave you pause or concern regarding following Jesus? If so what, and why?

- Are you becoming more in tune with Jesus' call in your life, and is
  your willingness increasing to say yes to the invitations of Jesus?
  Why, or why not?

Share your thoughts and feelings with God/Jesus, and when you
are finished, just be with Jesus, resting in his love for you, acknowledging his presence with you. Take a few moments to cease from
striving and be still in the presence of the One who is with you and
within you.

❧ SECTION 13 OF 15 ❧

During the next two sections (13 and 14) of Week 2, you will be focusing your attention on the seven "I Am" statements of Jesus. A series of
questions will help you ponder these statements during your prayer
time each day. As you make use of the questions, please remember that
the goal is not to get through them, but rather to use them as a means
of opening yourself to Jesus and discovering more about who you are as
his follower.

- What does this "I Am" statement communicate to you regarding
  who Jesus is? What are the feelings or thoughts that arise within you
  as you ponder this?

- Have you experienced Jesus in this way? If yes, take time to recall the experience. How did it make you feel? How did it, or does it, impact your life? If the answer is no, how does this make you feel? Take time to share your feelings with Jesus. Remember to be honest; even raw, angry honesty with God is welcomed by God.

- As you reflect on this "I Am" statement, are there feelings of disappointment, anger, frustration, confusion, hurt or pain that arise within you? What is the "why" behind these emotions? What is the impact of these emotions on your life and on your relationship with God/Jesus? Bring all this before God/Jesus through prayer, journaling, writing a letter to God, screaming at God—the means is not the important thing. What is important is that you bring all this to God.

- What might be the invitations, promises, encouragements and/or challenges for you found in this "I Am" statement?

- What are the needs and desires this "I Am" statement might meet in your life if you were fully able to embrace its truth in your heart and allow it to shape and mold you?

Allow this to flow into a time of talking with Jesus about whatever has been or is surfacing within you regarding Jesus' "I Am" statements.

The grace you are seeking this week is *to know Jesus intimately, to love him more intensely and to follow him more closely.*

Examen Questions

- How and when did you experience Immanuel (God with you) today?

- When were you aware of your love for Jesus today?

- When do you "follow Jesus" in your relationships, circumstances, reactive and proactive responses, and actions?

Start your time with a bow—slowly bending from your waist—as a visible sign of your reverence for and honoring of God, while asking God that everything in your day may more and more lead you to divine praise and service.

Process

☐ Opening   ☐ Closing

☐ Daily exercise   ☐ Noontime examen

☐ Journaling   ☐ Evening examen

Day 1. John 6:35
"I am the bread of life."

Day 2. John 8:12
"I am the light of the world."

Day 3. John 10:7
"I am the gate [or door]."

Day 4. John 10:11
"I am the good shepherd."

Day 5
Choose an "I Am" statement from a previous day, and ponder it further.

Day 6. John 11:25
"I am the resurrection and the life."

Day 7. Review this past week

• To which of these images are you most drawn? Why?

Reflect on your time in the "I Am" statements of Jesus, and imagine him asking you the question "Who do you say I am?" (Mk 8:29). Journal your response.

➤➤ SECTION 14 OF 15 ➤➤

The grace you are seeking this week is *to know Jesus intimately, to love him more intensely and to follow him more closely.*

Examen Questions

- How and when did you experience Immanuel (God with you) today?
- When were you aware of your love for Jesus today?
- When do you "follow Jesus" in your relationships, circumstances, reactive and proactive responses, and actions?

Start your time with a bow—slowly bending from your waist—as a visible sign of your reverence for and honoring of God, while asking God that everything in your day may more and more lead you to divine praise and service.

Process

☐ Opening   ☐ Closing

☐ Daily exercise   ☐ Noontime examen

☐ Journaling   ☐ Evening examen

Day 1. John 14:6
"I am the way."

Day 2. John 14:6
"I am the truth."
Spend some time pondering on how John 8:32—"Then you will know the truth, and the truth will set you free"—and Jesus' above declaration might tie together.

Day 3. John 14:6
"I am the life."

Day 4. Review
Read through your journal entries from the past couple of days, seeking something that resonated deep within you, something that was either drawing you or stirring resistance in you. Spend your prayer time pondering, unpacking and exploring whatever you come up with.

Day 5. John 15:5
"I am the vine."

Day 6

Draw a picture or create a collage that captures the images of the previous two sections (13, 14). Imagine yourself presenting your creation to God.

How does God respond?

Day 7. Review the past week

- To which of these images are you most drawn? Why?

Reflect on your time in the "I Am" statements of Jesus, and imagine him asking you the question "Who do you say I am?" (Mk 8:29). Journal your response.

⤙ SECTION 15 OF 15 ⤚

The grace you are seeking this week is *to know Jesus intimately, to love him more intensely and to follow him more closely.*

Examen Questions

- How and when did you experience Immanuel (God with you) today?
- When were you aware of your love for Jesus today?
- When do you "follow Jesus" in your relationships, circumstances, reactive and proactive responses, and actions?

Start your time with a bow—slowly bending from your waist—as a visible sign of your reverence for and honoring of God, while asking God that everything in your day may more and more lead you to divine praise and service.

Process

☐ Opening   ☐ Closing

☐ Daily exercise   ☐ Noontime examen

☐ Journaling   ☐ Evening examen

Day 1. Matthew 21:12-17

Imagine you are following Jesus.

- What are you feeling as you watch Jesus overturn tables?
- What are your feelings as he heals people?
- What is stirred within you as you hear the children and watch the interaction between Jesus and the Pharisees?
- How does watching all this make you feel about Jesus?
- How does this affect your desire and willingness to follow Jesus?

Day 2. Mark 11:1-11

Imagine you are one of the disciples.

What is going through your mind as you hear the shouts of the people and sense the popularity of Jesus, your teacher?

Colloquy. Freely speak out of your joy, thanks, wonder and praise to the triune God, earnestly beseeching God that God would enable you to know Jesus more closely and follow Jesus more nearly.

Day 3. Luke 21:1-4

Imagine you are watching as the woman gives her offering.

- What do you think of her and of her gift?
- What do you think of her and her gift after you hear the words of Jesus?

Now imagine that Jesus addresses his comments to you.

- What do his words touch within you?
- Look at your life, your pattern of giving to God and to others. Do Jesus' words challenge you, encourage you, embarrass you, etc.? Why, or why not?

Day 4. Review

Read through your journal entries from the past couple of days, seeking something that resonated deep within you, something that was either drawing you or stirring resistance in you. Spend your prayer time pondering, unpacking and exploring whatever you come up with.

Slowly pray the Lord's Prayer.

Day 5. Matthew 26:6-13

Imagine you are (A) one of the guests at the meal or (B) the woman who anoints Jesus' head with perfume, and answer the questions below that correspond to each option.

A

- What do you think and feel as this woman approaches Jesus?

- As you watch her pour expensive perfume on Jesus' head?

- As you hear the comments of the disciples?

- What, if anything, changes within you in terms of your feelings toward the woman, her actions and the response of the disciples as you hear Jesus' words to this woman? Why?

B

- What are you feeling as you decide to anoint Jesus' head?

- As you are on your way into the home that Jesus is visiting?

- As you enter the room and feel all the eyes of those there upon you?

- What do you feel as you pour the precious perfume on Jesus' head?

- As you hear the objections voiced by the disciples?

- As you hear the words of Jesus?

- As you look into the eyes of Jesus, and as he looks deeply into your eyes?

Day 6. Three kinds of humility

Read through the three kinds of humility listed below, seeking to name and discover which one would best indicate the level of your desire and commitment to follow Jesus. The goal is not to choose one over the other, but to discern where you currently are and to name and embrace that reality.

1. I desire to do nothing that would cut me off from God, not even were I put in charge of all creation or given more years of living here on earth. (obedience)

2. I do not desire riches rather than poverty, honor rather than dishonor, a long life rather than a short life. My desire is to do the will of God my Lord, to honor, praise and serve God. (indifference)

3. I desire the truth of Jesus' life to be fully the truth of my own life so that I find myself moved by grace, with a love and a desire for poverty, for insults, for being considered a worthless fool for Christ rather than wise and prudent according to the standards of the world. (transcendence of indifference)

- As you have reflected on the three kinds of humility, where do you currently find yourself?

- How do you feel about being there?

- What is your desire concerning these three kinds (not levels) of humility? Why?

Share your thoughts and feelings with Jesus, remembering that each kind of humility is acknowledging the greatness and supremacy of God and thus brings praise and honor to God.

Day 7. Review

- How did your time in Week 2 of the Exercises mold and shape your view of Jesus?

- Have you been able to know Jesus more intimately, to love him more intensely and to follow him more closely? If yes, how can this be seen in your life? If no, why not?

- What has drawn you to Christ, challenged you, amazed you?

- What has given you pause or caused resistance in you?

- Have you become more in tune with Jesus' call in your life and is your willingness to say yes to the invitations of Jesus increasing? Why, or why not?

Share your thoughts and feelings with God/Jesus, and when you are finished, just be with Jesus, resting in his love for you, acknowledging his presence with you. Take a few moments to cease from striving and be still in the presence of the One who is with you and within you.

CONCLUDING COMMENTS AND REFLECTIONS

You have made it through Week 2, the heart and soul of the Exercises. You have spent the past several months walking with and being with Jesus from his birth up until the Passion Week (Week 3). You have been growing in your experiential knowledge of Jesus, your love for Jesus and your desire to say yes to Jesus and to follow him more closely as you have faithfully journeyed through the daily exercises. You have asked God for the daily grace and practiced the prayer of examen. Through the meditations "Call of the King," the "Two Standards" and "Three Types of Humility," you have been challenged to consider the level of your desire for Jesus and your commitment to follow after him and embrace the life he offers. Week 2 has been a time of exploring and deepening your sense of who Jesus is and what it might mean for you to follow him at this stage of your life and during these circumstances of your life.

Now that Week 2 has come to an end, you are faced with another choice: do you continue on to Week 3; do you end your journey here; or do you continue your journey in the Exercises but instead of moving on to Week 3, go back through Week 2 or portions of it?

For some of you, this may mark the end of your journey, at least for now. For others, this may be an excellent time to slowly go back over your journal or even reenter a previous Week or section. Remember, the point is not to get through the Exercises, but rather to use them as a tool to open you up to God. If you are not sure where you are with Jesus, if you are unsure of the level of commitment you are willing to make in order to say yes to Jesus, I suggest you not move forward but spend time going back through Week 2.

As you ponder your decision I encourage you to work through the following material to discern whether or not you should move on to Week 3. There is nothing wrong with choosing to linger in Week 2 if that is where you are sensing God working in you. The spiritual transformation that God brings about during your journey through the Exercises is the result of time spent with God, not because you have worked your way through the entire Exercises.

As you go through the questions and continuums below to discern God's leading, take your time. Week 3 can be a very difficult journey for some, and it is certainly not meant for everyone. I suggest taking at least two to three days to journal about the following questions and work through the continuums. There is no need to move on to Week 3 if you are not sensing God's invitation to do so, and there is no rush to make your decision.

- How has your sense of Jesus changed during your journey through Week 2?

- What was lost and what has been gained as your image of Jesus changed?

- What is the level of your desire to follow Jesus?

- What price are you willing to pay to follow Jesus (would you be willing to take up your cross and die)?

- Are you more able to hear the call of Jesus in your daily life? Why, or why not?

- Are you more willing to say yes to the challenges and invitations of Jesus to follow? Why, or why not?

Spend time pondering where you find yourself on the continuums below, seeking to let go of internal pressure to move on to Week 3 and choosing to be open to God's leading regarding moving on. As you work through the continuums, endeavor to answer from your heart and not merely your head.

I live   Christ lives in me

|---|---|

Self-focused   Christ-focused

|---|---|

Follow world's ways   Follow Jesus

|---|---|

Earthly treasure	Treasure in heaven
├───┤

Riches, honor, significance	Humility, dependency, significance in Christ
├───┤

Disordered attachment	Indifference/freedom
├───┤

Follow Jesus if convenient	Follow Jesus
├───┤

Save life	Lose life
├───┤

Follow Jesus	Deeper identification with Jesus
├───┤

If you are leaning toward entering into Week 3, ask yourself this final question: Am I ready to walk to the cross with Jesus, to suffer with Jesus, to stand by Jesus as all others desert him? Week 3 will challenge you to enter into a new level, from following him to being with him in the midst of his Passion. It involves choosing to pick up the cross of Jesus, walking with him as Simon did on the Via Dolarosa. This is no walk in the park; it can be a grueling time of experiencing dryness and desolation during your prayer times. It can be a time of profound sorrow but also a time of surprising consolation.

Please consider carefully if God is leading you into Week 3. It is not for the weak, faint-hearted or timid in spirit. Week 3 is for those who feel the draw, call and desire to fully enter into the Passion of Christ, not as an interested spectator but as a participant willingly choosing to enter into the fellowship of Christ's sufferings.

Before making your final decision regarding moving on to Week 3, reentering Week 2 or concluding your journey through the Exercises, please speak with your spiritual director or listener, sharing your insights from the questions and continuums above.

If you are feeling that you are in a good internal place for moving forward, do one more thing: take time to recommit to your journey through the Exercises, pledging to give yourself wholly to God (as you are able) and to seek to gain nothing from God, but rather purpose to each day present yourself to God as "your spiritual act of worship," which is "holy and pleasing to God" (Rom 12:1).

Ash Wednesday and the spiritual exercises. If it is a few days or weeks before Lent begins (on Ash Wednesday), I would encourage you to wait before going forward in the Exercises, so you can begin Week 3 on Ash Wednesday. This is not always possible, but when it works out, it can be a powerful experience as you join millions of other Christians throughout the world who are also focusing on the Passion of Jesus during this time. If your own church intentionally participates in Lent, this can be a double blessing.

If you are able to sync your entry into Week 3 with the Lenten season, go to appendix 1, where you will find extra exercises for Ash Wednesday, the rest of that week and the final week leading to Easter.

JOURNEY TO THE CROSS

As you enter into this new unit of the Exercises, you will find yourself in what is traditionally referred to as Week 3. In Week 3, your focus shifts to the Passion Week (from the Last Supper through Jesus' death on the cross). Your prayer time during each day will involve walking with Jesus to the cross and being with him at the cross (even on the cross). The method for interacting with the Scriptures will primarily be imaginative prayer or lectio divina. The purpose of praying over the Passion is to experience it. This means you are not just to contemplate it, but to be with Jesus as it happens.

This week harkens you back to the Kingdom Meditation (section 1 of Week 2), when you heard Jesus declare, "It is my will to bring all the world into the glory of my Father's kingdom; therefore, all who would like to come with me must walk as I walk and live as I live, laboring with me, following me in the pain so that they may also follow me in the glory." This Week you follow Jesus "in the pain."

Week 3 might also remind you of Week 1, as the subject matter seems similar: the cross and sin. However, the focus of Week 3 is quite different. Whereas Week 1 was concerned with your ability to experience sorrow, tears and confusion over your choices to sin in light of God's limitless love, grace, mercy and faithfulness, Week 3 leads you into seeking to be able to enter into the sufferings of Jesus (*compassion:* to suffer with)—feeling the sorrow and pain of Jesus as he bore your sins and the sins of the world.

While this Week's focus does include the personal and cosmic reality of sin that is embedded in the cross of Christ, you are also to walk with Jesus to the cross, seeking to experience what he experienced. This Week is not about personal repentance but personal follow-ship of Jesus, who suffered and died because of your sins.

The goal is not to be overwhelmed by feelings of guilt and shame because your actions (sins) led to Christ's death, but to choose to join with Jesus in his suffering for the sins of the world, for your own sins—a grace that Paul deeply desired and wrote about in Philippians 3:10: "I want to know . . . the fellowship of sharing in his sufferings." This Week is about walking with Jesus in a deeper, more personal and intense way than in Week 2. It is entering into Jesus' journey as a companion in all he encounters. In a sense, it is a change of perspective. In sections leading up to Week 3, you have looked at Jesus. Now you are invited to look using Jesus' eyes to see. This focus continues into Week 4 as well.

Week 3 involves a deeper identification with Christ, an interior participation in his sufferings. This is a natural outflow of Week 2, during which you were asking God for the grace to know Jesus more intimately, to love him more intensely and to follow him more closely. This deeper identification with Jesus in his Passion is an outflow of a desire not only to follow Jesus but also to be with him as a companion, not merely as an observer.

Week 3 is about choosing to enter into solidarity with Jesus, whom you deeply love and care about. You will now walk with him through Week 3 as one walks with a friend—seeking to be present to Jesus, your friend, empathizing with him, seeing how he suffers through the words and actions of others. You no longer stand on the sidelines; you enter into the experience with Jesus, no longer watching but participating. This journeying with Jesus to the cross will continue the process of opening yourself to the depth of God's love.

Although Week 3 can lead you into a greater awareness of the depth and scope of God's love, it can also be a very difficult section of the Exercises. The daily exercises can be very dry and even agonizing, leading you to feel discouraged. There may be a time when the felt presence of God is nowhere to be found, a time of avoidance, of extreme distraction and even of unhealthy or destructive guilt. Seeing the depth of his pain and suffering, you might begin to assign yourself blame for what Jesus is going through.

As was stated earlier, Week 3 is not for the weak, timid or faint-hearted. This section may lead you into times when you feel powerless, humiliated, stressed and alone. These are the feelings Jesus encountered as he entered into the travails of his journey to the cross, so it should come as no surprise that you may experience these as you choose to journey with him to the cross.

Heed these words: the person ready for the third Week

> manifests a deepening desire for union with Christ, no matter what, and usually experiences a desire, although sometimes accompanied with hesitation and even fear, to move with Christ into a contemplation of his Passion and to glimpse what this will mean concretely after the retreat. . . . One's desire, one's whole thrust is to become so identified with Christ that suffering is inevitable.

If the above draws you, even though there may be internal resistance within, by all means move into Week 3. But if you are unable even to desire the desire for what is spoken of above, now is not the time for you to move on to Week 3.

If you are continuing on to Week 3, please carefully and prayerfully heed the warnings concerning the difficulties you may encounter. Your experience in Week 3 might mirror the helplessness and hardship that Jesus experienced in his Passion. But there is also great value found in meditating on the cross of Christ, on Christ crucified. Concerning the transforming power of meditating on the Passion of Christ, Martin Luther wrote,

> If one does meditate rightly on the suffering of Christ for a day, an hour, or even a quarter of an hour, this we may confidently say is better than a whole year of fasting, days of Psalm singing, yes, than even one hundred Masses, because this reflection changes the whole man and makes him new, as once he was in baptism.

The writings of apostle Paul also bear testimony to the importance and centrality of Christ crucified:

Jews demand miraculous signs and Greeks look for wisdom, but we preach Christ crucified: a stumbling block to Jews and foolishness to Gentiles, but to those whom God has called, both Jews and Greeks, Christ the power of God and the wisdom of God. (1 Cor 1:22-24)

For I resolved to know nothing while I was with you except Jesus Christ and him crucified. (1 Cor 2:2)

I have been crucified with Christ and I no longer live, but Christ lives in me. The life I live in the body, I live by faith in the Son of God, who loved me and gave himself for me. (Gal 2:20)

I want to know Christ and the power of his resurrection and the fellowship of sharing in his sufferings, becoming like him in his death. (Phil 3:10)

May I never boast except in the cross of our Lord Jesus Christ, through which the world has been crucified to me, and I to the world. (Gal 6:14)

Although the apostle Paul, Martin Luther and others stressed the importance and the transforming power of Christ crucified, this has not been embraced by Protestants as a whole. For Protestants, there is a tendency to ignore or at least minimize the reality of Christ crucified. Crosses in Protestant churches, if we have crosses, are almost always devoid of the pierced body of Christ. The focus tends to be on the resurrected Christ. Because of a lack of emphasis on Christ crucified in Protestant circles, you may have trouble staying with the focus of Week 3 if you are a Protestant.

Ironically, another hindrance to your ability to enter into the Passion narratives in Week 3—to be with Jesus as he walks to the cross—is your familiarity with these narratives. If you are very familiar with these passages, you likely will not be shocked, offended or appalled by the story. You also may find it difficult to name, let alone identify with, the pain Jesus endured on the cross, because it is beyond all our ability to comprehend. You may find yourself struggling to identify with how he suffered as his disciples slept, Judas betrayed him, Peter denied him, his own people turned against him, people bore false witness regarding him and God forsook him.

But do not lose heart. Simply continue to come into the prayer time each day, presenting your body as a living and holy sacrifice, asking for the grace for this Week, while trusting God and the process, endeavoring to receive whatever God has for you each day. If God has led you to continue, Week 3 will ultimately be a life-giving, spiritually transforming time.

ADDITIONS TO EXERCISES

As you work through the daily exercises, in addition to the questions given each day, there will be three considerations to make each day:

- What did Jesus suffer in his humanity in this narrative?

- How did Jesus hide (not use) his divinity in this narrative?

- What is your response to Jesus' sacrifice for you in terms of how you might view life, live life and interact with others?

During your prayer time, create an ambiance conducive to entering into the pain and sorrow of Jesus. For example, close your curtains or blinds, darken the room in which you will be spending the time, and use a candle as your light source. Consider using different postures during this time, such as kneeling or lying prostrate, to help you engage more fully with Jesus as you enter into the Passion narratives.

Sign of the cross. Making the sign of the cross will mark the beginning and end of your daily time through the duration of Week 3. This will serve as a physical declaration of your honoring of God and a presenting of yourself to God as you enter the prayer time as well as when you leave your prayer time to enter the world at large. The sign of the cross is yet another way to involve your body in the prayer process.

To make the sign of the cross, use your right hand. Beginning from the middle of your chest, raise your right hand and touch your forehead, saying out loud, "In the name of the Father." Then touch your chest (heart) while saying, "The Son," and touch your left shoulder, saying "and the Holy" and then your right shoulder, saying, "Spirit." (If you are a fan of the Eastern Church, do as they do, going from right shoulder to left shoulder.) Finally, put your hands together about chest height and say, "Amen."

Please make the sign of the cross slowly and prayerfully. One person, commenting on the speed at which many make this sign, said it has appeared to be less a practice of prayer and more a practice of swatting flies. Endeavor to make this an act of honoring the triune God and acknowledging the sacrifice and love of Jesus.

If you are wondering how to hold your fingers on your right hand while making the sign of the cross, there are generally two ways. The first and oldest way to position your fingers is by using your thumb and forefinger or your index and middle finger. Those in the Eastern Church put three fingers together (thumb, forefinger and middle), while the ring and little finger are folded back on the palm. I like this method because it was chosen to symbolize the Trinity (three fingers) and the two natures of Christ: fully God, fully man (the two fingers folded into the palm).

To the making of the sign of the cross you can add a slow bow, which you incorporated during Week 2, as you are saying amen.

Crucifix. A crucifix is a cross with a painted or sculpted image of Christ on it. Crucifixes first came into use around the fifth century, after the days of persecution for Christians in the West had come to an end. When the martyrdom ceased, Christians found it important to use crucifixes as a reminder of Jesus' suffering and death. Before this period, there was no need to be reminded, because Christians were martyred regularly. This religious art form developed over time, and from the ninth century on, the aim of medieval artists was to convey an increasingly realistic portrayal (if not at times a somewhat exaggerated picture) of Jesus' suffering.

Ignatius encouraged those entering and journeying through Week 3 to, upon rising, recall to mind the great sorrow and suffering of Jesus and then throughout the day to seek to take joyful thoughts or thoughts about the resurrection captive, endeavoring to foster an attitude of sorrow, suffering and heartache as the Passion narrative for the day is reflected upon. Carrying a crucifix can be a great aid in this practice.

I strongly encourage you to purchase a crucifix; they are available for as little as two dollars at Catholic supply stores. You may choose to carry your crucifix with you in a pocket or purse, and finger it as you pray. Display it during your daily prayer times as a reminder of the depth of Jesus' love for you. Use it as an aid to your times of meditation. Finger it as you do your nightly prayer of examen.

Rules for eating. Ignatius provided eight rules regarding eating. Rules 1-4 deal with what we eat and drink, while rules 5-8 provide suggestions regarding garnering spiritual profit from eating and drinking, bringing to mind Paul's admonition, "So whether you eat or drink or whatever you do, do it all for the glory of God" (1 Cor 10:31). Ignatius pointed out ways to develop a proper disposition toward food as well as ways to regulate the intake of food. He spoke not of extended fasts but rather of planning, focus and moderation regarding food. He encouraged focusing on the presence of Jesus, slowing down and using moderation when eating and drinking.

In short, Ignatius would encourage you to eat contemplatively while journeying through Week 3. You are invited to choose one meal (lunch or dinner) each week and apply any or all of the following: eating slowly, eating in silence, eating in moderation (eating less than you normally do), and drinking water and no other beverage.

Additionally, if you are physically able, fast (if in doubt, please visit your doctor before beginning a fast). I encourage you to seek to fast from food—having just water and fruit juice—for an entire day each week. Consider doing it on Friday each week to commemorate Jesus' death on the cross.

I also encourage you to use the Jewish rendering of a day when you fast, as this can help you have a successful and meaningful fasting experience. Start your fast at sunset on Thursday. In the late afternoon, have a light meal of fruit and vegetables, and then commence your fast. Conclude your fast the next day at sunset, having another light meal.

If you have health problems that would be triggered by not eating for a day, please do not fast from food. Instead, fast from such things as television, Internet, music, words, school or work.

Use the time you would normally be eating (or whatever you are fasting from) for prayer and reflection on the sacrifice, obedience and love of Jesus. In addition to food, you might want to also fast from television, music or other electronic distractions during this twenty-four-hour period so you can be singly focused. This would be a good time to carry around your crucifix or spend time meditating on the crucifixion.

Stations of the Cross. The Stations of the Cross (fourth century) is a meditative walk that takes you through various events associated with Jesus carrying his cross to Golgotha, as well as the crucifixion. Most Catholic churches and Catholic retreat centers have Stations of the Cross set up all year. These stations can include actual statues, artist depictions on canvas or simple placards. Each station has a Roman numeral associated with it and corresponding with Jesus' journey to the cross.

If you would like, download a guide for doing the Stations of the Cross and use it instead of following one of the prayer times during Week 3. I would suggest you wait a couple of weeks until you are fully into Week 3 before making use of this optional exercise. If you do decide to do this exercise, be aware that not every station on a Stations of the Cross will be found in your Bible.

These new additions for Week 3 could very well feel overwhelming to you, but do not worry. You will be prompted below when to make use of those components listed above. They are provided so you are not caught off-guard when they make their appearance during the daily exercises and to provide additional information regarding these components without interrupting the flow of the Exercises.

ENCOURAGEMENT

Even if you are not doing Week 3 during the Lenten season, I invite you to enter into the spirit of abstinence associated with Lent by choosing to give up something. As you bump up against your desire to partake of what you are choosing to abstain from, recall to your heart and mind Jesus' sacrifice and his own willingness to lay aside what was rightly his—equality with God—to instead empty himself.

Please continue to strive to make the noontime and evening examen part of your time in the Exercises. This is a very important part of the Exercises, so you are missing out if you are not incorporating the examen each day.

Also remember to recall throughout each day the topic of that day's prayer time.

As you enter into and journey through Week 3, my prayer for you is this:

> God, in your great mercy and grace, grant this beloved one the ability to enter into the fellowship of your sufferings, to journey with you not from afar but within your heart as you go to the cross, that this one may know something of your pain, your anguish, your suffering in order to begin to grasp the immeasurable depth of your love and, being filled with that love, spontaneously share it with others. (adapted from Col 3:12; Phil 3:10; Eph 3:18)

Exercises for Week 3

The grace you are seeking is *to sorrow with Christ in sorrow, anguish with Christ in anguish, with tears and interior suffering because of the suffering that Christ endured for you.*

Examen Questions

- Today did you recall to your mind Jesus' willingness to suffer physical, emotional and spiritual trauma for you? Why, or why not?

- How did the truth of Jesus' willingness to suffer and die for you and others impact how you interacted with others with whom you came in contact today?

- How did you die to self today?

Three Considerations

- What did Jesus suffer in his humanity in this narrative? Enter into Jesus' pain and suffering.

- How did Jesus hide (not use) his divinity in this narrative?

- Consider your response to Jesus' sacrifice for you in terms of how you might view life, live life and interact with others.

Start your time by slowly making the sign of the cross. Conclude with a bow, demonstrating your reverence for and honoring of God, while asking God that everything in your day may more and more lead you to divine praise and service.

Process

☐ Opening   ☐ Closing

☐ Daily exercise   ☐ Noontime examen

☐ Journaling   ☐ Evening examen

Day 1. 2 Corinthians 5:21

Spend time pondering "him [Jesus] who knew no sin," who became sin so you "might become the righteousness of God."

Colloquy. Spend time expressing thanksgiving and gratitude individually to God the Father, Jesus the Son, and the Holy Spirit for their investment, sacrifice and demonstration of love to you and to the world.

Day 2. John 13:1

Ponder the fact that Jesus knew the time had come, and "having loved his own who were in the world, he now showed them the full extent of his love."

Colloquy. Spend time expressing thanksgiving and gratitude individually to God the Father, Jesus the Son, and the Holy Spirit for their investment, sacrifice and demonstration of love to you and to the world.

Day 3. John 13:2-12

Imagine you are having your feet washed by Jesus.

- How do you feel? What is going on inside of you?

- What do you want to say to Jesus?

- What do you desire to hear Jesus say to you?

After Jesus has finished washing your feet, imagine you have an interchange with him.

- What do you say? What does Jesus say?

- How do you feel?

Day 4. Review the past three days

- What has really touched you during your prayer times? Why?

- How has the grace for which you have been asking impacted you these past few days?

Do something today for another, something that will cost you (time, money, comfort, security). Remember that Jesus, motivated by love, gave himself up for you.

Day 5. Matthew 26:20-30

Imagine you are with the disciples.

- What is going through your mind and arising in your heart as you hear Jesus speak of betrayal?
- As Jesus speaks of his body being broken and his blood poured out, what do you feel?
- As Jesus hands you the bread and the cup, your fingers touching his, what do you feel and sense deep within your being?

Day 6. Matthew 26:31-35

Imagine you are Peter.

- What are you feeling as you make your declaration?
- What do you feel when you hear Jesus' reply to you?

Contemplative Eating

Contemplative eating involves eating and drinking with a focus on the presence of Christ. Additionally, Ignatius would encourage you to eat slowly in silence while exercising moderation and drinking water. Please seek to employ these guidelines during one of your meals each week. (See "Rules for eating," p. 218.)

Day 7. Review this past week

- What has really touched you during your prayer times? Why?

- How has the grace for which you have been asking impacted you these past few days?

- What has surprised you during your prayer times this past week? Why?

⟶ SECTION 2 OF 5 ⟵

The grace you are seeking is *to sorrow with Christ in sorrow, anguish with Christ in anguish, with tears and interior suffering because of the suffering that Christ endured for you.*

Examen Questions

- Today did you recall to your mind Jesus' willingness to suffer physical, emotional and spiritual trauma for you? Why or why not?

- How did the truth of Jesus' willingness to suffer and die for you and others impact how you interacted with others with whom you came in contact today?

- How did you die to self today?

Three Considerations

- What did Jesus suffer in his humanity in this narrative? Enter into Jesus' pain and suffering.

- How did Jesus hide (not use) his divinity in this narrative?

- Consider your response to Jesus' sacrifice for you in terms of how you might view life, live life and interact with others.

Start your time by slowly making the sign of the cross. Conclude with a bow, demonstrating your reverence for and honoring of God, while asking God that everything in your day may more and more lead you to divine praise and service.

Process

☐ Opening   ☐ Closing

☐ Daily exercise   ☐ Noontime examen

☐ Journaling   ☐ Evening examen

Day 1. Matthew 26:36-41

Imagine you have been chosen by Jesus to go with him to the garden.

- What are you feeling as you and Jesus go to the garden?

- What are you feeling as you hear Jesus pleading with his Father (God)?

- What do you feel as Jesus rebukes you for falling asleep?

Day 2. Luke 22:39-44

Imagine that you are with Jesus as he is praying to his Father in heaven. Use the colloquy, asking God to help you experience the depth of feeling, love and compassion for Jesus and to be present with Jesus through everything that happens. Be with Jesus as he prays and as he returns to find those he brought with him sleeping.

- What do you do?

- What do you say?

  Conclude your time by saying the Our Father (the Lord's Prayer).

Fasting

If you are physically able (if in doubt, please visit your doctor before beginning a fast), I encourage you to seek to fast from food (you can have water and fruit juice) for an entire day each week. I would suggest you do so on Friday each week to commemorate Jesus' death on the cross.

Day 3. Matthew 26:47-54

Imagine you are with the disciples, unsure of what is happening as people are coming toward you with torches and weapons in hand. Listen to the words of Jesus. Watch his actions.

- What are you feeling and thinking?

- What do you want to do?

- What do you want to say to Jesus?

- To Judas?
- To those who have come to arrest Jesus?
- What do you do?

Day 4. Review the past three days

- What has really touched you during your prayer times? Why?
- How has the grace for which you have been asking impacted you these past few days?

Do something today for another, something that will cost you something (time, money, comfort, security). Remember that Jesus, motivated by love, gave himself up for you.

Day 5. Matthew 26:55-56

Imagine you are with Jesus and you hear his words spoken with courage, conviction and confidence.

What are you feeling about Jesus as you hear him speak to those who have come in the cover of darkness to arrest him?

You notice that the disciples are slowly backing away from Jesus and starting to flee. You feel yourself almost involuntarily following their lead.

- How do you feel about deserting Jesus?
- What do you think Jesus is feeling about you as you begin to leave his presence?

As you are leaving, you turn back and catch a glimpse of Jesus. Your eyes and his eyes meet.

- What do you see in his eyes?
- What does he say to you in that look?

Day 6. John 18:12-27

Imagine you are Peter, following Jesus and the crowd from a distance. As Jesus is taken inside, you are standing around the fire, waiting to see what will happen.

- What do you feel as you are asked if you are a disciple?

- What are you feeling as you deny that you are a disciple?

- What do you feel as you remember your words to Jesus: "Even if all fall away on account of you, I never will" (Mt 26:33)?

- What do you feel as he replies, "I tell you the truth, this very night, before the rooster crows, you will disown me three times" (v. 34)?

- How do you feel the second and third time you deny being a disciple of Jesus?

- What do you feel as you hear the cock crow after your third denial?

Day 7. Review this past week

- What has really touched you during your prayer times? Why?

- How has the grace for which you have been asking impacted you these past few days?

- What has surprised you during your prayer times this past week? Why?

Colloquy. Spend time expressing thanksgiving and gratitude individually to God the Father, Jesus the Son, and the Holy Spirit for their investment, sacrifice and demonstration of love to you and to the world.

⤫ SECTION 3 OF 5 ⤫

The grace you are seeking is *to sorrow with Christ in sorrow, anguish with Christ in anguish, with tears and interior suffering because of the suffering that Christ endured for you.*

Examen Questions

- Today did you recall to your mind Jesus' willingness to suffer physical, emotional and spiritual trauma for you? Why, or why not?

- How did the truth of Jesus' willingness to suffer and die for you and others impact how you interacted with others with whom you came in contact today?

- How did you die to self today?

Three Considerations

- What did Jesus suffer in his humanity in this narrative? Enter into Jesus' pain and suffering.

- How did Jesus hide (not use) his divinity in this narrative?

- Consider your response to Jesus' sacrifice for you in terms of how you might view life, live life and interact with others.

Start your time by slowly making the sign of the cross. Conclude with a bow, demonstrating your reverence for and honoring of God, while asking God that everything in your day may more and more lead you to divine praise and service.

Process

☐ Opening   ☐ Closing

☐ Daily exercise   ☐ Noontime examen

☐ Journaling   ☐ Evening examen

Day 1. Matthew 26:57-68

Imagine you are with Jesus. In conversational prayer (colloquy), ask God to help you experience the depth of feeling, love and compassion for Jesus and to be present with Jesus through everything that happens.

- What are you feeling as you watch Jesus being falsely accused, falsely testified against, remain silent, speak, get spit upon and hit in the face?

  Make your way over to Jesus and be with Jesus.

- What are you feeling?

- What do you desire to say and to do to Jesus?

  Conclude this time by saying the Our Father (the Lord's Prayer).

Day 2. Matthew 26:69-75

Imagine you are Peter.

- What are you feeling as you once again deny Christ, hear the cock crow and recall Jesus' words, "Before the rooster crows, you will deny me three times"?

- What are your tears about?

Now look at your own life. When do you find it difficult to make yourself known as a follower of Jesus? Why?

Ask God to show you if there are ways in which you explicitly or implicitly deny Jesus.

Conclude your time with conversation prayer (colloquy) with Jesus, sharing your feelings, discoveries and insights with him.

Day 3. Luke 23:1-7

Imagine that you are continuing to be with Jesus as they move him from place to place and take him to Pilate.

- What do you see and feel as Jesus is questioned by Pilate?
- As Jesus answers Pilate?
- As Jesus is pawned off by Pilate to Herod?
- What are you learning, discovering about Jesus as you walk this journey with him?

Day 4. Review the past two days

- What has really touched you during your prayer times? Why?
- How has the grace for which you have been asking impacted you these past few days?

Do something today for another, something that will cost you (time, money, comfort, security). Remember that Jesus, motivated by love, gave himself up for you.

Day 5. Luke 23:8-12

Imagine that you are continuing on with Jesus to Herod's palace.

- What are you feeling and thinking?
- As you watch Jesus remain silent before the mighty and powerful Herod, what do you think and feel?
- What do you feel as you watch Jesus ridiculed and mocked by the guards?

- What do you want to say to these guards?
- To Herod?
- To Jesus?

Day 6. Luke 23:13-25

Imagine that you are continuing on with Jesus from Herod's palace back to Pilate's.

- What are you feeling and thinking?
- When you hear Pilate desire to punish and then release Jesus, what do you feel inside?
- What do you feel as you hear a few shouts from some bystanders in the crowd saying, "Crucify him! Crucify him!"
- What do you feel as you notice that those shouts are growing in number and intensity?
- What do you feel as Pilate gives in to the crowd's demands and agrees to have Jesus crucified?

Day 7. Review this past week

- What has really touched you during your prayer times? Why?
- How has the grace for which you have been asking impacted you these past few days?
- What has surprised you during your prayer times this past week? Why?

Colloquy. Spend time expressing thanksgiving and gratitude individually to God the Father, Jesus the Son, and the Holy Spirit for their investment, sacrifice and demonstration of love to you and to the world.

Conclude this time by saying the Our Father (the Lord's Prayer).

⤙ SECTION 4 OF 5 ⤚

The grace you are seeking is *to sorrow with Christ in sorrow, anguish with Christ in anguish, with tears and interior suffering because of the suffering that Christ endured for you.*

Examen Questions

- Today did you recall to your mind Jesus' willingness to suffer physical, emotional and spiritual trauma for you? Why, or why not?

- How did the truth of Jesus' willingness to suffer and die for you and others impact how you interacted with others with whom you came in contact today?

- How did you die to self today?

Three Considerations

- What did Jesus suffer in his humanity in this narrative? Enter into Jesus' pain and suffering.

- How did Jesus hide (not use) his divinity in this narrative?

- Consider your response to Jesus' sacrifice for you in terms of how you might view life, live life and interact with others.

Start your time by slowly making the sign of the cross. Conclude with a bow, demonstrating your reverence for and honoring of God, while asking God that everything in your day may more and more lead you to divine praise and service.

Process

☐ Opening   ☐ Closing

☐ Daily exercise   ☐ Noontime examen

☐ Journaling   ☐ Evening examen

Day 1. Matthew 27:32-44

Read through the narrative two different times while taking turns imagining . . .

You are Simon, who is forced to carry Jesus' cross.

- What is Jesus' reaction as you take his cross?

- What do you see in his eyes?

- What goes through your mind and your heart as you take Jesus' cross on your back and walk with him?

- What do you want to say to Jesus?

You are a devoted follower of Jesus, who is following at a safe distance, seeking to go unnoticed, yet hearing and seeing all that is going on.

- What are you feeling?
- What do you want to say to Jesus?
- To God the Father?
- In which of the above do you most see yourself?
- Which one do you desire to be? Why?

Slowly read the following poem "The Cross" by Lois A. Cheney, and allow yourself to linger with each stanza. Stay with the words *wonder, fear, weep* and *rejoice.*

I stand before the cross
And wonder.

I stand before the cross
And fear.

I kneel before the cross
And weep.

I pray before the cross
And rejoice.

To know the cross
Is to know Christ.

To feel the cross
Is to feel Christ.

To gaze at the cross
Is to gaze at Christ.

To carry the cross
Is to be a Christian,

And not until then.
God, forgive me.

- What does each word—*wonder, fear, weep* and *rejoice*—say to you about God, yourself and the cross?

- How do they fit together?

- How does the cross help you to know Christ, feel Christ and see Christ?

- What does it mean for you to carry the cross in your life?

Day 2. Luke 23:33-44

Read the entire passage, then spend your time meditating on Jesus' words in verse 34. Afterward, imagine you are standing with others near the cross, and you hear Jesus' words about forgiveness.

What is your reaction?

Now imagine you are standing before the cross and Jesus looks at you, calls you by name and says, "Father, forgive [your name], for she/he did not know what she/he was doing."

- What goes on within you as you hear Jesus' words to you?

- To what degree are you able to internally embrace Jesus' forgiveness?

Spend time thanking God/Jesus for the forgiveness Jesus has provided for you through his suffering and death on the cross.

Day 3. Philippians 2:5-8

Read through the passage three times, allowing yourself to soak in the words. After a while, read the words below, taken from the passage, asking yourself which of these words, values or mindsets you are most resistant to and why:

- made himself empty

- servant

- humbled himself

- obedient

- died on a cross

Now go back through the above list and ask God to show you how manifesting each of these mindsets and values in your life could draw you into a closer relationship with God.

Day 4. Review the past three days

- What has really touched you during your prayer times? Why?

- How has the grace for which you have been asking impacted you these past few days?

Colloquy. Spend time expressing thanksgiving and gratitude individually to God the Father, Jesus the Son, and the Holy Spirit for their investment, sacrifice and demonstration of love to you and to the world.

Conclude this time by saying the Our Father (the Lord's Prayer).

Do something today for another, something that will cost you (time, money, comfort, security). Remember that Jesus, motivated by love, gave himself up for you.

Day 5. Luke 23:38-43

Imagine you are the criminal on the cross who rebukes the other criminal and says, "Jesus, remember me when you come into your kingdom."

- What are you feeling when you hear the other criminal hurling insults at Jesus?

- What is it about Jesus that makes you feel the need to defend him?

- What is it about Jesus that causes you to say, "Jesus, remember me when you come into your kingdom"?

- What goes on in your mind and heart when Jesus responds to you, "I tell you the truth, today you will be with me in paradise"?

- What makes you believe Jesus' words?

- What is your response to Jesus?

Additional imaginative exercise. Imagine you are Peter, standing near enough to the cross to hear what is going on between Jesus and the criminals. You are still feeling shame and disgust for your triple rejection of Jesus, and now you hear one of the criminals come to Jesus' aid. And you hear Jesus' promise that the criminal will join him in paradise that very day.

- What goes on in your head and heart?

- What do you want to say to Jesus? Why?

Day 6. John 19:25-27

Imagine you are John or Jesus' mother.

- What do you feel toward Jesus as you hear his words?

- What do they express to you about Jesus?

- What do they express to you about you (your value, worth, significance)? Why?

Day 7. Review this past week

- What has really touched you during your prayer times? Why?

- How has the grace for which you have been asking impacted you these past few days?

- What has surprised you during your prayer times this past week? Why?

Colloquy. Spend time expressing thanksgiving and gratitude individually to God the Father, Jesus the Son, and the Holy Spirit for their investment, sacrifice and demonstration of love to you and to the world.

◆ SECTION 5 OF 5 ◆

The grace you are seeking is *to sorrow with Christ in sorrow, anguish with Christ in anguish, with tears and interior suffering because of the suffering that Christ endured for you.*

Examen Questions

- Today did you recall to your mind Jesus' willingness to suffer physical, emotional and spiritual trauma for you? Why, or why not?

- How did the truth of Jesus' willingness to suffer and die for you and others impact how you interacted with others with whom you came in contact today?

- How did you die to self today?

Three Considerations

- What did Jesus suffer in his humanity in this narrative? Enter into Jesus' pain and suffering.

- How did Jesus hide (not use) his divinity in this narrative?

- Consider your response to Jesus' sacrifice for you in terms of how you might view life, live life and interact with others.

Start your time by slowly making the sign of the cross. Conclude with a bow, demonstrating your reverence for and honoring of God, while asking God that everything in your day may more and more lead you to divine praise and service.

Process

☐ Opening   ☐ Closing

☐ Daily exercise   ☐ Noontime examen

☐ Journaling   ☐ Evening examen

Day 1. Mark 15:33-36

Sit with the words in verse 34. Imagine the anguish and pain as Jesus, who has been one with the Father, now feels separated from God. Notice that Jesus does not use the word *Father* to address God, but rather the more distant term *God*.

Using conversational prayer (colloquy), ask God to help you experience the depth of feeling, love and compassion for Jesus and to be present with Jesus as he experiences separation from the Father.

Day 2. Isaiah 53:3-6

Spend your time meditating on this passage, especially focusing on what Jesus went through for you—he was despised, rejected, smitten, afflicted, crushed for you—and what Jesus took on for you: your transgressions, your infirmities, your sorrows, your iniquities, your punishment.

Conclude your time with prayers of gratitude and thanksgiving, for by his wounds you have been healed.

Day 3. Luke 23:44-46

Imagine you are standing before the cross, hearing the last few words of Jesus. You just heard him cry out in an anguished voice, "My God, my God, why have you forsaken me?" and now you hear him say, "Father, into your hands I commit my spirit."

- What has changed?
- Why does Jesus now address God as "Daddy"?
- What is the invitation and the challenge for you in these two statements of Jesus?

Day 4. Review the past three days

- What has really touched you during your prayer times? Why?
- How has the grace for which you have been asking impacted you these past few days?
- What has surprised you during your prayer times this past week? Why?

Colloquy. Spend time expressing thanksgiving and gratitude individually to God the Father, Jesus the Son, and the Holy Spirit for their investment, sacrifice and demonstration of love to you and to the world.

Do something today for another, something that will cost you (time, money, comfort, security). Remember that Jesus, motivated by love, gave himself up for you.

Day 5. John 19:30

Reflect on Jesus' words, "It is finished."

Imagine you are a disciple hearing this.

- What are your immediate feelings?
- What do you do?
- What do you think this means for you and the rest of the disciples?
- What do these final words of Jesus mean? What is finished?
- What do you long to say to Jesus, now departed?

Day 6. Luke 23:47-49

Imagine you are the centurion.

- What did you see in Jesus as he suffered on the cross that caused you to praise God and say, "Surely this was a righteous man"?

As you have meditated these past several days on the seven sayings of Jesus on the cross, what stands out to you? Why?

What challenges you? Why?

Slowly read the following poem "The Cross" by Lois Cheney, and allow yourself to linger with each stanza. Stay with the words *wonder, fear, weep* and *rejoice*.

I stand before the cross
And wonder.

I stand before the cross
And fear.

I kneel before the cross
And weep.

I pray before the cross
And rejoice.

To know the cross
Is to know Christ.

To feel the cross
Is to feel Christ.

To gaze at the cross
Is to gaze at Christ.

To carry the cross
Is to be a Christian,

And not until then.
God, forgive me.

- What does each word—*wonder, fear, weep* and *rejoice*—say to you about God, yourself and the cross?

- How do they fit together?

- How does the cross help you to know Christ, feel Christ and see Christ?

- What does it mean for you to carry the cross in your life?

Day 7. Review this past week

- What has really touched you during your prayer times? Why?

- How has the grace for which you have been asking impacted you these past few days?

- What has surprised you during your prayer times this past week? Why?

Colloquy. Spend time expressing thanksgiving and gratitude individually to God the Father, Jesus the Son, and the Holy Spirit for their investment, sacrifice and demonstration of love to you and to the world.

Conclude by saying the Our Father (the Lord's Prayer).

Note: If you started this section on Ash Wednesday, you will now be entering Holy Week (the week leading up to Easter) before you work your way through the section below. Go to Ash Wednesday and Holy Week Exercises on page 268. When you complete these exercises, return here and read through the following section. If you did not start Week 3 on Ash Wednesday or if Holy Week is not next week, then continue on with the following section.

CONCLUDING COMMENTS AND REFLECTIONS

You have completed Week 3, which can be a very dry and arduous time in the Exercises. You have spent the past several weeks walking with Jesus through the events leading up to the cross and climaxing in his crucifixion. You have been asking God for the grace of experiencing sorrow with Christ in sorrow and anguish with Christ in anguish. You have been transformed from a follower of Jesus to a companion with Jesus, seeking to see as he saw and experience what he experienced, even though painful and disheartening. You wrestled with bringing the reality of Christ crucified to the table of your everyday life and experiences. You discovered to a greater degree what it meant for Jesus to humble himself by not regarding equality with God a thing to be grasped and by choosing to come into this world as a human and to willingly endure suffering as he refused to make use of the attributes resident in his divinity.

Now it is time to discern if you will continue into Week 4, the final section of the Exercises. There are some who get to this point and, because of weariness, decide God does not desire them to move on to Week 4. I strongly urge you not to make your decision on that basis. If you sense God has more for you in Week 3 or is telling you your season in the Exercises has come to an end, then God bless you. But if that is not the case, I encourage you to enter into Week 4.

You may be caught a little off-guard by my new tone regarding entering the new Week. There also are no questions or continuums to help you discern if you should enter into Week 4. This is in part because Week 3 and 4 are from the same spiritual formation phase, known as the Unitive Way. So it is not a matter of if you are ready to enter into Week 4. Instead, the question is, what is your sense of God's leading and your own internal desire?

So the choice is yours, and whatever you choose is perfectly okay. But, instead of strongly cautioning you not to go forward, this time I am encouraging you to enter into Week 4 and its focus on the resurrection of Jesus.

WEEK 4

RESURRECTION OF JESUS

WELCOME TO THE FOURTH AND FINAL Week of the Exercises. During Week 2 and 3, your focus has been on the life and passion of Jesus. Now you will focus on the resurrection of Christ, or more precisely, Jesus' post-resurrection experiences and interactions. You have moved out of a time of meditating on the suffering, agony and death of Christ to enter into a period of embracing the joy and consolation that flows out of the reality of his resurrection. Additionally, Week 4 has a component known as Contemplation to Attain Love of God, which is the final piece of your journey through the Exercises and encourages you to engage with the world as an active contemplative.

As you begin your time in Week 4, your sole focus will be on the resurrection, which is the linchpin of the Christian faith. The apostle Paul rightly reminds us,

> If Christ has not been raised, our preaching is in vain and so is your faith. . . . And if Christ has not been raised, your faith is futile; you are still in your sins. . . . If only for this life we have hope in Christ, we are to be pitied more than all men. But Christ has indeed been raised from the dead. (1 Cor 15:14, 17, 19-20)

> He appeared to Peter, and then to the Twelve. After that, he appeared to more than five hundred of the brothers at the same time, most of whom are still living, though some have fallen asleep. Then he appeared to James, then to all the apostles, and last of all he appeared to me also, as to one abnormally born. (1 Cor 15:5-8)

Jesus' resurrection did occur within time and space, and in Week 4 this resurrection takes center stage. We move away from the agonized suffering of Jesus in Week 3 and into the glorious light of an empty tomb and our resurrected Lord and Savior. The goal of Week 4 is to enter into the joy of the resurrection while also affirming the reality of the crucifixion, for there is no resurrection of Jesus without the crucifixion of Jesus. Week 4 and Week 3 are two sides of the same coin, linked and inseparable from one another.

Week 4 does not proclaim that you are forever safe within the protective bubble of the resurrected Christ but that there will be ultimate victory in and through Christ. You who journey with the resurrected Christ will experience evil, heartache and possibly even agonizing death, but these will no longer have the final word in your life. Week 4 is all about freedom—freedom to be, freedom to become the person God has created you to be and freedom from paralyzing fears and doubts. Jesus' resurrection removes the constricting boundary of death from your life and allows the expanse of life everlasting to cascade on you, filling your heart and spirit with the joy of Jesus.

As you make your way through the exercises of Week 4, you will discover that there are two pivotal points found in it: the resurrection appearances of Jesus, and Jesus' consoling presence. The post-resurrection Jesus brings consolation to those who are hurting and struggling in their faith. Jesus frees Mary Magdalene from despair, those on the road to Emmaus from their spiritual pessimism, Thomas from his doubts and Peter from his remorse and guilt. Week 4 is a time of consolation, a time for entering into the joy of Jesus, a joy that becomes an inner strength for proactively living and dealing with life.

The desired grace of Week 4 is the ability to rejoice and be intensely glad because of the great glory and joy of Jesus, your risen Lord. In Week 4 you move from weeping with Jesus as he wept (Week 3) to rejoicing with Jesus as he rejoiced (Rom 12:15). You have moved from enduring the cross with Jesus to entering into the joy of Jesus (Heb 12:2).

The joy of Jesus brings life-giving freedom to those who follow him. This is the consolation of Jesus, namely, Jesus resurrected. This Week you are called to be present to and embrace the triumph of love and life in Jesus, broadcasted throughout the universe by his resurrection. Week 4 is a time to celebrate, to sing and dance—so do it! Be happy! Christ is risen; he was dead but now he is alive! It is time to celebrate!

ADDITIONS TO EXERCISES

Conclude your opening prayer time by saying the following: "Jesus is risen. Jesus is risen indeed. Alleluia. Amen."

As you get up each morning during this Week, recall Ephesians 5:14: "Wake up, O sleeper, rise from the dead, and Christ will shine on you."

Questions for sections 1-3. These questions are to be used after you have entered the daily passage using imaginative prayer.

- How does Jesus now manifest his divine attributes, his true self, following his resurrection?

- How does Jesus console those he encounters?

- What do you experience as you encounter the resurrected Christ?

Create an ambiance that is conducive to entering into the happiness and spiritual joy that flows from the resurrection of Jesus. Allow the sunshine to fill your room, and place potted plants or cut flowers or other things around the room that communicate beauty, joy and hope to you.

Do your best to enter into the narrative as one who does not know the whole story. Try to imagine what you would be feeling, knowing that Jesus, whom you had watched, listened to and followed for three years, was dead. Seek to allow yourself to experience the confusion, wonder, joy and delight as he begins to appear and interact with you and the others. Ask God to help you to do this.

The above could feel overwhelming to you, but do not worry. You will be prompted below when to make use of those components listed above. They are provided so you are not caught off-guard when they make their appearance during the daily exercises and to provide additional information regarding these components without interrupting the flow of the Exercises.

REMINDER AND ENCOURAGEMENT

It is very helpful to journal through these exercises. It allows you to see patterns in your prayer times and to recall what God has spoken to you. Often as you journal, God expands on what you have discovered or been made aware of. I *strongly* encourage you to journal. It will deepen your experience with the Exercises.

Please continue to strive to make the noontime and evening examen a part of your time in the Exercises. And remain faithful to showing up each day and presenting yourself to God as a living and holy sacrifice. You have almost completed your season in the Exercises.

As you enter into and journey through Week 4, my prayer for you is this:

> God, bless and honor these ones as they have faithfully journeyed with you all these weeks. Help them to sense your presence with them and your delight in them. Grant them wisdom and insight, that they may come to know something of the power and joy associated with the glorious resurrection of Jesus. I pray that they may come to experience the power that is theirs, the power that raised Christ from the dead, and that the joy associated with the resurrection would become itself a strength that would enable them to live a life worthy of their calling, a life of love, a life that pleases and honors you their God. (adapted from Phil 3:10; Eph 1:19-20; Neh 8:10; Eph 5:1)

Exercises for Week 4

⤙ SECTION 1 OF 4 ⤚

The grace you are seeking this week is *the ability to rejoice and be intensely glad because of the great glory and joy of Jesus, your risen Lord.*

Examen Questions

- How did the joy and power of Jesus' resurrection impact how you viewed your life, your self and your circumstances today?

- How did it impact how you dealt with others today?

- How did the truth of Jesus' resurrection bring consolation and the ability to experience the reality of Jesus in the happenings of your life today?

Come to prayer, conscious of the reverence God deserves, while asking God that everything in your day may more and more lead you to divine praise and service.

Process

☐ Opening: Conclude your opening prayer time by saying the following: "Jesus is risen. Jesus is risen indeed. Alleluia. Amen."

☐ Daily exercise

☐ Journaling

☐ Closing

☐ Noontime examen

☐ Evening examen

Questions for Sections 1-3

These questions are to be used after you have entered the daily passage using imaginative prayer.

- How does Jesus now manifest his divine attributes, his true self, following his resurrection?

- How does Jesus console those he encounters?

- What do you experience as you encounter the resurrected Christ?

These questions can be used after you work through the daily passage using imaginative prayer and the suggested questions for the day.

Day 1. Mark 16:1-16

Read slowly through this passage two to three times.

- To what aspects of the story are you drawn? Why?

- With which of the participants do you readily identify? Why?

- What feelings are stirred within you as the narrative unfolds?

Day 2. Luke 24:1-9

Imagine you are one of the women going to the tomb.

- What is going on in your mind and heart as you travel to the tomb to prepare Jesus' body?

- When you discover the stone is rolled away and the body of Jesus missing?

- When you see the angels, and when you hear the angels speak to you?

- What is it like to interact with the angel and hear the angel say to you, "Do not be so surprised. You're looking for Jesus the Nazarene, who was crucified. He is not here! He has been raised from the dead!"

- What are you thinking and feeling? Why?

Day 3. Luke 24:10-11

Imagine you are one of the women who went to the tomb.

Setting the Stage

Create an ambiance that is conducive to entering into the happiness and spiritual joy that flows from the resurrection of Jesus. Allow the sunshine to fill your room, and place potted plants or cut flowers or other things around the room that communicate beauty, joy and hope to you.

🙣🙣

- As you head back to tell the disciples about the empty tomb and the message of the angels, what is going on in your head and heart?

- What happens within you, especially as a woman who is looked down on in your society, as the disciples say your story is nonsense and they laugh in your face?

- What do you think Jesus was feeling about this exchange between the women who went to the tomb and the disciples? Why?

Day 4. Review your past three days

- What has really touched you during your prayer times? Why?

- How has the grace for which you have been asking impacted you these past few days?

Day 5. Luke 24:1; John 20:3-10

Imagine you are Peter. Although you do not believe the story told by the women, you are drawn to visit the tomb.

- Why are you drawn to the tomb?

- What is going on in your mind and heart as you travel to the tomb?

- What do you feel or think as you notice the stone has been rolled away and you peer into the tomb and discover Jesus' body is gone while the linens remain?

- Now, as belief slowly rises within you, what emotions also arise as you realize that this is all in harmony with Scripture?

Day 6. John 20:11-18

Imagine you are Mary.

- What are you feeling as you interact with the angel and the gardener?
- Why do you have such a strong desire to attend to Jesus' body?
- Now listen for Jesus to call you by name. What do you feel as you hear Jesus call your name?
- As you hold onto Jesus, and he says to you, "Don't cling to me, for I haven't yet returned to the Father," what are you feeling? Why?
- What do you think Jesus was feeling about the above exchange with Mary? Why?

Day 7. Review this past week

- What has really touched you during your prayer times? Why?
- How has the grace for which you have been asking impacted you these past few days?
- What has surprised you during your prayer times this past week? Why?

Colloquy. Spend time expressing thanksgiving and gratitude individually to God the Father, Jesus the Son, and the Holy Spirit for their investment, sacrifice and demonstration of love to you and to the world.

SECTION 2 OF 4

The grace you are seeking this week is *the ability to rejoice and be intensely glad because of the great glory and joy of Jesus, your risen Lord.*

Examen Questions

- How did the joy and power of Jesus' resurrection impact how you viewed your life, your self and your circumstances today?
- How did it impact how you dealt with others today?

- How did the truth of Jesus' resurrection bring consolation and the ability to experience the reality of Jesus in the happenings of your life today?

Come to prayer, conscious of the reverence God deserves, while asking God that everything in your day may more and more lead you to divine praise and service.

Process

☐ Opening: Conclude your opening prayer time by saying the following: "Jesus is risen. Jesus is risen indeed. Alleluia. Amen."

☐ Daily exercise

☐ Journaling

☐ Closing

☐ Noontime examen

☐ Evening examen

Questions for Section 1-3

These questions are to be used after you have entered the daily passage using imaginative prayer.

- How does Jesus now manifest his divine attributes, his true self, following his resurrection?

- How does Jesus console those he encounters?

- What do you experience as you encounter the resurrected Christ?

Day 1. Luke 24:13-24

Imagine you are one of the two people walking on the road to Emmaus.

- What are you feeling as you are walking down the road?

- What are you thinking about?

- As another joins you, what goes through your mind? Are you glad another has joined you and is walking with you, or do you feel that this is an unwelcome intrusion? Why?

- What are you thinking and feeling as you speak with this person and as you share the events and reports of the past few days? Why?

Day 2. Luke 24:25-32

Imagine you are one of the two people walking on the road to Emmaus.

- As you hear the other (Jesus) reply to you, what is going on inside you?

- As he goes through the Scriptures, highlighting truths about the Messiah, what is stirring within you?

- What do you feel the moment you realize it is Jesus speaking to you and he disappears from your presence?

- What do you think Jesus was feeling about the above exchange with these two individuals? Why?

Day 3. John 20:19-23

Imagine you are with the disciples, hiding behind locked doors, afraid and confused.

- What do you feel as Jesus appears before you and as he shows you his hands and feet?

- What do you think Jesus was feeling about the above exchange with the disciples? Why?

Day 4. Review the past three days

- What has really touched you during your prayer times? Why?

- How has the grace for which you have been asking impacted you these past few days?

Day 5. John 20:24-25

Imagine you are Thomas.

- What are you feeling when you return to hear the story of Jesus' appearance while you were gone?

- How does it make you feel that Jesus possibly showed himself to the others but not you?

- Why have you decided not to believe their reports?
- What are your feelings toward Jesus, who has not shown himself to you? Why do you feel this way?

Day 6. John 20:26-29

Imagine you are Thomas.

- What have you been feeling during this past week as you have heard over and over again about Jesus' appearance but have not seen Jesus yourself?
- What are your feelings toward the disciples?
- Toward Jesus?
- Why is it so hard for you to believe?

Now Jesus appears before you and the others.

- What are you feeling as you see Jesus alive?
- What are you feeling when Jesus walks toward you, saying, "Put your finger here; see my hands. Reach out your hand and put it into my side. Stop doubting and believe"?
- What are you feeling when you hear Jesus say, "Because you have seen me, you have believed; blessed are those who have not seen and yet have believed." Why?
- What do you think Jesus was feeling about the above exchange with Thomas? Why?

Day 7. Review this past week

- What has really touched you during your prayer times? Why?
- How has the grace for which you have been asking impacted you these past few days?
- What has surprised you during your prayer times this past week? Why?

Colloquy. Spend time expressing thanksgiving and gratitude individually to God the Father, Jesus the Son, and the Holy Spirit for their investment, sacrifice and demonstration of love to you and to the world.

⟡ SECTION 3 OF 4 ⟡

The grace you are seeking this week is *the ability to rejoice and be intensely glad because of the great glory and joy of Jesus, your risen Lord.*

Examen Questions

- How did the joy and power of Jesus' resurrection impact how you viewed your life, your self and your circumstances today?

- How did it impact how you dealt with others today?

- How did the truth of Jesus' resurrection bring consolation and the ability to experience the reality of Jesus in the happenings of your life today?

  Come to prayer, conscious of the reverence God deserves, while asking God that everything in your day may more and more lead you to divine praise and service.

Process

☐ Opening: Conclude your opening prayer time by saying the following: "Jesus is risen. Jesus is risen indeed. Alleluia. Amen."

☐ Daily exercise

☐ Journaling

☐ Closing

☐ Noontime examen

☐ Evening examen

Questions for Sections 1-3

These questions are to be used after you have entered the daily passage using imaginative prayer.

- How does Jesus now manifest his divine attributes, his true self, following his resurrection?

- How does Jesus console those he encounters?

- What do you experience as you encounter the resurrected Christ?

Day 1. John 21:1-14

Imagine you are one of the disciples who were fishing. You have been fishing all night and have caught nothing.

- What are you feeling as the sun rises in the morning?
- What are you feeling as you hear a stranger yell out from the shore to cast your net on the other side?
- What are you feeling as you make such a huge catch of fish?
- As John recognizes that it is Jesus on the shore?
- As you watch Peter jump out of the boat and start to swim ashore?
- What do you want to do and to say?

Now imagine you are back on shore, and Jesus is walking toward you. He is bringing you some bread and fish. As he stands before you, he looks deep into your eyes and you into his.

- What do you want to say and to do?
- What does Jesus say to you?

Sit in this scene for a few minutes.

Day 2. John 21:15-19

Imagine you are Peter. You are eating with the others, and Jesus walks over to you and says, "Peter, we need to talk." As you get up, you are well aware of the three times you denied him, even after you swore you would never do such a thing.

- As you and Jesus walk away from the others, what are you feeling about yourself and about Jesus?
- What do you long to say to Jesus?

As you move away from the others, Jesus turns to you and asks you three different times, "Do you love me?"

- What are you thinking and feeling as Jesus repeatedly asks you if you truly love him? Why?
- What do you feel when Jesus tells you to "Follow me"? Why?

Day 3. Matthew 28:16-20

Imagine you are one of the disciples. As you stand there, worshiping Jesus, you can see in the eyes of some of the others that they still doubt.

- What do you think about those who still doubt?

- What do you feel toward them?

- How do you think Jesus feels toward them?

- As you hear the words, the commission of Jesus, what do you feel?

- When you hear Jesus' promise, "I am with you always, to the very end of the age," how does that make you feel about him?

Day 4. Review the past three days

- What has really touched you during your prayer times? Why?

- How has the grace for which you have been asking impacted you these past few days?

Day 5. Luke 24:44-53

Imagine you are one of the disciples.

- What are you thinking and feeling as you hear Jesus explain to you from the Scriptures how all this (his death and resurrection) has been foretold by Moses, the prophets and himself?

- What does his promise of sending the Holy Spirit with power upon you mean to you?

- What do you feel as you watch Jesus ascend into heaven? Why?

Day 6. Acts 1:3; 1 Corinthians 15:3-9

Even at the end, there were those who doubted.

- Do you believe that Jesus died and rose again? Why?

- What difference does your belief make in how you live your life, spend your time and money, and interact with others?

- How is your life different because you believe Jesus died and rose again?

Day 7. Review this past week

- What has really touched you during your prayer times? Why?

- How has the grace for which you have been asking impacted you these past few days?

- What has surprised you during your prayer times this past week? Why?

Colloquy. Spend time expressing thanksgiving and gratitude individually to God the Father, Jesus the Son, and the Holy Spirit for their investment, sacrifice and demonstration of love to you and to the world.

CONTEMPLATION OF DIVINE LOVE

You have arrived at the final days of Week 4. The focus of this final week will be on contemplating the love of God. You will be focusing on God's gift to you, God's self-giving to you, God's labor for you and God's unceasing giving and gifting.

The goal of this small section is to plunge you into the love of God, which will in turn teach and empower you to love and serve God in all things: "to be a contemplative in action, finding God in all things: to be able always to recognize the Love that surrounds us, the Love in which we are immersed, the Love from which everything comes and to which everything goes."

Ignatius stated at the beginning of this section that "love ought to be more in deeds than words." This is reminiscent of the words of the apostle John, "Dear children, let us not love with words or tongue but with actions and in truth" (1 Jn 3:18). Here Ignatius made it clear that this journey through the Exercises does not result in a privatized faith but in a life of loving service, of active contemplation.

⟫⟫ SECTION 4 OF 4 ⟪⟪

The grace you are seeking is *an intimate knowledge of all the goods that God lovingly shares with you so that, filled with gratitude, you may be empowered to respond just as totally in your love and service to God.*

Examen Questions

- How has your awareness of God's unceasing giving to you and God's continual laboring for you impacted how you viewed your life, your self and your circumstances today?

- How did it impact how you dealt with others today?

- How did it enable you to more fully enter into and manifest the fullness of God in your life?

Process

☐ Opening   ☐ Closing

☐ Daily exercise   ☐ Noontime examen

☐ Journaling   ☐ Evening examen

Day 1

Today spend time with the two prayers below. One is taken from the Spiritual Exercises and the other is from John Wesley's writings. Both of these prayers are an expression of the indifference communicated in the Principle and Foundation, which marked the beginning of Week 1. Read the prayers three times, paying attention to what you are drawn to in the prayers, as well as to what you are resistant toward. Then work through the questions that follow the prayers.

> Take, Lord, and receive all my liberty, my memory, my understanding, my entire will—all is yours; do with it what you will. Give me only your love and your grace. That is enough for me.
> —*Ignatius of Loyola*

> I am no longer my own, but thine. Put me to what thou wilt, rank me with whom thou wilt; put me to doing, put me to suffering; let me be employed for thee or laid aside for thee, exalted for thee or brought low for thee; let me be full, let me be empty; let me have all things, let me have nothing; I freely and heartily yield all things to thy pleasure and disposal.
> —*John Wesley's Covenant Prayer*

- What were you drawn to and resistant toward in these prayers? Why?

- Is God's love and grace enough for you? Why, or why not?

Conclude your time by reading Psalm 73:25-28 and talking to God about why God is or is not enough for you.

Day 2

> His divine power has given us everything we need for life and godliness through our knowledge of him who called us by his own glory and goodness. Through these he has given us his very great and precious promises, so that through them you may participate in the divine nature and escape the corruption in the world caused by evil desires. (2 Pet 1:3-4)

> For no matter how many promises God has made, they are "Yes" in Christ. And so through him the "Amen" is spoken by us to the glory of God. (2 Cor 1:20)

> God made him who had no sin to be sin for us, so that in him we might become the righteousness of God. (2 Cor 5:21)

Make a list of all that God has done, is doing and will do for you (God's gifts to you).

Spend time resting in God's love for you and presence with you.

Colloquy. (This colloquy will be used on days 2, 3, 5 and 6.) Spend time expressing thanksgiving and gratitude individually to God the Father, Jesus the Son, and the Holy Spirit for rooting you and establishing you in love. Thank them also for all that they have done, are doing and will do on your behalf, which communicates their investment, sacrifice and demonstration of love to you.

Consider what you have to give to the Divine Majesty (God). Conclude by praying the following: "Take, Lord, and receive all my liberty, my memory, my understanding, my entire will—all is yours; do with it what you will. Give me only your love and your grace. That is enough for me."

Day 3. Acts 17:28

"For in him [God], we live and move and have our being." And I might add, "And in you. God lives and has his being."

Spend your time pondering how God dwells in creation, giving and sustaining life, making you his temple (dwelling place), creating you in God's own image, and God's self-giving to you.

Spend time resting in God's love for you and presence with you.

Colloquy. Spend time expressing thanksgiving and gratitude individually to God the Father, Jesus the Son, and the Holy Spirit for rooting you and establishing you in love. Thank them also for all that they have done, are doing and will do on your behalf, which communicates their investment, sacrifice and demonstration of love to you.

Consider what you have to give to the Divine Majesty (God). Conclude by praying the following: "Take, Lord, and receive all my liberty, my memory, my understanding, my entire will—all is yours; do with it what you will. Give me only your love and your grace. That is enough for me."

Day 4

Spend your time resting in God's love, thanking God for God's goodness to you and adoring God for who God is, not for what God has done. You might want to take a walk as you do this.

Day 5. Isaiah 64:4

"Since ancient times no one has heard, no ear has perceived, no eye has seen any God beside you, who acts on behalf of those who wait for him." Spend time pondering how God works and labors for you in all created things on the face of the earth.

Spend time resting in God's love for you and presence with you.

Colloquy. Spend time expressing thanksgiving and gratitude individually to God the Father, Jesus the Son, and the Holy Spirit for rooting you and establishing you in love. Thank them also for all that they have done, are doing and will do on your behalf, which communicates their investment, sacrifice and demonstration of love to you.

Consider what you have to give to the Divine Majesty (God). Conclude by praying the following: "Take, Lord, and receive all my liberty, my memory, my understanding, my entire will—all is yours; do with it what you will. Give me only your love and your grace. That is enough for me."

Day 6. James 1:17

"Every good thing and perfect gift is from above, coming down from the Father of the heavenly lights, who does not change like shifting shadows." Spend time pondering how all good things and gifts descend from above.

Spend time resting in God's love for you and presence with you.

Colloquy. Spend time expressing thanksgiving and gratitude individually to God the Father, Jesus the Son, and the Holy Spirit for rooting you and establishing you in love. Thank them also for all that they have done, are doing and will do on your behalf, which communicates their investment, sacrifice and demonstration of love to you.

Consider what you have to give to the Divine Majesty (God). Conclude by praying the following: "Take, Lord, and receive all my liberty, my memory, my understanding, my entire will—all is yours; do with it what you will. Give me only your love and your grace. That is enough for me."

Day 7. Reflect on and review your week

- What has really touched you during your prayer times? Why?
- How has the grace for which you have been asking impacted you these past few days?
- What has surprised you during your prayer times this past week? Why?

Spend your time today resting in God's love for you and presence with you.

Colloquy. Spend some time expressing thanksgiving and gratitude individually to God the Father, Jesus the Son, and the Holy Spirit for rooting you and establishing you in love. Thank them also for all that they have done, are doing and will do on your behalf, which communicates their investment, sacrifice and demonstration of love to you.

FINAL WORDS

You have made it to the end of this journey, but your adventure of faith will continue. At this point you cannot yet fully know how God has, is and will use your experience in these exercises in your life and the lives of others. As a result of the time you have spent in the Spiritual Exercises of St. Ignatius of Loyola, God was and is at work in you and will continue to bring fruit into your life and the lives of those with whom you journey.

You have used many different prayer methods throughout your time in the Exercises, methods you can continue to draw from and make use of in the days, weeks and years ahead. At some time it would be beneficial for you to review the journal you kept as you journeyed through these exercises. This can bring to mind prayer practices you may want to make use of, or specific days or experiences in the Exercises you want to ponder or reenter. To help you in your review process, there are a series of questions provided in appendix 5.

Finally, as you move on in your journey, I encourage you to continue to employ some of the tools you have used and attitudes you have fostered during your time in the Exercises. The examen, imaginative prayer and the practice of intentionally presenting yourself to God are powerful tools to help you as you embrace a new chapter in your adventure of faith. The attitudes of indifference, being the beloved of God and finding God in all things can give you the focus and the strength needed to fight the good fight of faith. Seek to carry with you those things that God has used in your life as you have journeyed through the Exercises. The value of these various practices and attitudes extends far beyond the Exercises, and they are profitable to you who continue to intentionally partner with God in being conformed to the image of Christ.

PART FOUR

RESOURCES

BIOGRAPHY OF
ST. IGNATIUS OF LOYOLA

THE EXERCISES WERE BIRTHED OUT OF Ignatius's own adventure of faith. As he walked with God, read about Jesus and interacted with others who shared their spiritual experiences, he incorporated these learnings into what was to become the Exercises. Thus it is important to have at least a snapshot of his life and times.

Ignatius was born and baptized Íñigo López de Loyola in 1491, one year before Columbus set sail from Spain. He was the youngest of seven sons and one of thirteen children. He was in his mid-twenties when the Protestant Reformation began and would become a major figure in the counter-reformation.

Ignatius was raised in nobility and at an early age began to serve in the court of Don Juan Velázquez de Cuéllar, during which time he learned poetry, Christian devotion and the use of weaponry. On his departure he was given a horse, weapons and a sack of gold, and he set off to pursue a life of fame and fortune as well as gambling, womanizing and general mischief.

Ignatius's conversion did not result from hearing the Gospels read or experiencing a crucifix speak to him. God used a French cannonball. The shattering of Ignatius's leg by a cannonball at the Battle of Pamplona marked the beginning of his conversion process.

During an extended time of convalescing, Ignatius became overwhelmed with boredom and asked that books on chivalry be brought to him. Instead, he was given two religious books: Ludolph the Carthusian's *Life of Christ* and Jacobus de Voragine's *The Book of the Lives of the Saints.* For the next several months, these two books became his constant companions and the means God would use to woo and draw him. *Life of Christ* in particular was formational for Ignatius; he spent close to a year reading it, meditating on it and journaling what he discovered within its pages.

This was the beginning of an inner purging for Ignatius. The focus of his loyalty and desire to serve was gradually changing from loyalty to an earthly kingdom, with its fame and glory, to Christ the King and the fame and glory that might be his through that avenue of service. Ignatius was still externally focused, but things within were slowly beginning to change. His life was on the verge of launching on a new trajectory, one firmly fixed on the person of Jesus.

In 1522, Ignatius left Loyola physically healed but very much spiritually a work in progress. He was still Íñigo, seeking after fame and fortune but now seeking to serve Christ the King, desiring to perform severe penances and do great and glorious works as the saints before him had done. He was becoming a knight of Christ—a theme seen in the meditations he designed for those going through the Exercises.

Ignatius arrived in Montserrat, where he accepted the hospitality of Benedictine monks and secured a confessor. His written confession took three days to complete. After his confession, he slipped away at night for a vigil of arms, which was traditionally done by new knights as they entered into the service of an earthly lord or king. On March 24, 1522, Ignatius gave his fine clothes to a beggar, put on a pilgrim's tunic and spent the whole night in prayer at the altar. When he was finished, he left his sword and dagger at the altar. Ignatius was now a knight of Christ.

From there Ignatius journeyed to Manresa, a league (three-and-a half miles) away, where he was planning to stay a few days and write some notes about what had been taking place. Instead he stayed in Manresa for about eleven months, and it was there that God met him powerfully, shaping and molding him into a true knight of Christ.

Upon arriving in Manresa, Ignatius began to wholeheartedly embrace the ascetic lifestyle. He begged for alms, ate no meat, drank no wine, did not comb or cut his hair, and allowed his fingernails and toenails to grow. Ignatius was fighting against the vainglory that had directed so much of his life and consumed so much of his thinking. During this time, he prayed seven hours a day.

As his stay in Manresa lengthened, Ignatius endured many physical, mental, emotional and spiritual hardships. Some of his hardships were self-generated through his ascetic practices, especially of fasting, while others were results of battles with the world, the flesh and the devil. This practice did much physical damage to him, which he battled throughout his life. Ignatius's own struggles with temptations, his scruples and his own practices of spiritual disciplines during this time gave shape to various components within his Exercises.

For Ignatius, the time in Manresa was one of deep, profound and lasting consolation and agonizing despair. It was also a time of great devotion and supreme testing. Manresa was a refining crucible for Ignatius, purifying him from the inside out, bringing clarity and insight and helping to put flesh on the skeletal pieces of the Exercises that had begun with his reading and note taking while at Loyola.

From Manresa, Ignatius journeyed to Barcelona and then on to Jerusalem, where he arrived destitute. He planned on praying at the holy sites and helping souls, but he was eventually ordered to leave by the Franciscans, who feared for his life. Ignatius eventually returned to Barcelona and began a ten-year period of study, teaching others using the Exercises, having spiritual conversations with people and numerous run-ins with those of the Inquisition (a dozen times he was arrested, and he ended up in jail on a couple of those occasions). Although Ignatius was confronted by those of the Inquisition for teaching the Exercises, the material he taught was never called into question. The problem was that he had not been officially trained and sanctioned by the church to teach such things—true or otherwise.

Ignatius began preparation for his formal theological education by studying Latin grammar alongside grade-school boys in Barcelona while continuing to teach the Exercises. After learning the basics of

Latin grammar, he began taking classes at Alcala (during this time he was jailed for forty-two days) and then Salamanca (where he was jailed for twenty-two days) and eventually ended up in Paris, first at Montaigu and then in Sainte Barbe, where he concluded his studies in 1535. His roommates at Sainte Barbe were Pierre Favre and Francis Xavier, who would become his first permanent companions. In 1528, Ignatius started giving the Exercises to non-Spanish-speaking people and was forced to begin to translate the Exercises into a rudimentary Latin.

On August 15, 1534, Ignatius and six followers gathered at Montmartre and swore a vow of poverty and chastity and to embrace a life of missionary work in Jerusalem (Ignatius still desired to return to Jerusalem), and if that did not work out, to journey to Rome and offer their service to the pope in whatever way he deemed best.

They all gathered in 1537 in Venice as ordained priests and began giving the Exercises as they awaited the opportunity to journey to Jerusalem. They were unable to secure passage that year and spent their time giving the Exercises, teaching in churches and helping the sick and poor. When the year was up, true to their vow, they went to Rome to have an audience with the pope and pledge their service to him.

On his way to Rome, Ignatius stopped at a church at La Storta. There Ignatius experienced himself as intimately united with Christ. This experience affirmed his desire to found an order dedicated to Christ, bearing the name of Christ and being about the work of Christ for the service and glory of God and the spiritual well-being of others.

On September 3, 1539, Ignatius presented the materials to the pope for the forming of a religious order, and on September 27, 1540, he and his ten followers were officially sanctioned as an order: the Society of Jesus, known as the Jesuits. The Spiritual Exercises of St. Ignatius received official approval of the church in 1548. Ignatius died on July 31, 1556.

There is much more that can be said about Ignatius's life. The Exercises arose from the laboratory of life and not the hallowed halls of academia, and thus have a down-to-earth, honest feel to them. The Exercises reflect the insights of Ignatius's own spiritual saga with God, beginning with a cannonball and culminating in the acceptance and publishing of the Exercises and the founding of the Society of Jesus.

Resources

Ganss, George E., ed. *Ignatius of Loyola: Spiritual Exercises and Selected Works*. Classics of Western Spirituality. Mahwah, N.J.: Paulist Press, 1991.

Tylenda, Joseph N. *A Pilgrim's Journey: The Autobiography of St. Ignatius of Loyola*. Fort Collins, Colo.: Ignatius Press, 2001.

Ash Wednesday
and Holy Week Exercises

ASH WEDNESDAY

These exercises are for you if you begin Week 3 on Ash Wednesday or start on the first Monday of the Lenten season following Ash Wednesday. If you are starting Week 3 on Ash Wednesday, please start with the exercises designated "Ash Wednesday" below and continuing through Sunday. When you have completed these five days of exercises, go to Week 3, section 1, and continue on in Week 3.

Process

☐ Opening   ☐ Closing

☐ Daily exercise   ☐ Noontime examen

☐ Journaling   ☐ Evening examen

Start your time by slowly making the sign of the cross. Conclude with a bow, demonstrating your reverence for and honoring of God, while asking God that everything in your day may more and more lead you to divine praise and service.

The grace you are seeking this week is *to sorrow with Christ in sorrow, anguish with Christ in anguish, with tears and interior suffering because of the suffering that Christ endured for you.*

Examen Questions

- Today did you recall to your mind Jesus' willingness to suffer physical, emotional and spiritual trauma for you? Why, or why not?

- How did the truth of Jesus' willingness to suffer and die for you and others impact how you interacted with others with whom you came in contact today?

- How did you die to self today?

Three Considerations

- What did Jesus suffer in his humanity in this narrative? Enter into Jesus' pain and suffering.

- How did Jesus hide (not use) his divinity in this narrative?

- Consider your response to Jesus' sacrifice for you in terms of how you might view life, live life and interact with others.

Ash Wednesday. Isaiah 53:3-5

Thursday. Philippians 3:10

Friday. 1 Peter 2:22-24

Saturday. 1 John 4:9-10

Sunday. Review this past week

- What has really touched you during your prayer times? Why?

- How has the grace for which you have been asking impacted you these past few days?

- What has surprised you during your prayer times this past week? Why?

Colloquy. Spend time expressing thanksgiving and gratitude individually to God the Father, Jesus the Son, and the Holy Spirit for their investment, sacrifice and demonstration of love to you and to the world.

Conclude by saying the Our Father (the Lord's Prayer).

Now go to section 1 of Week 3 (p. 221) and continue through the exercises. When you get to the end of section 5, return and begin the section below. This will take you up to Easter (Resurrection) Sunday.

FINAL DAYS OF WEEK 3 (HOLY WEEK)

This section is for those who started Week 3 on the first Monday of Lent. When you have finished these, return to Week 3 and read through the final section of Week 3, titled "Concluding Comments and Reflections" (p. 239).

Final Days of Week 3

This begins the Monday after Palm Sunday. If you did not begin Week 3 either on Ash Wednesday or the following Monday, these exercises are not for you. Just journey through Week 3 as found in the earlier part of this book.

Spend your time during the next few days sitting in the Gospel narratives of the crucifixion of Christ. Use the colloquy, asking God to help you experience the depth of feeling, love and compassion for Jesus and to be present with Jesus through everything that happens. Use your imagination to more fully enter into what is happening. As you explore the Scripture passage for each day, choose whose perspective you will take: try being a different individual (such as a criminal, a disciple, a centurion, Jesus' mother, John).

- How does your experience change with the different roles you take in the story?
- To which of the Gospel depictions are you most drawn? Why?
- What are your feelings as you watch Jesus being nailed to the cross, being insulted, being pierced by the spear?
- What are you feeling as you hear his words?
- Which of his words from the cross do you find most challenging? Why?
- Which of his words from the cross do you find most hope producing? Why?

    I encourage you to
- fast on Good Friday
- attend a Maundy Thursday service

- attend a Good Friday service
- attend an Easter Vigil service, which is on Saturday night
- celebrate Easter!

PART 6 (HOLY WEEK)

Start your time by slowly making the sign of the cross. Conclude with a bow, demonstrating your reverence for and honoring of God, while asking God that everything in your day may more and more lead you to divine praise and service.

Process

☐ Opening   ☐ Closing

☐ Daily exercise   ☐ Noontime examen

☐ Journaling   ☐ Evening examen

The grace you are seeking this week is *to sorrow with Christ in sorrow, anguish with Christ in anguish, with tears and interior suffering because of the suffering that Christ endured for you.*

Examen Questions

- Today did you recall to your mind Jesus' willingness to suffer physical, emotional and spiritual trauma for you? Why, or why not?
- How did the truth of Jesus' willingness to suffer and die for you and others impact how you interacted with others with whom you came in contact today?
- How did you die to self today?

Three Considerations

- What did Jesus suffer in his humanity in this narrative? Enter into Jesus' pain and suffering.
- How did Jesus hide (not use) his divinity in this narrative?
- Consider your response to Jesus' sacrifice for you in terms of how you might view life, live life and interact with others.

Monday. Slowly read the following poem, allowing yourself to linger with each stanza. Stay with the words *wonder*, *fear*, *weep* and *rejoice*.

The Cross

I stand before the cross
And wonder.

I stand before the cross
And fear.

I kneel before the cross
And weep.

I pray before the cross
And rejoice.

To know the cross
Is to know Christ.

To feel the cross
Is to feel Christ.

To gaze at the cross
Is to gaze at Christ.

To carry the cross
Is to be a Christian,

And not until then.
God, forgive me.

- What does each word—*wonder*, *fear*, *weep* and *rejoice*—say to you about God, yourself and the cross?
- How do they fit together?
- How does the cross help you to know Christ, feel Christ and see Christ?
- What does it mean for you to carry the cross in your life?

Tuesday or Wednesday. Stations of the Cross. You can visit a local Catholic Church to go through the stations, or go online, where you will find a pictorial Stations of the Cross with text at <www.metamorpha.com>.

Now begins what is referred to as the Triduum: Holy Thursday, Good Friday and Holy Saturday.

Thursday. Lord's Supper. John 13:1-38. Put yourself in the story.

- Where are you sitting, and who are you sitting next to?

- What is your sense or experience of Jesus?

- What is your experience of the meal?

- The foot washing?

- Jesus' words?

- What is your internal reaction when Jesus says one of you will betray him?

Friday (Good Friday). Crucifixion. John 19:28-42. Put yourself at the foot of the cross, seeking to truly be with Jesus in his pain and agony—physical, emotional and spiritual.

- What are you feeling for Jesus?

- What are you feeling as you help take the body down from the cross?

- As you hold his lifeless body?

Spend some time thanking Jesus for his willingness to die for you. Conclude your time with the Lord's Prayer.

Saturday (Holy Saturday). Put yourself in the place of the disciples. You have been following Jesus for three years. You have watched as he performed miracles. You have been stirred by his teachings. You have come to believe that God was with Jesus in a special way, so much so that when others ceased to follow him, you continued believing he had the words of eternal life. Now you sit with the other disciples. Jesus has been crucified and buried. Your hope, dreams and beliefs are as dead as Jesus.

- What are you feeling? What is going on in your heart and head?

Spend time journaling.

Resurrection Sunday. *He is risen. He is risen indeed! Rejoice and be glad!* Return to the end of Week 3, and read through "Concluding Comments and Reflections" on page 239.

Shorter Options for Journeying

Through the Exercises

I have designed three formats of varying durations you may choose from in order to interact with the Exercises in an abbreviated way. Ignatius originally designed the Exercises to be entered into for a period of thirty days or about nine months. The nine-month format is the one used in this book and is often referred to as the 19th Annotation, or the retreat in everyday life. The shorter retreats (seven and seventeen weeks) outlined below do not incorporate the intensity of the thirty-day retreat or the longevity of the nine-month retreat, which are each key components in bringing profound depth and transforming power to your experience in the Exercises.

If you are leaning toward choosing an option with a shorter time frame (seven and seventeen weeks), I urge you to explore the reasons for your decision. As you process through the following questions, remember that these Exercises are not for everyone.

- Why are you willing or desiring to enter into a journey through the Exercises that will be somewhat limited in what it can accomplish in your life?

- Why are you unable to make the longer commitment to the Exercises at this time?

- Why not wait for a time when the 19th Annotation format (a nine-month journey, as presented in this book) might work for you?

• What has convinced you that now is the time to go through the Exercises and the shorter option is the best for you?

If you are convinced that God would have you enter the Exercises at this time and that a shorter version of the Exercises would be the best fit for you, I have designed a seven-week and a seventeen-week option, as well as a third option (which I consider to be the most viable) for you to choose from. As far as choosing between the seven-week and seventeen-week options, I would suggest the seventeen weeks, because there is something that happens in terms of the spiritual breadth and depth of the journey that results from an extended time in the Exercises.

Before you choose, consider the third option, which I believe is a much better choice than either of the first two choices. This third option incorporates all the Exercises as laid out in this book, but broken into bite-size pieces, which will give you the opportunity to eventually enjoy the whole banquet contained in each of the sections rather than just getting a taste. This method affords you the ability to take breaks between each of the Weeks while still allowing you to journey through the Exercises in their entirety.

THE ALTERNATIVE JOURNEYS

Seven-Week Exercises

Please read the introduction to each of the sections below before you enter into them. When you are finished, please read the final portion of the section you just completed. The beginning and ending portions of each section contain valuable information that will help you. And although not everything will pertain to those who choose to use the shorter format, it still has value for you.

Preparatory Exercises

1. Section 1—Day 1 and 2 combined

2. Section 1—Day 5

3. Section 1—Day 6

4. Section 2—Day 1 and/or optional exercise

5. Section 2—Day 2

6. Section 2—Day 5

7. Section 3—Day 6

Principle and Foundation

1. Section 1—Day 1 and 2 combined

2. Section 2—Day 2

3. Section 3—Day 1

4. Section 4—Day 5

5. Section 5—Day 1 (Read special introduction to section 5.)

6. Section 5—Day 3

7. Section 5—Day 7

Week 1

1. Section 1—Day 2

2. Section 1—Day 5

3. Section 2—Day 2

4. Section 2—Day 3

5. Section 2—Day 4

6. Section 2—Day 5

7. Section 3—Day 6

Week 2

1. Section 4—Day 3

2. Section 5—Day 5

3. Section 6—Day 1

4. Section 6—Day 3

5. Section 6—Day 5

6. Section 7—Day 1

7. Section 6—Day 7

8. Section 7—Day 3

9. Section 7—Day 5

10. Section 8—Day 2

11. Section 8—Day 5

12. Section 9—Day 1

13. Section 9—Day 2

14. Section 9—Day 7

15. Section 10—Day 5

16. Section 10—Day 6

17. Section 11—Day 1 and 2

18. Section 11—Day 5

19. Section 12—Day 1 and 2

20. Section 13 and 14 (Read beginning section of 13 and then choose one of the "I Am" statements of Jesus from section 13 or 14 to spend your prayer time with.)

21. Section 15—Day 7

Week 3

1. Section 1—Day 1 and 2

2. Section 1—Day 6; Section 2—Day 2

3. Section 4—Day 1

4. Section 4—Day 2

5. Section 5—Day 1 and 3

6. Section 5—Day 2

7. Section 5—Day 7

Week 4 is not included. If you would like to extend your time by seven days, feel free to use Week 4, section 2—All (seven days).

Seventeen-Week Exercises

Please read the introduction to each of the sections below before you enter into them. When you are finished, please read the final portion of the section you just completed. The beginning and ending portions of each section contain valuable information that will help you. And although not everything will pertain to those who choose to use the shorter format, it still has value for you.

Preparatory Exercises

Section 1—All (seven days)
Section 2—All (seven days)

Principle and Foundation

1. Section 1—Day 1 and 2
2. Section 2—Day 2
3. Section 3—Day 1
4. Section 3—Day 6
5. Section 4—Day 2
6. Section 4—Day 5
7. Section 4—Day 7
8. Section 5—All (seven days)

Week 1

Section 2—All (seven days)
Section 3—All (seven days)
Section 4—All (seven days)

Week 2

Section 1—All (seven days)
Section 2—All (seven days)
Section 5—All (seven days)
Section 6—All (seven days)
Section 9—All (seven days)
Section 10—All (seven days)
Section 11—All (seven days)

Week 3
Section 2—All (seven days)
Section 4—All (seven days)
Section 5—All (seven days)

Week 4
Section 2—All (seven days)

Third Option
The third option uses the full expression of the 19th Annotation found in this book. This format allows you to journey through the entire experience in the Exercises while taking breaks between each section. After completing your break, I encourage you to review your journal, covering the previous section before reentering the Exercises in the new section. During your review, be open to God inviting you to sit with something or even to go back through one or more of the exercises from the previous section.

Before entering into the next section, work through the questions and continuums at the end of the section you are finishing. This will help you discern if it is a good time for you to move on. Remember, the point is not to finish the Exercises but to encounter God through the Exercises as God leads you. This third option provides you the opportunity to journey through the Exercises yet incorporates a more manageable time frame and flexibility for doing so.

Please read the introduction to each of the sections below before you enter into them. When you are finished, please read the final portion of the section you just completed. The beginning and ending portions of each section contain valuable information that will help you.

Preparatory Exercises (21 days)
Principle and Foundation (35 days)
Week 1 (35 days)
Week 2 (105 days)
Week 3 (35 days)
Week 4 (28 days)

For Spiritual Directors
and Listeners

Y OU HAVE HAD A GREAT HONOR BESTOWED UPON YOU. You have been offered a front-row seat to witness firsthand the spiritual journey of another. This person has chosen you because she feels you can be trusted with her heart, because she believes you have the spiritual maturity and deepening relationship with God needed for this endeavor.

However, before you say yes, please consider if you are truly up to the challenge. Read through all that follows and see if this is something you are willing to commit to. This journey, though quite amazing and satisfying, will not be a walk in the park for the person going through the Exercises or for you. Besides meeting with the person two to four times a month (as you mutually decide) for about an hour, you will also need to prepare before each session. So as you read through this section prayerfully, consider if this is a journey God is inviting you on.

As you start meeting, it is important for you to read through the section the retreatant will be entering. Also familiarize yourself with the Rules of Discernment that apply to that section and be aware of the "grace" and the examen questions the retreatant will be asking God for and interacting with.

The information that follows will help you as you prepare to meet with your retreatant. It includes insights gathered from people who have taken others through the Exercises. Many of the insights are taken from a section in the Exercises known as the "Annotations," which was written for spiritual directors. As you make your way through this section, if you come across a term or concept you are not familiar with, please check the glossary.

NOTES FROM IGNATIUS'S EXERCISES 1-20

It is important for you to discern if the retreatant possesses great courage and generosity toward God. This is the focus of the Preparatory Exercises as well as the Principle and Foundation. If the retreatant does not possess these requisite qualities in his walk with God, he may not be ready to proceed into Week 1.

There will be an ebb and flow to the retreatant's experiences in the Exercises. There will be times of consolation, desolation, dryness and nothingness. This is how it should be, and if the ebb and flow is not there, make sure the retreatant is spending the specified time in prayer each day and is doing the examens, as well as journaling.

When the retreatant is struggling, be gentle, giving her courage and strength, helping her to process the whys of her desolation (see "Rules of Discernment" in the introduction to Week 1).

If you perceive that your retreatant is struggling with evil taking on the appearance of good, take him through the Rules of Discernment for Week 2.

If the retreatant is going through times of extreme consolation, caution her from making a hasty promise or vow to God or another.

Help your retreatant see if there is any disordered attachment that is keeping him from coming fully before God.

Note to spiritual directors: I am well aware that some of you reading this are trained spiritual directors who have developed a level of expertise when it comes to companioning with others. The following sections are not designed to teach you, but rather they'll expose you to the type of questions that are important as you journey with someone going through the Spiritual Exercises—and they'll provide you with an overall feel regarding what the Exercises entail (see "Brief Overview of Weeks" on p. 285). So even if you are trained in the art of spiritual direction, I would strongly encourage you to keep reading

through the following sections and even to visit the website <www
.metamorpha.com>.

GENERAL QUESTIONS TO ASK A RETREATANT

- How have your prayer times with God been since we last met?
  Why?

- What are you feeling during your prayer times regarding God, Jesus
  and yourself? Why?

- What stands out to you regarding your time spent in the Exercises
  since the last time we met? If something is shared, take time to process this with your retreatant. Ask questions such as, What feeling(s)
  did this stir within you? How did this make you feel toward God,
  Jesus and/or yourself? What has been the impact of this time on
  your heart? In your life?

- What might be God's current invitation or challenge for you? How
  do you feel about that invitation or challenge?

- How are the examens going for you—the noontime one, the evening
  one? Which is easier for you? Why? What difference do these seem
  to be making in your life?

- How is your journaling going? Why? Have you tried different approaches to journaling? Why, or why not? What are you noticing
  during your journaling times?

- Are your times in the Exercises beginning to impact the rest of your
  day? If yes, how? If no, why not? How do you feel about this?

- During this period of your journey, do you feel that it is predominately a time of desolation or of consolation? Why? What is
  the source of your desolation or consolation? What is the suggested response to your current situation in the Rules of Discernment?

- Is there any one overall theme or invitation or life/heart change that
  you have noticed rising within you since the last time we met?

- How can I pray for you until our next time together?

HELPING A RETREATANT UNPACK
AN EXPERIENCE WITH GOD

- How would you describe this experience with God? How did you feel during the experience? What was God like? What were you like? What seem to be the results of your experience?

- As you are now reflecting on that previous experience: What are you feeling? What, if any, new insights or feelings are arising? As you continue to reflect on your experience, what feelings concerning God arise within you? How does that make you feel about God, about you and God?

HINDRANCES TO LISTENING TO OTHERS

- If you "know" what the person will say, you stop paying close attention.

- If you share your own story (so you feel important, interesting, helpful, experienced), this brings the focus off the retreatant and onto you.

- A drive to fix the situation keeps you from listening and instead occupies your mind with seeking solutions or similarities to the person you are listening to.

- If you "know" what a person means, you stop seeking to understand. For example, if a retreatant tells you about a painful situation, and you automatically assume that would make her feel sad, you stop seeking to understand and you move forward in the conversation instead of taking time to ask her how that situation made her feel.

- Your own woundedness, fear of or discomfort with pain, struggles and feelings can lead to non-listening and therefore not being fully present to the journey of the retreatant.

GOOD QUESTIONS

- are open ended.

- cause one to reflect, ponder, explore, get in touch with self, God and feelings.

- focus attention on feelings (movement), God and self-discovery.

- focus on resistance, places the retreatant is not willing to explore. This may be a conscious or unconscious choice on the part of the retreatant, but if you notice resistance, gently invite the retreatant to enter into it. Resistance can be a place of great divine and self-discovery when entered into.

- help the person pay attention to her internal movements.

- help the person deepen, explore and sink into his experience.

- help the person move from head to heart.

- invite raw honesty and unhindered exploration of God and self.

- help the retreatant get in touch consciously and/or subconsciously with internal feelings, energy and movements that lead her in divine and self-discovery.

BAD QUESTIONS

- are closed-ended questions, needing only a yes or no answer.

- focus on circumstances alone.

- lead the person in the way you want him to go.

- move person from heart to head.

- have one right answer.

- are birthed by curiosity.

- stop reflection.

- are questions asked too quickly without the proper time given for reflection.

- flow from your own discomfort and/or desire to control, fix, correct or make the retreatant think a certain way about something.

Listening is a gift you are giving to the retreatant. As you journey together, you will become a better listener. Remember that the person's growth is God's responsibility, not yours. You are to show up, create a safe, caring place, and let the retreatant share his heart while you listen to what is said and not said. Yours is not an easy task, but with God's help, you will be able to do beyond all you ask, think or even imagine. Trust God and trust the process, and seek to do no harm.

BRIEF OVERVIEW OF WEEKS

It would be very beneficial for you as a spiritual director or listener to read through each section, beginning to end, before your retreatant enters it, paying attention to the grace(s) she will be asking for and the examen questions she will be considering each day.

As the retreatant nears the end of a section, become familiar with the materials he will make use of to make his decision whether to move forward into the next section of the Exercises or not. It is important for you to assist him in discerning his readiness to enter into a new part of the Exercises. As you help him, it is key for you to remember, and to remind him, that the important thing is not to get through the Exercises but to use the Exercises to present himself before God as a living and holy sacrifice.

Preparatory Exercises: Section 1

During this week, the retreatant will be seeking to embrace and internalize the unconditional love God has for her. The grace she is seeking from God is a deeper awareness of God's love. This can be a difficult section for those who realize they do not believe, at a deep level, that God loves them, or who come face to face with situations where they did not experience God's love and care. It is important for them to honestly process these issues. It is also very important that they do not leave this section until they have a deep and abiding sense of God's love.

Principle and Foundation: Section 2

In this section, the retreatant will focus on God as creator and spend time pondering, reverencing and praising God. Then he will seek to understand and embrace the role of indifference in his spiritual life. The grace he is seeking will change weekly, but the emphasis of this section is on developing a healthy concept of God.

The Weeks

Week (uppercase W) does not refer to a seven-day period but is a section possibly lasting many weeks.

Week 1

This can be a difficult section of the Exercises for the retreatant. Pay special attention to her feelings in terms of her own worth and value. Be alert to signs that she is struggling with self-condemnation or shame. The focus of this section is on sin: the sin of Adam and Eve, the sin of the angels, the sin of the world and our own sin. The grace the retreatant is asking for is the ability to experience sorrow, tears and confusion over her choices to sin in light of God's limitless love, grace, mercy and faithfulness.

It is important that the retreatant keep the truths of his own sinfulness and God's unlimited love and grace tightly tethered together. If things get difficult for him, consider having him revisit some of the Preparatory Exercises. Making a confession is an optional exercise during this week.

Week 2

This section focuses on Jesus, from birth to Palm Sunday. It is a time of discovering one's willingness to follow Jesus. The grace the retreatant is asking for in Week 2 is the ability to know Jesus intimately, to love him more intensely and to follow him more closely. The retreatant will be asked again and again to ponder the depth and level of her desires. This section can be a place where she begins to experience dryness, discouragement and may struggle to do the daily exercises. She may begin to realize that there are days when God feels far away. Remind her that the key to the Exercises is "showing up" and presenting herself as a living and holy sacrifice to God. This is what is important, not what does or does not happen during these times. Also, encourage her to continue the practice of the examen at noontime and night.

There are four meditations especially designed by Ignatius for this Week, and there are three cautions listed on page 149. Please take a look at the meditations and the cautions. There are many retreatants for whom Week 2 will mark the end of their journey through the Exercises, and that is as it should be. They are not ready to continue to the greater level of commitment required for Week 3.

Week 3

This section follows Jesus through Holy Week, ending with his crucifixion. Those entering this Week are choosing not merely to follow Jesus but also to be with Jesus in his pain and suffering. The Week is not for everyone. The grace that is asked for is sorrow with Christ in sorrow, anguish with Christ in anguish, with tears and interior suffering because of the suffering that Christ endured for them. The discipline of fasting is encouraged during this Week, as well as instructions regarding eating food contemplatively. The experience of retreatants in the section varies greatly.

Week 4

The post-resurrection encounters of Jesus are the focus of this section. The grace sought during Week 4 is the ability to rejoice and be intensely glad because of the great glory and joy of Jesus, their risen Lord. For many, it is difficult to fully enter into the joy of Week 4. The "Contemplation to Attain Love of God" serves as an encouragement to put faith into action. The retreatant is encouraged to become an active contemplative who loves God and others in word, deed and truth.

FINAL THOUGHTS

It is an honor to be chosen to journey with another as a spiritual director or listener, but it is also a good bit of work. If you can be patient with yourself, give yourself grace, trust in God and take one leg of the journey at a time, you will do well. This will be an incredible journey for you too.

Using the Exercises
with a Group

Going through the Exercises as a group could be a very beneficial experience. A group of three to five people (no bigger) can provide accountability, encouragement, insight and support to each other as you journey through the Exercises. The group does not necessarily take the place of an individual spiritual director or listener but certainly augments that resource. What follows are some general insights regarding forming a group and some ideas regarding the format of a group meeting.

MEMBERS OF THE GROUP
Besides being actively involved as participants in the Exercises, it would be important for the members to

- be open and honest with God, themselves and each other
- be trusted by each other, keeping confidences, speaking from a place of love
- know Jesus and have a deep desire for God and the things of God
- fully participate in the group through prayerful listening, sharing and attendance

FORMAT FOR MEETINGS

- Time frame—about two hours.

- Prayer—committing time to God, asking for an openness to God and to each other.

- Sharing—each person takes a turn sharing about his experience in the Exercises (about ten minutes), and everyone else prayerfully listens.

- Silence (about three minutes)—everyone sits together in silence listening for God's still small voice on behalf of the person who just shared.

- Response (about ten minutes)—the group shares responses (questions, comments, images, senses received) with the person who shared. These are not "thus says the Lord" statements but merely offerings.

- Prayer (about five minutes)—the groups prays silently for the person who shared.

- The process—sharing, silence, response and prayer are completed by each person in the group. It helps the sharing to flow if you designate a leader and the group members become familiar with the insights in appendix 3, "For Spiritual Directors and Listeners."

Finally, because this is a group that is journeying through the Exercises together, it would be helpful to check in with each other about whether you are putting the time in each day, practicing the examen at noontime and evening, and seeing a listener or spiritual director. The point is not condemnation but positive accountability. Check to see if anyone feels he is in a period of desolation or consolation, so that you may remind each other what Ignatius encourages you to do during those times.

Going through the Exercises with a group can be a very meaningful and beneficial journey. Just choose your companions wisely.

Reviewing Your Journey Through the Exercises

Once you finish your journey through the Exercises, it can be very beneficial to revisit what took place during your sojourn. This is akin to looking at your pictures after you return from a trip. I suggest you take a month or so after completing your time with the Exercises, and then set aside time to begin to revisit your time in the Exercises. I have suggested two methods of doing so. Please feel free to adapt, modify and tweak them as you see fit. The goal is to help you reconnect with your experience in hopes that God may reinforce and deepen your learning while encouraging you regarding what God has formed and shaped in you.

PLAN 1

Day 1
Review your journal for the Preparatory Exercises (God's love). As you begin your review, remind yourself of the grace you asked for during that section.

- What stands out to you from that time?

- What was the invitation, challenge, reminder or encouragement from God that flowed out of that section to you?

Conclude your day with a colloquy with Jesus, sharing your insights, thoughts and feelings about your experience in the Preparatory Exercises.

Day 2

Go back and review your journal for the Principle and Foundation exercises, which dealt with praising, honoring and serving God, as well as indifference. As you begin your review, remind yourself of the grace you asked for during that section.

- What stands out to you from that time?
- What was the invitation, challenge, reminder or encouragement from God that flowed out of that section to you?

Conclude your day with a colloquy with Jesus, sharing your insights, thoughts and feelings about your experience in the Principle and Foundation.

Days 3 and 4

Review your journal for Week 1 of the Exercises, which dealt with sin. As you begin your review, remind yourself of the grace you asked for during that Week.

- What stands out to you from that time?
- What was the invitation, challenge, reminder or encouragement from God that flowed out of that Week to you?

Conclude your day with a colloquy with Jesus, sharing your insights, thoughts and feelings about your experience from Week 1.

Days 5 and 6

Review your journal for Week 2 of the Exercises, which dealt with Jesus' life. As you begin your review, remind yourself of the grace you asked for during that Week.

- What stands out to you from that time?
- What was the invitation, challenge, reminder or encouragement from God that flowed out of that Week to you?

Conclude your day with a colloquy with Jesus, sharing your insights, thoughts and feelings about your experience from Week 2.

Days 7 and 8

Review your journal for Week 3, which dealt with Jesus' death. As you begin your review, remind yourself of the grace you asked for during that Week.

- What stands out to you from that time?

- What was the invitation, challenge, reminder or encouragement from God that flowed out of that Week to you?

Conclude your day with a colloquy with Jesus, sharing your insights, thoughts and feelings about your experience from Week 3.

Days 9 and 10

Review your journal for Week 4, which dealt with Jesus' resurrection. As you begin your review, remind yourself of the grace you asked for during that Week.

- What stands out to you from that time?

- What was the invitation, challenge, reminder or encouragement from God that flowed out of that Week to you?

Conclude your day with a colloquy with Jesus, sharing your insights, thoughts and feelings about your experience from Week 4.

PLAN 2

Instead of a daily focus as in plan 1, this plan employs a week-long focus (feel free to take longer), which encourages you to once again sit with the material of a given section while reviewing your journal entries that cover that section. This plan also has an artistic expression aspect to it.

Spend a week on each of the sections you went through (Preparatory Exercises, Principle and Foundation, Week 1 and so on), reflecting on the grace(s) asked for, the examen questions and your journal entries. During your review, make a note of feelings that arise within you regarding God. Also make a note of insights you receive and words that seem to grab hold of you.

When you have completed your review of a specific section, use what you have gathered to create a collage, or use another artistic expression to capture the essence of your time in that section.

This can be a powerful way to revisit your experience in the Exercises and can be stretched over an extended period.

ABOUT THE WEBSITE

An additional tool to assist you on your journey through the Exercises is Metamorpha, a website with a designated area that is designed to be a resource for you and your spiritual director or listener as you journey through the Exercises. The website, though composed of many static pieces, also has a dynamic component through which new material will be added, such as frequently asked questions.

Notes

Introduction

page 10   "If you . . . make": Dallas Willard, *The Divine Conspiracy* (San Francisco: HarperCollins, 1998), p. 370.

page 12   published in Fleming's book: David L. Fleming, SJ, *Draw Me into Your Friendship* (St. Louis: Institute of Jesuit Sources, 1996).

page 12   translation of George Ganss: George E. Ganss, SJ, *The Spiritual Exercises of Saint Ignatius* (St. Louis: Institute of Jesuit Sources, 1992).

page 16   "finding God in all things": This phrase is not only a goal of the Exercises but also a succinct articulation of Ignatian spirituality.

PART ONE

Chapter 1: The Daily Elements of the Exercises

page 24   "Opening": David L. Fleming, SJ, *Draw Me into Your Friendship* (St. Louis: Institute of Jesuit Sources, 1996), no. 46.

page 24   "Ask for desired grace": Ibid., no. 49.

page 25   the Soul of Christ: This prayer is often attributed to St. Ignatius but was written the century before him. It has become a part of the Exercises.

page 25   "Noontime examen": Fleming, *Draw Me*, nos. 32-43.

page 30   steps for the General Examen of Conscience: Though originally referred to as Examen of Conscience by Ignatius, today many refer to it as the examen of consciousness—both are correct.

page 31   Particular Examen of Conscience: Fleming, *Draw Me*, nos. 24-31.

page 35   "Lectio divina is not": Quoted in James L. Wakefield, *Sacred Listening* (Grand Rapids: Baker Books, 2006), p. 22.

page 37   "We begin to enter": Richard J. Foster, *Prayer* (San Francisco: Harper-Collins, 1992), p. 147.

page 37   "For Christians whose": Eugene H. Peterson, *Under the Unpredictable Plant* (Grand Rapids: Eerdmans, 1992), pp. 169, 171.

PART TWO

Chapter 1: The History of Preparatory Exercises

page 58   Principle and Foundation: David L. Fleming, SJ, *Draw Me into Your Friendship* (St. Louis: Institute of Jesuit Sources, 1996), no. 23.

page 58   great courage and generosity: Ibid., no. 5.

page 60   "rules for perceiving": Ibid., nos. 313-327.

Chapter 2: God's Love

page 64   "Neither knowing God": David G. Benner, *The Gift of Being Yourself* (Downers Grove, Ill.: InterVarsity Press, 2004), p. 49.

page 64   "Genuine transformation requires": David G. Benner, *Surrender to Love* (Downers Grove, Ill.: InterVarsity Press, 2003), p. 76.

page 68   "I am convinced": Benner, *The Gift*, p. 48.

page 69   "We have the formula": Evelyn Underhill, *The Spiritual Life* (Harrisburg, Penn.: Morehouse, 1996), p. 59.

page 70   "Divine love is absolutely": Benner, *The Gift*, p. 49.

page 75   "In order for our knowing": Ibid., p. 49.

Chapter 3: Principle and Foundation

page 79   To mitigate against: Joseph A. Tetlow, SJ, *Choosing Christ in the World* (St. Louis: Institute of Jesuit Sources, 1989), p. 128.

page 80   "Human Beings are *created*": David L. Fleming, SJ, *Draw Me into Your Friendship* (St. Louis: Institute of Jesuit Sources, 1996), p. 26.

page 94   "It is necessary to": Ibid., no. 23.

page 94   "enkindles the heart": Quoted in Gerald G. May, *Addiction and Grace* (San Francisco: HarperCollins, 1988), p. 15.

page 94   "great unbounded love": Ibid., p. 144.

pages 94-95   "structured for the purpose": Fleming, *Draw Me*, no. 21.

page 96   "We cannot see things": Thomas Merton, *Thoughts in Solitude* (Boston: Shambhala, 1993), p. 4.

PART THREE

Week 1

page 103   You have now reached: David L. Fleming, SJ, *Draw Me into Your Friendship* (St. Louis: Institute of Jesuit Sources, 1996), nos. 23-90.

page 104   intense sorrow and even tears: Ibid., nos. 48, 55.

page 104   Ignatius has built into: Ibid., nos. 53-54, 61, 63, 71.

page 104   A series of meditations: Ibid., nos. 239-243.

page 106   confusion over your choices: Ibid., nos. 48, 62.

page 107   Ignatius describes the practice: Ibid., no. 54.

page 110   the second section: Ibid., nos. 328-336.

page 110   Timothy Gallagher came up: Timothy M. Gallagher, OMV, *The Discernment of Spirits* (New York: Crossroads, 2005), pp. 16-25.

page 111   "The word further signifies": Ibid., p. 33.

page 111   "From the point of view": Thomas Green, *Weeds Among the Wheat* (Notre Dame, Ind.: Ave Maria Press, 2000), p. 104.

page 112   encounters with the evil spirits: Ignatius, in his writing, uses "evil spirit" or "enemy" to refer to the legions of Satan while the good spirits referred to the emissaries of God.

page 114   The first is the spoiled child: The spoiled child imagery is not found in the original Exercises but in Fleming, *Draw Me*, p. 257.

page 121   *Colloquy.* Spend time: Ibid., no. 60.

page 133   *Colloquy.* Today use your: Ibid., no. 61.

page 137   those whom God has: Ibid., no. 60.

Week 2

page 144   The method for interacting: David L. Fleming, SJ, *Draw Me into Your Friendship* (St. Louis: Institute of Jesuit Sources, 1996), no. 112.

page 144   "application of the senses": Ibid., nos. 122-125.

page 145   "Call of the King": Ibid., nos. 91-100.

page 145   "Two Standards": Ibid., nos. 136-148.

page 145   "Three Classes of Persons": Ibid., nos. 149-157.

page 147   to not be deaf: Ibid., no. 91.

page 147   to know Jesus intimately: Ibid., no. 104.

page 148   "Eternal Lord and King": Ibid., no. 98.

page 148   consider downloading the entire: To download an audio version of *The Imitation of Christ*, go to <http://christianaudio.com/advanced_search_result.php?keywords=kempis>.

page 148   The final new addition: Fleming, *Draw Me*, no. 130.

page 150   Ignatius provides key discernment: Ibid., nos. 326-336.

page 151   These rules, like the first: Timothy M. Gallagher, OMV, *The Discernment of Spirits* (New York: Crossroads, 2005), pp. 16-25.

page 151   When you are living: Fleming, *Draw Me*, no. 329.

page 152   However, in rule 8: Ibid., no. 330.

page 152   Wisdom and discernment are: Ibid., no. 332.

page 155   is "to not be deaf": Ibid., no. 91.

page 155   Start your time with a bow: Ibid., no. 55.

page 155   "Day 1. Will You?": This section is an adaptation of the meditation entitled the Two Kingdoms; ibid., nos. 91-100.

page 158   Recall the focus: Ibid., no. 130.

page 167   Be still and be: Ibid., no. 117.

page 169   "to not be deaf" : Ibid., no. 91.

page 170   "Days 1-2. Who will it be": This is an adaptation of the Two Standards; exercises 136-146.

page 171   "Days 3-4. Three Classes of People": Fleming, *Draw Me*, nos. 149-155.

page 206   "Day 6. Three Kinds of Humility": Ibid., nos. 165-168.

Week 3

page 212   referred to as Week 3: David L. Fleming, SJ, *Draw Me into Your Friendship* (St. Louis: Institute of Jesuit Sources, 1996), nos. 190-218.

page 212   "It is my will to bring": Ibid., no. 95.

page 212   feeling the sorrow and pain: David L. Fleming, SJ, *Draw Me into Your Friendship* (St. Louis: Institute of Jesuit Sources, 1996), no. 193.

page 214   "manifests a deepening desire": Marian Cowan, CSJ, and John C. Futrell, SJ, *Companions in Grace* (St. Louis: Institute of Jesuit Sources, 2000), p. 124.

page 214   "If one does meditate rightly": Quoted in Calvin Miller, *The Book of Jesus* (New York: Simon & Schuster, 1996), p. 417.

page 216   What did Jesus suffer: Ibid., nos. 195-197.

page 216   create an ambiance: Ibid., no. 229.

page 216   Consider using different postures: Ibid., no. 79.

page 217   to take joyful thoughts: Ibid., no. 206.

page 218   "Rules for eating": Ibid., nos. 210-217.

page 221   "to sorrow with Christ": Ibid., no. 203.

page 221   "Three Considerations": Ibid., nos. 195-197.

page 232   "The Cross": Lois A. Cheney, *God Is No Fool* (Nashville: Abingdon, 1969), p. 105. Reprinted by permission.

page 238   "The Cross": Ibid.

Week 4

page 241   Week 4: David L. Fleming, SJ, *Draw Me into Your Friendship* (St. Louis: Institute of Jesuit Sources, 1996), nos. 218-229.

page 241   Contemplation to Attain Love: Ibid., nos. 230-237.

page 242   The post-resurrection Jesus: Ibid., no. 306.

page 242   The desired grace of Week 4: Ibid., no. 221.

page 255   contemplating the love of God: Ibid., nos. 230-237.

page 255   "to be a contemplative": Marian Cowan, CSJ, and John C. Futrell, SJ, *Companions in Grace* (St. Louis: Institute of Jesuit Sources, 2000), p. 133.

page 255   an intimate knowledge: Fleming, *Draw Me,* no. 233.

page 256   expression of the indifference: Ibid., no. 23.

page 256   "Take, Lord, and receive": Ibid., no. 234.

PART FOUR

Ash Wednesday and Holy Week Exercises

page 272   "The Cross": Lois A. Cheney, *God Is No Fool* (Nashville: Abingdon, 1969), p. 105. Reprinted by permission.

GLOSSARY

This glossary contains a list of terms and concepts employed in this book, along with explanations for each, all of which are uniquely pertinent to the Exercises. Additionally, if these terms and concepts are covered more fully in other sections of the book, directions on where to find this information will be given after the word's explanation.

19th Annotation. The annotation that allows the Exercises to be administered in a format other than the traditional thirty-day format. Those who are journeying through the Exercises outside the thirty-day format often refer to their experience as the "19th Annotation," or the retreat in everyday life.

All is gift. An important attitude for retreatants to bring with them into the Exercises. It is the awareness that it is not our effort but God's grace that is the determining factor in our experience in a given prayer time or on a given day.

Annotation(s). Notes written by Ignatius to aid those taking others through the Exercises. There are twenty annotations that precede the material the retreatant will be journeying through.

Colloquy. "Little conversation," a type of prayer that is one of simply conversing with God, Jesus and the Holy Spirit as directed. They flow from the heart and are somewhat informal.

Consolation. A deep connection with God that does not necessarily have anything to do with emotions (see "Rules of Discernment: Week 1" on p. 109).

Desolation. A disconnection with God that does not necessarily have anything to do with emotions (see "Rules of Discernment: Week 1" on p. 109).

Discernment of spirits. Discovering which spirit is behind the inner movements you are feeling.

Disordered attachment. Anything that you become attached to in a way that takes away your freedom to freely respond to God.

Evil spirits. Primarily used for spirits from Satan or Satan, but for the purposes of this book "the evil spirit," "evil one," and so on, refer to that which seeks to take a person away from following God's call or invitation.

Examen. Exercise used to help people to review and explore their life, seeking to discern what God has been up to and how well they are able to cooperate with God (see "Prayer of Examen" on p. 28).

Exercises. When the word *Exercise(s)* appears with an uppercase E, it refers to the Spiritual Exercises of St. Ignatius of Loyola. When the word *exercise(s)* appears with a lowercase E, it refers to the daily prayer times spent in the Exercises.

Finding God in all things. A five-word summary of Ignatian spirituality and a natural outcome as a person journeys through the Exercises.

Good spirits. Spirits from God, angels.

Grace. The gift for which the retreatant is asking God during prayer time. Each Week has a unique grace that is tied to that Week, something the retreatant asks God for.

Lectio divina. "Sacred reading"; refers to a fourfold approach to entering into the Scriptures (see "Lectio divina" in chapter 1).

Imaginative prayer. A way of entering into the Scriptures with Jesus. This style of prayer is a component unique to the Exercises (see "Imaginative prayer" in chapter 1, p. 36).

Indifference. An attitude that does not desire one thing over the next but seeks to be open to whatever comes, discerning God's invitation or challenge in each event and circumstance of life (see pp. 94-95).

Listener. One who has agreed to accompany the retreatant on the journey through the Exercises (see also "Spiritual director").

Preparatory prayer. The ways retreatants holistically ready themselves to intentionally enter into the presence of God.

Optional exercises. Exercises that are not a part of the original Exercises but added by the author as aids in helping the retreatant more fully experience a truth. These exercises are optional.

Repetition. Days that occur weekly and give the retreatant the opportunity to revisit something that was stirred within them on the prior days. It gives space for the retreatant to go deeper with God in a particular experience.

Retreat in everyday life. Another name for a 19th Annotation retreat.

Retreatant. A person who is journeying through the Exercises.

Rules of Discernment. Rules that Ignatius developed to help people discern what is going on within them and which spirit is behind it. There are two sets of these rules: those written for those in Week 1 of the Exercises and those written for those in Week 2. These rules have much to say on the topic of consolation and desolation.

Slowdown. A method designed to help retreatants release the internal stuff they carry in order to be better able to enter into the daily prayer time. It is not a part of the original Exercises (see "Slowing Down" in chapter 1, p. 26).

Spiritual director. One who is mature and trained in the art of spiritually companioning another.

Week(s). When the word *Week(s)* appears with an uppercase W, it refers to the fourfold division of the Exercises. It does not refer to our traditional week of seven days. When the word *week(s)* appears with a lowercase W, it refers to the daily prayer times spent in the Exercises.

ACKNOWLEDGMENTS

THERE IS MUCH THAT WENT INTO writing this book and many who played small and large roles in its development. It is a delight to be able to name a few of those who helped the idea of this book to become a reality.

My first words of thanks go to my lovely wife, Donna. I often referred to this as her book, especially as I struggled to write it, for she believed in the value of this project long before I did. She has been a support and encouragement during the long hours that went into writing *Journey with Jesus*, and she willingly helped me to create the space and time needed for its completion, even as we were in the process of moving to a new city.

I am also indebted to Jan Johnson, who recommended me for this writing project after reading through the materials I had put together on the Exercises. Her belief in this project and in my ability to write it helped to convince me to say yes and move foreword.

Celia Bradley was a godsend. She graciously agreed to edit the rough draft, which at one point was well over 225 pages, offering her wisdom and insight along the way. Her hard work in the initial editing stages helped me to feel much better about all I submitted to InterVarsity Press and saved me much work in the rewrite stages.

Rich and Katy Murray, true friends in the richest sense of the term, allowed me to use their cabin at a critical time in the writing of this book. I was able to work uninterrupted for hours and days on end. This was a huge gift.

Cindy Bunch, my editor at InterVarsity Press, who believed in the value of this project, expanded the reach of the material and gently guided me each step of the way. Her efforts helped the manuscript to take shape and form in ways that would be beneficial for all those who choose to journey through the Exercises. She was a much-needed support to my writing process.

I am thankful to Father Albert Haase and Marilyn Stewart who each read my original manuscript and whose comments and insights were encouraging and extremely helpful. I listened to your wisdom and incorporated much that you suggested. I believe the book is much better because of the input you shared with me.

Finally, I thank Mick and Carol Berberian. God used this couple to bring me into the kingdom more than thirty years ago. I learned and witnessed grace and freedom at their feet and in their home. God has used them greatly to help me to become who I am today by embracing me and freeing me to be the one-of-a-kind creation God created me to be.